# Spatial Evolution of Manufacturing:
# Southern Ontario 1851-1891

UNIVERSITY OF TORONTO
DEPARTMENT OF GEOGRAPHY
RESEARCH PUBLICATIONS

1.  THE HYDROLOGIC CYCLE AND THE WISDOM OF GOD: A THEME
    IN GEOTELEOLOGY by Yi-Fu Tuan

2.  RESIDENTIAL WATER DEMAND AND ECONOMIC DEVELOPMENT
    by Terence R. Lee

3.  THE LOCATION OF SERVICE TOWNS by John U. Marshall

4.  KANT'S CONCEPT OF GEOGRAPHY AND ITS RELATION TO
    RECENT GEOGRAPHICAL THOUGHT by J. A. May

5.  THE SOVIET WOOD-PROCESSING INDUSTRY: A LINEAR
    PROGRAMMING ANALYSIS OF THE ROLE OF TRANSPORTATION
    COSTS IN LOCATION AND FLOW PATTERNS by Brenton M. Barr

6.  THE HAZARDOUSNESS OF A PLACE: A REGIONAL ECOLOGY OF
    DAMAGING EVENTS by Kenneth Hewitt and Ian Burton

7.  RESIDENTIAL WATER DEMAND: ALTERNATIVE CHOICES FOR
    MANAGEMENT by Angelo P. Grima

8.  THE ATMOSPHERIC ENVIRONMENT: A STUDY OF THERMAL
    COMFORT AND PERFORMANCE by Andris Auliciems

9.  URBAN SYSTEMS DEVELOPMENT IN CENTRAL CANADA:
    SELECTED PAPERS edited by L. S. Bourne and R. D. MacKinnon

10. SPATIAL EVOLUTION OF MANUFACTURING: SOUTHERN ONTARIO
    1851-1891 by James M. Gilmour

# Spatial Evolution of Manufacturing: Southern Ontario 1851-1891

James M. Gilmour

Published for the University of Toronto
Department of Geography
by the University of Toronto Press

© University of Toronto Department of Geography
Published by University of Toronto Press
Toronto and Buffalo, 1972
Printed in Canada
ISBN 0-8020-3295-8
Microfiche ISBN 0-8020-0264-1

To Gillum

# Acknowledgments

This monograph is a modified and much shortened version of a doctoral dissertation presented to the University of Toronto in 1970. My efforts to complete both these endeavours owe much to the aid and encouragement of my instructors, colleagues, and friends.

Many thanks are due to the supervisor of my doctoral programme, Professor Donald Kerr, for his encouragement, interest, and kindness extending over many years, and to Professors Neil Field, John Britton, and Cole Harris for their painstaking reading of several manuscripts and their many helpful suggestions. I also wish to express my thanks to several other people who kindly listened to me and talked with me about doubts and problems related to my research. In particular I wish to thank Professors Percy Silva, Lyn Collins, Peter Holland, David Walker, Brenton Barr, and John Marshall, and equally to Terence Lee, Tam Taylor, and Rick Guty.

Finally, I wish to express my gratitude to Mrs. Lydia Burton and her staff for their time and effort in making this a more consumable product, and to Mr. Geoffry Matthews, Miss Jenny Wilcox, and Miss Jane Ejima for their excellent cartographic work.

McGill University                                    James M. Gilmour
April, 1972

# Contents

ACKNOWLEDGMENTS  /  vii

TABLES  /  x

FIGURES  /  xii

MAPS  /  xiii

I        INTRODUCTION  /  3

II       EXPORT-BASE THEORY AND
         GENERAL ECONOMIC GROWTH  /  12

III      STRUCTURE OF MANUFACTURING
         IN SOUTH ONTARIO: 1851 - 1891  /  26

IV       SPATIAL VARIATION IN THE
         STRUCTURE OF MANUFACTURING  /  41

V        DISTRIBUTIONAL PATTERNS OF MANUFACTURING:
         THEORETICAL CONSIDERATIONS  /  70

VI       SPATIAL PATTERNS IN SOUTH ONTARIO:
         1851 - 1891  /  121

VII      PROCESS IN SELECTED INDUSTRIES  /  153

VIII     CONCLUSION  /  189

         APPENDIX:  CLASSIFICATION OF MANUFACTURING BY
                    MARKETS FOR OUTPUT AND AREAL
                    ALLOCATION OF DATA  /  195

BIBLIOGRAPHY  /  206

# Tables

1. Structure of the regional economy 1851–1891. Absolute employment in the primary, secondary, and tertiary sectors, and percentage share of total regional employment in each sector / 27

2. Absolute and percentage structure of manufacturing employment by major groups, 1851–1891 / 27

3. Structure of secondary manufacturing: 1851–1891 absolute employment / 35

4. Value of output of consumer and producer goods industries as a percentage of total manufacturing in Canada, 1870–1949 / 38

5. Sample of industries introduced into Ontario between 1850 and 1890 / 109

6. Major manufacturing groups: coefficients of localization / 132

7. Manufacturing subgroups: coefficients of localization / 132

8. Cotton mills in South Ontario, 1891 / 134

9. Share of employment and population in the "manufacturing belt" and the rest of South Ontario, 1851 and 1891 / 143

10. Brewing industry characteristics: 1851–1891 / 154

11. Estimates of the market of selected brewing centres: 1881 / 160

12. Estimates of the market of selected brewing centres: 1891 / 161

13. Scale increases in brewing: 1871–1891 / 163

14. Average employment per plant by output share of areal units: 1891 / 164

15. Output–labour share ratios by output share of areal units: 1871 and 1891 / 165

16. Output–capital share ratios by output share of areal units: 1891   /   165

17. Brewing: relative distribution.  Manufacturing belt versus the rest of the region   /   166

18. Average employment per establishment   /   167

19. Brewing: average value of output per establishment   /   168

20. Brewing: output shares in the manufacturing belt, 1871 and 1891   /   168

21. Agrcultural implements: characteristics   /   169

22. Agricultural implements: average size of establishment by output share, 1871   /   175

23. Agricultural implements: output–labour share ratios by output share, 1871   /   177

24. Agricultural implements: industry characteristics by output share, 1891   /   178

25. Agricultural implements: output–labour share ratios and output–capital share ratios by output shares, 1891   /   179

26. Agricultural implements: relative distribution. Manufacturing belt versus the rest of the region   /   179

27. Agricultural implements: average employment per establishment   /   180

28. Engraving and lithographing: industry characteristics by areal units, 1871   /   184

29. Engraving and lithographing: industry characteristics, 1871–1891   /   184

30. Engraving and lithographing: relative distribution. Manufacturing belt versus the rest of the region, 1891   /   185

31. Saw and file cutting: industry characteristics, 1871–1891   /   186

32. Saw and file cutting: relative distribution. Manufacturing belt versus the rest of the region, 1871 and 1891   /   186

# Figures

1.  Hypothetical variation in the relative importance of primary manufacturing through time and space  / 44

2.  Hypothetical variation in the relative importance of consumer goods and producer goods industries through time and space  / 45

3.  Relative importance of the primary, secondary, and tertiary sectors in the areal units along line A-B  / 54

4.  Relative importance of the primary, secondary, and tertiary sectors in the areal units along line E-F  / 54

5.  Relative importance of the primary, secondary, and tertiary sectors in the areal units along line K-L  / 56

6.  Relative importance of secondary manufacturing, 1851, 1861, 1871, and 1881 for the areal units along line A-B  / 56

7.  Relative importance of secondary manufacturing, 1851, 1861, 1871, and 1881 in the areal units along line E-F  / 61

8.  Relative importance of consumer and producer goods industries in South Ontario and selected areal units for 1851, 1861, 1871, 1881, and 1891  / 62

9.  Relative importance of consumer goods industries in 1851, 1861, 1871, 1881, and 1891 in the areal units along line A-B  / 62

# Maps

1. The study area / 4

2. Settlement in southern Ontario / 47

3. Relative importance of the primary sector, 1851 / 50

4. Relative importance of the primary sector, 1861 / 50

5. Relative importance of the primary sector, 1871 / 50

6. Relative importance of the primary sector, 1881 / 51

7. Settlement cross-sections / 51

8. Relative importance of the secondary sector, 1851 / 51

9. Relative importance of the secondary sector, 1881 / 52

10. Relative importance of the tertiary sector, 1851 / 52

11. Relative importance of the tertiary sector, 1881 / 52

12. Relative importance of secondary manufacturing in the total economy, 1851 / 60

13. Relative importance of secondary manufacturing in the total economy, 1881 / 60

14. Relative importance of consumer goods in secondary manufacturing, 1851 / 63

15. Relative importance of consumer goods in secondary manufacturing, 1891 / 63

16. Relative importance of clothing and footwear in secondary manufacturing, 1851 / 64

17. Relative importance of clothing and footwear in secondary manufacturing, 1891 / 64

18. Relative importance of unfinished producer goods in secondary manufacturing, 1851 / 65

19. Relative importance of unfinished producer goods in secondary manufacturing, 1891 / 65

20. Magnitude of secondary manufacturing, 1851 / 122

21. Magnitude of secondary manufacturing, 1891 / 122

22. Growth of secondary manufacturing, 1851-1891 / 122

23. Secondary manufacturing: output share, 1851 / 124

24. Secondary manufacturing: output share, 1891 / 124

25. Secondary manufacturing: growth output share, 1851-1891 / 124

26. Magnitude of primary construction industries, 1851 / 125

27. Magnitude of primary construction industries, 1891 / 125

28. Employment in brick and tile manufacturing, 1851 / 126

29. Employment in brick and tile manufacturing, 1891 / 126

30. Employment in sawmilling, 1851 / 127

31. Employment in sawmilling, 1891 / 127

32. Magnitude of consumer goods industries, 1851 / 128

33. Magnitude of consumer goods industries, 1891 / 128

34. Growth of consumer goods industries, 1851-1891 / 129

35. Magnitude of producer goods industries, 1851 / 129

36. Magnitude of producer goods industries, 1891 / 129

37. Growth of producer goods industries, 1851-1891 / 130

38. Secondary manufacturing: location quotients, 1851 / 136

39. Secondary manufacturing: location quotients, 1891 / 136

40. Consumer goods: location quotients, 1851 / 137

41. Consumer goods: location quotients, 1891 / 137

42. Producer goods: location quotients, 1851 / 138

43. Producer goods: location quotients, 1891 / 138

44. Real concentration: secondary manufacturing, 1851 / 140

45. Real concentration: secondary manufacturing, 1891 / 140

46. Real concentration: consumer goods, 1851 / 141

47. Real concentration: consumer goods, 1891 / 141

48. Real concentration: producer goods, 1851 / 142

49. Real concentration: producer goods, 1891 / 142

50. Real concentration: household goods, 1851 / 144

51. Real concentration: household goods, 1891 / 144

52. Real concentration: unfinished producer goods, 1851 / 145

53. Real concentration: unfinished producer goods, 1891 / 145

54. Employment in brewing, 1871 / 157

55. Employment in brewing, 1891 / 157

56. Brewing: output share, 1871 / 158

57. Brewing: output share, 1891 / 158

58. Brewing: plant appearance and disappearance, 1871-1891 / 159

59. Brewing: changes in manufacturing employment, 1871-1891 / 159

60. Employment in agricultural implement manufacturing, 1871 / 169

61. Employment in agricultural implement manufacturing, 1891 / 169

62. Agricultural implement manufacturing: output share, 1871 / 170

63. Agricultural implement manufacturing: output share, 1891 / 170

64. Agricultural implements: changes in manufacturing employment, 1871–1891 / 171

65. Agricultural implements: plant appearance and disappearance, 1871–1891 / 171

66. Employment in engraving and lithography, 1871 / 183

67. Employment in engraving and lithography, 1891 / 183

68. Engraving and lithography: changes in manufacturing employment, 1871–1891 / 183

69. Employment in saw and file cutting, 1871 / 187

70. Employment in saw and file cutting, 1891 / 187

71. Saw and file cutting: changes in manufacturing employment, 1871–1891 / 187

Spatial Evolution of Manufacturing:
Southern Ontario 1851-1891

# I

# Introduction

The concern of the pages to follow is with the changing distributional patterns of manufacturing industry in developing regions, and more specifically with the forces which lead to the localization of manufacturing and the creation of highly industrialized areas.

Three major sets of objectives are sought. First, the study is intended to improve understanding of the changing spatial patterns of manufacturing in regions which initially developed on the basis of exports from the primary sector. Second, it is designed to determine whether or not functional relationships exist between (a) the growth and structure of the manufacturing sector and the general economic development of a region, and (b) the growth and structure of the manufacturing sector and the distribution of manufacturing. Last, the study attempts to augment our understanding of the geography of South Ontario.

Realization of these objectives will be achieved by means of a consideration of economic growth theory and location theory, and an analysis of the changing structure and distribution of manufacturing in South Ontario between 1851 and 1891. Map 1 depicts this area and the areal subdivisions within it that were used for purposes of analysis.

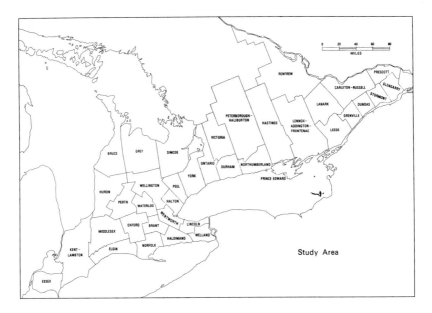

Map 1. The Study Area

## THE CHOICE OF GROWTH THEORY

There are many theories and models of economic growth. The purpose of this short section is to explain why the export-base model should be singled out for consideration when relating distributional change and economic development in Canada. The full elucidation of the model is not provided at this point.

The growth model selected has to meet certain conditions. A regional economic growth model that recognizes intra-regional spatial variation, or a non-spatial regional model that can be modified to accommodate spatial variation is needed. This rules out all supra-national-scale models such as Prebisch's[1] model of international economic development, and most of the models described by Keeble[2] as national-scale non-spatial models. The

[1] R. Prebisch, The Economic Development of Latin America and Its Principal Problems (Lake Success: 1950); and "Commercial Policy in the Underdeveloped Countries," American Economic Review 49 (1959): 251-273.

[2] D. E. Keebel, "Models of Economic Development" in Models in Geography, eds. R. J. Chorley and Peter Haggett (London: Methuen and Co., 1967), pp. 248-256.

best-known example of these is the Rostow model, which outlines growth as a set of discrete stages.[3] This heavily criticized model is the only one of this type which attempts to be universally applicable. It is this quality, in fact, that has been the source of much criticism, and has led to the formation of models of more limited applicability, such as the model designed by Fairbank, Eckstein, and Yang[4] to fit contemporary underdeveloped countries. Given the general criticisms aimed at Rostow's model by economists such as Cairncross[5] and more especially the charges by Bertram[6] based on an analysis of Canadian manufacturing that a stage analysis is not relevant to Canada, and that a take-off cannot be found, there seems little point in attempting to give this national model spatial dimensions.

The many mathematical models of national economic growth seem no more promising at the present time. These can be divided into "aggregate" and "inter-industry"[7] models. Representative of the former is work by Klein[8] and of the latter, work by Chenery and Clark.[9] The aggregate models are normally highly abstract and not suited for the accommodation of spatial dimensions. The inter-industry models, although falling under the category of growth models are not usually dynamic and hence are unsuited to examining the economic evolution of a specific area.

[3]W. W. Rostow, "The Take-Off into Self-Sustained Growth," Economic Journal 66 (1956): 25-48; "The Stages of Economic Growth," Economic History Review, Second Series 12 (1959): 1-16; The Stages of Economic Growth: A Non-Communist Manifesto (Cambridge: Cambridge University Press, 1960). A good survey of the stage approach to the study of growth and history is Bert F. Hoselitz, "Theories of Stages of Economic Growth" in Theories of Economic Growth, ed. Hoselitz (New York: The Free Press of Glencoe, 1960).

[4]J. K. Fairbank, A. Eckstein, and L. S. Yang, "Economic Change in Early Modern China: An Analytic Framework," Economic Development and Cultural Change 9 (1960): 1-26.

[5]A. K. Cairncross, "The Stages of Economic Growth" in Factors in Economic Development by Cairncross (London: Allen and Unwin Ltd., 1962), pp. 131-144.

[6]G. W. Bertram, "Economic Growth in Canadian Industry, 1870-1915: The Staple Model and the Take-off Hypothesis," The Canadian Journal of Economics and Political Science 29 (1963): 159-184.

[7]Keeble, "Models of Economic Development," p. 254.

[8]L. R. Klein, "A Model of Japanese Economic Growth," Econometrica 29 (1961): 277-292.

[9]Hollis B. Chenery and P. G. Clark, Interindustry Economics (New York: John Wiley and Sons, Inc., 1959).

The two remaining major sets of models are described by
Keeble as the national-scale spatial models and the sub-national-
scale models. The majority in the first category are spatial in
the sense that they are concerned with inter-regional variations
in economic development within the nation. Income inequality
models are prominent. Notable among them is Myrdal's model.[10]
This incorporates the concept of "cumulative causation" which
is very relevant to spatial concentration, and the concept of
spread effects. Equally important is Hirschman's[11] model in
which the key role in differential growth is accorded "...to
spatial interaction between growing 'Northern' and lagging
'Southern' regions in the form of 'trickling-down' and 'polariza-
tion' effects."[12] Many empirical studies have been undertaken
to test the ideas and concepts of these models.[13]

Another category of the national-scale spatial models is the
export-base model, which at the present time is most strongly
associated with the American economist D.C. North.[14] This
model is discussed separately after this general review. National-scale spatial models are not really concerned with intra-
regional variations in economic development. However, because
the scale of regions varies so greatly, they are frequently applicable to regions.

The second category of spatial models, sub-national-scale
models, is unquestionably concerned with intra-regional variation. Included here is the regional multiplier concept[15] which
is strongly related to the export-base model. Also in this category is the growth-pole model that has been developed by many

[10] G. M. Myrdal, Economic Theory and Underdeveloped Regions (London: Gerald
Duckworth, 1957).

[11] Albert O. Hirschman, The Strategy of Economic Development (New Haven: Yale
University Press, 1958).

[12] Keeble, "Models of Economic Development," p. 260.

[13] A lengthy bibliography is provided by Keeble, ibid., pp. 261-266.

[14] D. C. North, "A Note on Professor Rostow's 'Take-Off' Into Self-Sustained Growth,"
Manchester School of Economic and Social Studies 26 (1958): 68-75; "Location Theory
and Regional Economic Growth," Journal of Political Economy 63 (1955): 243-258; The
Economic Growth of the United States, 1790-1860 (Englewood Cliffs, N.J.: Prentice-
Hall, 1961).

[15] At the present time regional multiplier analysis normally consists of an application
of the input-output model, for example, see W. Isard and R. Kuenne, "The Impact of
Steel Upon the Greater New York-Philadelphia Industrial Region: A Study in Agglomeration
Projection," Review of Economics and Statistics 35 (1953): 289-301.

researchers, but is most frequently associated with the French economist Perroux.[16]

Although several of the models and, more especially, aspects of the national and sub-national models are highly relevant to the aim of relating economic growth and spatial distribution in a specific area, as recognized by the attention paid to some of their concepts in later pages of this study, there are strong reasons why the export-base model should be the favoured construct.

In the first place it appears to have a high degree of "fit" to the Ontario case and to the Canadian growth experience in general. Ontario provides a classic example of an area which until recently was unpopulated and "unused," but with the initiation of settlement quickly developed into a prosperous urban industrial area. As in all Canadian regions, primary exports have been vitally important to economic development, a fact which immediately encourages consideration of export-base theory. The Canadian historian, Harold Innis, in his studies of the fur trade [17] and cod fisheries [18] in Canada was the pioneer of this line of thinking. Watkins describes the staple approach to the study of economic history as primarily a Canadian innovation:

...indeed, it is Canada's most distinctive contribution to political economy. It is undeveloped in any explicit form in most countries where the export sector is or was dominant. The specific terminology--staple or staples approach, or theory or thesis--is Canadian, and the persistence with which the theory has been applied by Canadian social scientists is unique.[19]

Two great continuous threads have built coherence and consistency into Canadian economic history. The first uniting theme is the role of the staple in promoting economic growth through the extension of settlement, trade, and transportation and the reciprocal relationships between the staple and the other elements of the economy. The other theme is the preservation of Canada's political independence from the United States, a factor which was inseparable from the westward extension of the country and the production of new staple products.

[16]F. Perroux, "Note sur la notion de pôle de croissance," Economie Appliquée 8 (1955): 307-320.

[17]Harold Innis, The Fur Trade in Canada: An Introduction to Canadian Economic History (New Haven: Yale University Press, 1930).

[18]Harold Innis, The Cod Fishery: The History of an International Economy (New Haven: Yale University Press, 1940).

[19]Melville Watkins, "A Staple Theory of Economic Growth," The Canadian Journal of Economics and Political Science 29 (May, 1963): 141.

It is difficult, therefore, to ignore the great significance the staples have had in Canada's development. Morton writes of Canada in the 1850's:

The staples of timber and wheat, then, still dominated the Canadian economy. It was for their transport that the canals had been dug and that the new railways were being driven across the farmlands and through the forests. It was to move the men and supplies into the shanties, and send the rafts and drives down flooding spring rivers and to draw the wheat from the granaries to the ports for barge and schooner that the banks strung their branches up the rivers and lakes from Montreal, and inland from Toronto. [20]

Third, and equally important in making the export-base model attractive is the recent clean "bill of health" given it by some Canadian economists. Watkins believes that exports are one of the basic determinants of Canadian growth at the present time, and with regard to the past he states:

The closeness of the link between the staple approach and Canadian historical research makes it unlikely that the application of a more explicit theory will add much to our understanding of Canadian economic development. [21]

Bertram comes to substantially the same conclusion [22]. Even more recently, two Canadian economists, N. H. Lithwick and Gilles Paquet [23] enlisted the support of export-base theory in an attempt to tie together regional economic growth and the interaction between city and region, thus putting the export-base model in a spatial setting. They conjoin the notion of the export base with an input-output model to explain the spatial-economic connections between cities and their primary resource-oriented hinterlands. The concept of the growth pole is also introduced to explain intra-regional disparities in development. Their exciting discussion strongly implies that relating the export-base model to spatial distribution is a very worthwhile exercise.

In Canada there exists, therefore, a strong precedent for the use of the export-base model as the explanatory framework of economic growth. Support for this step, however, exists beyond Canada's boundaries. In the United States, the model has

---

[20] W. L. Morton, The Critical Years (Toronto: McClelland & Stewart Ltd., 1964).

[21] Watkins, "A Staple Theory of Economic Growth," p. 153.

[22] Bertram, "Economic Growth in Canadian Industry, 1870-1915."

[23] N. H. Lithwick and Gilles Paquet, "Urban Growth and Regional Contagion" in Urban Studies: A Canadian Perspective, eds. Lithwick and Paquet (Toronto: Methuen, 1968), pp. 18-39.

received some of its strongest criticisms, but also some of its strongest support.

Tiebout has been the major critic.[24] In an article criticizing a paper by North,[25] he voices the suspicion that exports may not be the only or most important variable in determining regional income. Business investment, government expenditures, and the volume of residential construction, are cited as possible independent variables.[26] Such criticism, however, does not invalidate the model; rather it calls for modification, which may or may not be necessary when the model is applied to particular regions. Where exports are far less important than other variables, then the validity of the model is more questionable. Tiebout also argues it is possible that the nature of residentiary industries could be a crucial factor in economic development, for lack of growth in them may prohibit the development of the export industries. This is a possibility, but it seems unlikely that any residentiary industry will develop until exports have met with some success and created a market for residentiary industry.

Another major criticism of Tiebout is that the size of the region is very important. The larger the region, the less important exports are likely to be in promoting development. One can see the point of the argument. A large region may commence its development by exporting to other regions, but as it is settled, the new areas of settlement may sell to the early settled, more developed areas, thus reducing the relative importance of exports. However, if we accept North's definition of an export-base region as an area held together by its development around a common export base, the problem seems to be minimized.[27]

Despite these criticisms there is a considerable body of support in the United States for the model. Friedmann and Alonso state that "...it is supported by considerable evidence and is most successful in explaining the origins of regional growth."[28] They add however that it is not so applicable to"...explaining

[24] C. M. Tiebout, "Exports and Regional Economic Growth," Journal of Political Economy 64 (1956): 160-164 and 169.

[25] North, "Location Theory and Regional Economic Growth."

[26] Tiebout, "Exports and Regional Economic Growth," p. 161.

[27] North, "A Reply," Journal of Political Economy 64 (1956): 165.

[28] John Friedmann and William Alonso, "Introductory Note" in Regional Development and Planning, eds. Friedmann and Alonso (Cambridge, Mass.: The MIT Press, 1964), p. 210.

the mechanics of sustained and cumulative growth."[29] After a
good start there are so many things that can go wrong, such as
resource exhaustion, demand changes, and technological change
that place the region in a disadvantageous situation.

It is most interesting that two major studies [30] based on the
export-base model have been undertaken on the Pacific Northwest
which has been so similar in its economic growth characteristics
to certain Canadian regions. The work of Tattersall on this area
was the final inducement to the author to employ the export-base
model. Tattersall was interested in the spatial consequences of
multiplier growth stimulated in the first place by regional exports.
Responding to North's plea for the joining of growth theory and
locational models, he tries to show the connections between the
spatially dispersed primary industries and the spatially concentrated secondary and tertiary activities which are the product of
a multiplier process stemming from the export sector. Keeble's
comment on Tattersall's work provides the starting point of this
study.

Tattersall's model, although extremely simple, is interesting both for its
identification of the spatial consequence of multiplier growth, and for the way
in which it dovetails into North's export base model--a feature which clearly
reflects the interest of both authors in the same region, the Pacific Northwest.
However, much more work on this subject aiming in particular at the integration of multiplier analysis with location theory does appear to be needed. [31]


THE STUDY PERIOD

The limits of the study period were imposed as much as they
were chosen. The ideal study period would have been one that
started earlier in Ontario's history and ended in the 20th century.
It would then have been possible to trace the spatial developments
of South Ontario from its origins as a simple primary economy
through to the time when it is unmistakably clear that it would be
a provider of manufactured goods and services rather than a

---

[29] Ibid.

[30] J. H. Tattersall, "Exports and Economic Growth: The Pacific Northwest 1880 to 1960,"
Papers and Proceedings of the Regional Science Association 9 (1962): 215-234. Richard
L. Pfister, "External Trade and Regional Growth: A Case Study of the Pacific Northwest,"
Economic Development and Cultural Change 11 (1963): 134-151.

[31] Keeble, "Models of Economic Development," p. 281.

primary exporter. Data limitations, however, imposed closer
boundaries on the period studied, and in so doing reduced it to
more manageable proportions.

The analysis undertaken in this work requires data that are
almost non-existent for South Ontario before 1850. An abundance
of statistical data is available for the period after 1891, but
unfortunately they are so incomplete for small areas, such as
counties, that it is impossible to determine either the structure
of the economy or the structure of the manufacturing sector
within them. This state of affairs has continued up to the present
so that it is possible to do for the census year 1881 what is not
possible for that of 1971.

These remarks are not meant to imply that the period is
unworthy of detailed examination from a geographical point of
view. This period has been but thinly researched by geographers,
and hardly any work has been done on establishing a picture of
total spatial patterns. The transitional nature of the period endows
it with considerable geographic interest. In 1850 most parts of
the area were at least thinly settled and only a few areas still
awaited their first settlers. The railway network was not yet
started but would be substantially completed by 1891. This closing
date is very close to the period defined by Rostow as the Canadian
take-off, viz. 1896-1914.[32] Although his delineation is questionable
there is no doubt that it was from 1890 to 1920 that South Ontario
emerged as an industrial area.

This gives the study period especial interest. One question
in particular invites investigation. Had the spatial organization
of the region already assumed a fixed form in 1890 prior to the
industrialization and urbanization yet to come? This raises two
broader questions. First, do the spatial forms of the primary
phase of the economy determine the spatial forms of the urban-
industrial economy if and when it emerges? Second, are the
seeds of present-day regional development problems sown at
this early phase of growth?

---

[32]W. W. Rostow, The Stages of Economic Growth: A Non-Communist Manifesto, p. 38.

# II

# Export-base theory and general economic growth

Export-base theory of regional economic growth is applicable only to areas that are export-orientated and that meet the following requirements: suffer from no population pressure problems; have an absence of inhibiting traditions; have grown up within a framework of capitalist institutions responding to profit-maximizing opportunities in which factors of production have been relatively mobile.[1]

The central premise of this theory is that a region's export sector is the key factor in promoting economic growth and in determining the nature of that growth. A successful export sector sets in motion a cumulative multiplier mechanism which expresses itself in growth of the other sectors of the economy and in a general increase in prosperity. The growth stimulated by the export sector may eventually cause other sectors of the

---

[1] The first two conditions are recognized by Melville Watkins, "A Staple Theory of Economic Growth," The Canadian Journal of Economics and Political Science 29 (May, 1963): 143. The first and third conditions are recognized by Douglas North, "Location Theory and Regional Economic Growth," Regional Development and Planning, eds. John Friedmann and William Alonso (Cambridge, Mass.: The MIT Press, 1964), p. 240.

economy to develop to the point where the export sector no longer acts as the major stimulant to growth.

This is not a deterministic theory. Inevitability of events is neither implicitly nor directly stated. Regions whose growth commences with the sale of primary or other commodities in foreign or other regional markets [2] may remain conspicuously backward and unprosperous.

The literature of export-base theory, however, does set down the likely conditions for successful economic growth. In the first place the export sector must be successful, meaning that demand for a region's staple or staples must be considerable, long-lived, and growing. Given that condition there may or may not be a series of impacts or spread effects on the domestic economy, resulting in diversification around the export base.

Spread effects and diversification are directly related, with two principal factors uniting them: the technology of the export industries, and the distribution of income from the export sector. As we shall see these two factors are in themselves strongly related. The first factor is the more important and plays a significant role in shaping the character of the other. The technological conditions of production of export commodities are particularly important in conditioning the potential for growth in newly settled regions, for they determine the nature of inputs and outputs. As Watkins expresses it:

The important determinant is the technology of the industry, that is, the production function, which defines the degree of factor substitutability and the nature of returns to scale. With the production function specified and the necessary ceteris paribus assumptions—including the demand for goods and the supply of factors—a number of things follow: demand for factors; demand for intermediate inputs; possibility of further processing; and the distribution of income. [3]

In a staple economy, the production of a staple export acts as the leading edge of the economy, exerting pressures and demands on the other sectors. The degree to which growth is induced partly depends upon the nature of the staple's production process. Leading export industries in the early years of development are most likely to be extractive, e.g., mining, fishing, lumbering, and farming. Each of these four broad categories contains within itself innumerable staple production possibilities and each commodity can be produced

[2] The markets for the export sector may lie in other regions of the same country. Outstanding in this respect is the United States where much of the produce of her expanding western regions was absorbed by the more highly developed regions of the northeast.

[3] Watkins, "A Staple Theory of Economic Growth, " pp. 144-145.

13

in many different ways. Although it may be a matter of chance that one extractive industry is developed rather than another, and one method of production (e.g., labour-intensive) is preferred over others, the long-term implications for development can be very great.

The nature of the production function affects the distribution of income. This, again, has varying effects upon the domestic investment potential and also upon the spatial organization of a region. Robert Baldwin[4] points out how some production functions will lead to an inequitable distribution of income while others promote relative equality. The latter condition enhances domestic growth opportunities while the former tends to inhibit. Baldwin illustrates his point with two contrasting examples. In the first case he describes a region which relies heavily on the production of a plantation crop on a labour-intensive basis. Organization of production in this way results in income becoming concentrated in the hands of a relatively small number of plantation owners and merchants, while most of the population lives only just above the subsistence level. Such a skewed distribution of income severely diminishes domestic growth opportunities in the consumer goods sector, because the majority of potential consumers generates a very low effective demand for goods and services. The wealthy minority, on the other hand, satisfies its material demands by importation of expensive articles. Other effects include the discouragement of voluntary migration and the direction of entrepreneurial energies along the same old channels related to primary resource exploitation. Lack of consumer goods industries associated with the labour-intensive nature of primary production discourages producer goods production -- the sector most likely to be the basis of a future industrial economy. It is also of interest to note that the poor development of consumer goods production and the provision of services will inhibit the development of towns and cities.

In contrast to the above, Baldwin selected a region characterized by family-size farms. An economy with these origins is much more likely to break out of a predominantly export orientation. Distribution of income is more equitable and the incentives and opportunities exist for farmers to re-invest in their farms and

[4]Robert E. Baldwin, "Patterns of Development in Newly Settled Regions," Regional Development and Planning, eds. John Fiedmann and William Alonso (Cambridge, Mass.: The MIT Press, 1964), pp. 266-284.

to improve efficiency. This provides a growth potential, for as Thomas argues:

Economic growth is possible in a region when there is a growth in per capita output as a result of increases in the quantities and/or the efficiency of use of the factors of production.[5]

The growth of individual incomes simultaneously with increase in regional aggregate income promotes growth in effective demand for certain products and services which eventually becomes strong enough to attract entrepreneurs into domestic production.

There is no primary resource activity which will totally fail to induce any growth in the domestic economy. But it is argued here that if initial growth is based on mining, lumbering, or fishing, the regional growth potential is not as good as initial development based on agriculture with a "favourable" production function.

In the first place there is the question of the extent to which the area of a region is occupied, i.e., the areal distribution of production. This is an important point, for it conditions the nature of spatial demand for goods and services that develops as the staple industry brings income into the region. Agriculture is unique in being characterized by the existence of many small production units which in their contiguity blanket the space economy and may eventually occupy the greater part of it. Of course, the extent to which this occurs is dependent upon the distribution of potential agricultural land. In striking contrast is mining, which usually manifests itself in a comparatively small number of production centres within small local concentrations. There is, in effect, no space economy, only a series of localized production points. Fishing on the other hand is characterized by a linear distribution along coasts. The significance of the distribution of the staple industry lies first of all in the nature of the transportation system that is necessary to serve it. The blanket distribution of agriculture may eventually call forth a system that services the entire agricultural area with a network of transportation linkages.[6]

[5] Morgan D. Thomas, "The Export Base and Development Stage Theories of Regional Economic Growth," Land Economics 40 (1964): 122.

[6] D. W. Meinig has examined the development of railnets in regions with economic origins similar to those of Ontario. In both the Columbia Basin and in South Australia the railway nets developed to link grain farming areas with the ports serving the regions. See D. W. Meinig, "A Comparative Historical Geography of Two Railnets: Columbia Basin and South Australia," Annals of the Association of American Geographers 52 (December, 1962): 394-413. Transport development in underdeveloped areas is examined by E. J. Taaffe, R. L. Morrill, and P. R. Gould, "Transport Expansion in Underdeveloped Countries: A Comparative Analysis," Geographical Review 53 (October, 1963): 503-529.

Mining on the other hand, creates a series of frequently unconnected routes that extend from the mine to a port or other shipping point. Fishing may generate no transportation links at all other than routes connecting fishing ports or villages, for the staple export can be shipped directly to the export market.

The relationship between the distribution of an economic activity and tranportation is an important factor for growth. It is to the advantage of a developing region if the staple export exerts pressure for an extensive transportation system, for:

Theory and history suggest that the most important example of backward linkage is the building of transport systems for collection of the staple, for that can have further and powerful spread effects.[7]

But the total importance of the relationship does not rest here. The more widely and evenly an economic activity is distributed, the greater the likelihood that many service centres will develop. Services for mining and its related population will be provided at the small number of mining centres, and in the case of fishing at the fishing ports. Agriculture, however, will encourage the growth of many service centres which are as widely distributed as the agricultural areas they serve. Before the development of railways or the rise of predominantly industrial centres one would expect to find the smallest service centres distributed only a few miles from each other throughout the agricultural area. Construction of service centres is another important influence of the staple industry; as with transportation, the growth of a system of towns and villages has powerful spread effects.

There are many other implications for growth which bear no relation to the distribution pattern of the staple industry. Space permits only brief discussion of some major factors.

An important point is the number of persons a particular resource exploitation activity can sustain above subsistence level. It is very reasonable to argue that agriculture in general will support more people than other primary activities. Of course, from preceding statements it will be understood that the number of persons supported by an activity is dependent upon the nature of its production function. However, if we specify that agriculture is organized on a family-farm basis and that the potential agricultural area occupies at least half the total area of the region, as in South Ontario, there is little doubt that farmers and their employees and dependents will vastly outnumber employees and their dependents in other primary industries. Accordingly, a

[7]Melville Watkins, "A Staple Theory of Economic Growth," p. 145.

developing region with an agricultural staple will more likely generate a greater aggregate effective demand for goods and services.

The renewability or non-renewability of primary resource commodities has many implications for a region's resource potential. Mining exploits exhaustible resources or, at least, resources whose exploitation eventually becomes uneconomic. Lumbering, in the past at any rate, has had qualities of impermanence, using timber resources with no thought to the future and continually moving on to new virgin forest areas. Once again, agriculture exhibits advantages. While it is true that soil structure and certainly fertility can be destroyed through "crop mining," the natural resource -- soil -- is normally maintained or even improved in quality with the passing of time. There is a permanence in agriculture which history shows has been lacking in lumbering and fishing, and an impermanence in mining which economy dictates. Impermanence of the primary resource activity, while not necessarily totally discouraging domestic activity in other sectors, does to some degree inhibit it, and may encourage entrepreneurs to concentrate on the export sector, with an attitude of "make the best of it as long as it lasts." In addition, agriculture, unlike some primary activities, and to a much greater extent than any other, is able to switch production from one staple commodity to another. Whether or not this is possible depends on a number of factors, but the physical environment is particularly important. A region producing a staple crop may be able to switch to another commodity if the demand for the first declines, or if its competitive situation weakens, but only if soil, climatic, and other physical factors permit the economic production of other commodities in demand on foreign markets. The important point is, however, that the possibility of switching production does exist and the study region -- South Ontario -- provides an example, moving from wheat as the dominant agricultural export to dairy products and livestock at a later date.

Ideally, a new region is better placed for future growth if it can avoid reliance on one staple commodity and is able to change its staple emphasis if the need arises or advantages accrue from it. The ability to do this depends on three main sets of factors. First, the wider a region's resource base, the greater is the probability of that region constantly finding and producing marketable commodities. This leads to the second major factor. Irrespective of the breadth of the resource base, the market must exist for the commodities which a region can produce. With no markets for its products, a region may be forced to exist at a subsistence level until the situation changes. Or, there may be a demand for a commodity which has only slight spread effects. The fur trade in New France is a case in point. Finally, a variety of resources, and market demand for commodities derived from them, is no guarantee that a region is free from growth problems. It is also necessary for a region to be competitive in extra-regional markets, a consideration which greatly depends upon a region's location. Many other factors are significant to development but those discussed are the most important and they go a long way towards explaining why a region may commence its growth with production of a staple which preceding paragraphs have shown may be far less than ideal.


THE IMPACT OF THE EXPORT SECTOR ON MANUFACTURING

The summary above concerns the general conditions for growth based on a staple export. We now turn to the theoretical development of secondary manufacturing in a region possessing a staple commodity with a favourable production function. In fact, since the greater part of South Ontario relied on family-farm agriculture it is assumed that the staple commodity's production function is of that nature.

A successful export commodity will bring income into the developing region. This income will be expended on goods and services. As demand increases in response to growth of population and rising incomes, successive thresholds will be reached for the domestic production of goods and services. Spread effects from the export sector will be felt in the construction of transportation links and in local residential and commercial construction. These developments in turn will provide further manufacturing investment opportunities as new thresholds are reached for a widening range of manufactured commodities. Secondary manufacturing, therefore, develops upon the heels of primary export activity. The more successful the export sector, the more favourable its production function, the greater will be the growth of manufacturing. As primary activities grow and an increasing number of productive agents pass from subsistence farming, or enter directly into supplying some commodity for export, as more people enter the area attracted by the income opportunities of primary activities

18

and related services, two interconnected long-term trends will manifest themselves: 1) there will be growing effective demand for a wider variety of goods and services; 2) specialization of labour will develop.

Several writers accepting the staple hypothesis, discuss the relations between the staple industry and the development of manufacturing. Only Douglas North, however, has attempted to classify the manufacturing that develops in response to the success of the export sector.[8] North's classification distinguishes four different types of manufacturing. His first category consists of materials-oriented industries. In general these are weight-loss industries and are more economically located at the source of raw materials than close to the market for the processed raw material. The second group consists of service industries to the export sector, e.g., logging and lumbering equipment. Residentiary industry producing for local consumption constitutes the third group. His last group consists of footloose industries for which transfer costs are of little significance in location.

These groups are scarcely a satisfactory basis for a more detailed classification, mainly because they are not mutually exclusive. There is the possibility, for example, that an industry could have the characteristics of two or more groups.

Watkins does not classify manufacturing into groups as such, but the linkage effects of the export sector which he describes, i.e., the inducements to invest in different sectors of the economy, have strong affinities with the first three groups in North's classification. In Hirschmann's terms, the inducement to domestic investment resulting from the increased activity of the export sector can be broken down into three linkage effects: backward linkage, forward linkage, and what we shall call final demand linkage.[9] North's first group, materials-oriented industries, are in many cases related to the forward linkage effect. In this case the effect is expressed by an inducement to invest in industries using the produce of the staple export industries as an input. Thereby, the values of the staples are increased before export. Milling of wheat and sawmilling are two examples of the crudest type of forward linkage. Production of pulp from wood is a more advanced form requiring much greater capital investment. Such developments would, of course, have many potential spread effects, for given the growth of manufacturing utilizing the output of primary industries

[8]Douglas North, "Location Theory and Regional Economic Growth," p. 250.

[9]Melville Watkins, "A Staple Theory of Economic Growth," p. 145.

as inputs, investment opportunities would exist for the production of a variety of producer goods, such as tools, machinery, office furniture, transportation equipment, etc.

Backward linkage effects are the result of growth and changing production techniques in primary industries. It is easy to appreciate, for instance, that as farm exports gain momentum, accompanied by rising farm incomes, farmers may increase their investment in the form of machinery, fertilizer, buildings, etc. Although at first, as with all linkage effects, this may simply increase the region's imports, thresholds for the domestic production of various goods may be reached. But Hirschmann suggests that those commodities to be first produced domestically may well be those which are imported in the greatest quantities.[10] It was pointed out earlier that backward linkage effects also include the construction of transport systems as well as other social overhead capital invest- ments such as harbours and their ancillary services. Such devel- opments can have further strong spread effects that impinge upon manufacturing.

The industries representing final demand linkage effects produce a very broad range of goods for the final consumer market. Growth of this group as well as others will encourage the production of intermediate goods. Boot and shoe makers will purchase leather from tanneries; brewers will commence buying barrels and casks and so on.


TESTING THE GENERAL THEORY

It is obvious that this idealized theoretical industrialization of a region growing through the impact of its successful export sector upon the rest of the economy is very general and rather imprecise. This is only to be expected, however, because the theory can only be general if it is to encompass all the eventualities and circum- stances, social and economic, that make the development of real regions unique in character. For this reason the theory contains little reference to the timing of the process of industrialization and we are left wondering how long or how quickly the process operates. We know of different linkage effects promoting the growth of different kinds of industry, and this knowledge prompts many questions. Does each linkage effect operate with equal force

[10]Albert O. Hirschman The Strategy of Economic Development (New Haven: Yale University Press, 1958), p. 121.

all the time? Do industrial groups emerge simultaneously, or do they appear at different times, growing at different rates? And do they each have a varying importance within the total industrial structure?

It is unreasonable to expect answers to questions of this nature to be included within the general body of the theory. It postulates on the processes of growth for export-oriented regions. Although the processes may possess generality, the circumstances under which they operate do not. Each region is unique internally, and the external conditions which each meets vary with time and place. Regions do not contain similar bundles of resources distributed in an exactly similar manner. For that matter, they are unlike in size and ethnic composition and, therefore, in the customs, mores, and drives of their populations. Political decisions of manifold character have to be made in each region. Such decisions can impinge on economic development. This, in fact, may be their intention. In this respect again each region is unique. For these reasons it is impossible to describe a general path of development to be followed by export-based regions. There are too many variables to be considered, and it is doubtful if the behaviour of any one is predictable.

The examination of South Ontario, the content of succeeding chapters, will consequently be largely exploratory. Attention is focused on establishing what industries developed, when they developed, and where they developed. By examining structural change in manufacturing we can proceed backwards to the processes described by export-base theory. The presence or absence of various types of manufacturing will provide insights into what processes were operating, and at what times, and of the sequence in which they occurred. In this way a rudimentary testing of the theory can be made.

STRUCTURAL CLASSIFICATION OF MANUFACTURING

In order to relate the industrialization of South Ontario to the postulates of export-base theory, it is imperative that manufacturing industries be allocated to groups that represent the various linkages and impacts of the export sector. At the same time it is also important to have a classification that is of value in examining the distribution of manufacturing, for a major aim is to find relationships between distribution and the processes of economic growth.

While the conventional classifications employed by geographers are suitable for examining distributions, [11] they do not have much relevance to regional economic growth. They are not designed to provide insights into the immaturity or maturity of manufacturing; its complexity or lack of it; or more broadly, the degree of development of manufacturing.

North's classification meets some of the required characteristics, but his groups seriously overlap and are very broad and imprecisely defined. More precision and finer subdivisions are necessary, but at the same time the groups must relate to the growth process. These requirements are met by a structural classification that groups manufacturing industries according to the market for their commodity output. Using employment and occupation data from the five censuses taken during the period 1850-1891, all manufacturing establishments have been classified into one or more of the following groups of a classification developed by Shaw[12] and later modified by Dales. [13]

I. Secondary Manufacturing

    A. Consumer goods

        A1 food, drink, tobacco
        A2 consumer sundries
        A3 clothing and footwear
        A4 household goods
        A5 consumer durables

    B. Finished producer goods

        B1 construction materials
        B2 supplies to primary and tertiary sectors
        B3 investment goods

    C. Unfinished producer goods

II. Primary Manufacturing

    1. food
    2. construction
    3. unfinished producer

[11] The classifications most frequently used by geographers are partially based on raw material inputs, and partially based on production processes and on use of output. Data are allocated to establishment industries which are conceptually quite distinct from the commodity industries employed by economists in their models of economic growth.

[12] William Howard Shaw, Value of Commodity Output Since 1869 (New York: National Bureau of Economic Research, 1947).

[13] J. H. Dales, "Estimates of Canadians Manufacturing Output by Markets, 1870-1915," Papers, Canadian Political Science Association, Conference on Statistics 1962 and 1963.

The consumer goods group of this classification corresponds to the final demand linkage effect of the export sector, while primary manufacturing industries are indicative of a forward linkage effect. It should be added, however, that primary manufacturing also includes industries producing for the domestic market, for example, the brick, tile, lime, and cement industries. Producer goods give evidence of a backward linkage effect. At the same time they can indicate spread effects from primary manufacturing and consumer goods. As these grow, thresholds will be created for the production of both finished and unfinished producer goods. This statement stems from the recognition that the various groups do not correlate perfectly with the linkage effects of the export sector. The classification assumes a simplicity that probably never exists, and ignores the increasing complexity of an economy as it develops. The problem is that there seems no way of differentiating between the direct linkage effects from the export sector and the linkage effects from activities initially stimulated by the export sector. To separate direct from indirect effects, as well as the unrelated effects of other activities, requires data from the past that our predecessors did not collect. We can only recognize that to talk in terms of simple direct relationships between the export sector and various groups is begging the issue with regard to growth mechanisms. The validity of the structural analysis, however, remains unimpaired. The classification is perfectly adequate for describing the structural development of the manufacturing sector, and is closely related to the growth mechanisms postulated by export base theory.

This classification possesses distinct advantages for this research. In the first place, manufacturing industries can be arranged into broad or narrow groups. At the broadest level there is quite simply secondary and primary manufacturing. As can be seen above these are then sub-divided into narrower groups such as consumer and producer goods and these in turn are broken into subgroups according to the markets for commodity outputs. The subgroups, for example, household goods, are composed of individual commodity[14] industries. The Appendix lists all industries employed in the study and shows how they have been grouped.

The second major advantage of this classification is that it permits the detection of industrialization. It is arguable that true industrialization exists only where we find the production of the

---

[14]This and other terms used in the present section are fully discussed in the Appendix.

more durable types of consumer goods as well as finished producer goods. Also, relative growth in intermediate or unfinished producer goods is indicative of an increasingly mature industrial economy with increasing specialization and agglomeration. Classifications normally used by geographers, namely, those based on principal component material or "purpose" of finished goods are of limited value in exploring the processes of industrialization and their spatial manifestations.

The Appendix provides a detailed explanation of the concepts underlying the classification of manufacturing and the methods employed for allocating establishment industries to the various groups.

The most important and laborious stage of data manipulation consisted of transforming data collected for establishment industries into commodity industries. In performing this transformation recourse was made to the estimating procedures developed by Shaw and Dales. In view of his concern with the Canadian national economy from 1871 onwards, the work of the latter is more relevant. His estimating procedures are relied on heavily but unfortunately his manipulated data could not also be employed. He aggregated his data for Canada as a single statistical unit while this work is confined to South Ontario. In the second instance, this research is concerned with the industrial structure of small areal units, reflecting the interest in spatial developments within the region. Consideration of spatial variation in structure was not encompassed by Dale's work. Therefore he was untroubled by the boundary change problems which arise in dealing with census units smaller than provinces and by the data problems associated with small area units. Just as today, the 19th century data for small areas do not match large area data either in range or quantity. The censuses of 1851 and 1861 are particularly difficult to employ; they provide detailed information at the county level for only a very small number of industries. This renders the data inadequate for the purposes of establishing the structure of manufacturing. Fortunately, data on occupations are reasonably complete, and there was no alternative but to use them rather than the manufac- turing employment data. As regards the censuses covering the period 1870 to 1890, the manufacturing employment data were quite satisfactory.

In looking at the structure of Canadian manufacturing, Dales used wages and salaries figures in preference to net value of product figures, suspecting that the latter were more susceptible to serious reporting errors. While the research could have used the same for the period 1870 to 1890, it was quite impossible for the censuses of 1851 and 1861. The only means whereby structure could be compared throughout the study period was by utilization of employment and occupation data.[15] Although most geographers normally prefer to use value-added data, it is generally conceded that employment data constitute a second best.

As mentioned above, in establishing the structure of manufacturing in South Ontario, a serious problem arose from inconsistency in the boundaries of the areal units for which data are presented. This would not have been regarded as too serious if the analysis of small area units had been confined to total manufacturing. The research, however, intended to derive utility from disaggregating manufacturing in order to uncover critical trends in growth and spatial distribution which may be masked when a more highly aggregative approach is used. At this more detailed level, boundary changes in data collection units can seriously distort results. Consequently, much time was devoted to creating consistent areal units and re-allocating the data to fit their boundaries. For the most part those units approximate the present-day counties. To use smaller units is unfortunately impossible and to use larger units courts the risk of important spatial trends remaining undetected. The Appendix discusses the question of boundary change and areal units in more detail.

[15] Almost as important in influencing this choice was the difficulty in re-allocating value added figures between areal units in those cases where the census changed the boundaries of the census subdivisions. The directories used to aid in making re-allocations gave information on employment but none on value of output.

# III

# Structure of manufacturing in south Ontario: 1851-1891

GENERAL NATURE OF THE ECONOMY

Throughout the study period primary activity dominated the Ontario economy. Between 1851 and 1871, the primary sector was more important, and in the next twenty years was just slightly less important, than the secondary and tertiary sectors combined. All sectors grew continually (see Table 1) but at different rates. Except for the first decade, the primary sector had the lowest growth rate of the three and at no time did it sur-pass that of the tertiary sector.

The general picture presented by Table 1 is that of an economy dominated by the extractive activities from which its exports were derived. It was not a static economy. Between 1851 and 1891, the primary sector grew approximately three times, the secondary five times, and the tertiary seven times. As a result of these different growth rates, the relative importance of sectors was altered: the primary sector fell approximately 10 per cent, or slightly more, if the peak of 1861 is considered. On the other hand, the tertiary sector increased its relative importance by about eight per cent, while the secondary sector remained vir-

TABLE 1    STRUCTURE OF THE REGIONAL ECONOMY 1851-1891.  ABSOLUTE
EMPLOYMENT IN THE PRIMARY, SECONDARY AND TERTIARY SECTORS, AND
PERCENTAGE SHARE OF TOTAL REGIONAL EMPLOYMENT IN EACH SECTOR

| Year | Primary Employment | Per Cent | Secondary Employment | Per Cent | Tertiary Employment | Per Cent | Total Employment |
|------|--------------------|----------|----------------------|----------|---------------------|----------|------------------|
| 1851 | 87,598 | 56.9 | 31,121 | 20.2 | 35,264 | 22.9 | 153,983 |
| 1861 | 136,305 | 58.1 | 41,679 | 17.8 | 56,439 | 24.1 | 234,423 |
| 1871 | 228,708 | 49.3 | 98,871 | 20.3 | 140,845 | 30.4 | 463,424 |
| 1881 | 304,630 | 48.3 | 130,214 | 20.6 | 195,918 | 31.1 | 630,762 |
| 1891 | 344,791 | 47.2 | 158,833 | 21.8 | 226,603 | 31.0 | 730,227 |

SOURCE:  Censuses of Upper and Lower Canada, 1851 and 1861.  Censuses of Canada,
1871, 1881, and 1891.  Data transformed by author.  Source for all other
tables is the same, except when another source is specified.

TABLE 2    ABSOLUTE AND PERCENTAGE STRUCTURE OF MANUFACTURING
EMPLOYMENT BY MAJOR GROUPS, 1851-1891

| Group | 1851 Employment | Per Cent | 1861 Employment | Per Cent | 1871 Employment | Per Cent | 1881 Employment | Per Cent | 1891 Employment | Per Cent |
|-------|-----------------|----------|-----------------|----------|-----------------|----------|-----------------|----------|-----------------|----------|
| Consumer goods | 17,397 | 59.7 | 19,775 | 52.1 | 34,742 | 46.1 | 46,657 | 45.5 | 66,148 | 47.2 |
| Producer goods | 7,339 | 25.2 | 9,767 | 25.7 | 20,012 | 26.5 | 29,602 | 28.4 | 39,593 | 28.2 |
| Primary | 4,426 | 15.2 | 8,402 | 22.1 | 20,689 | 27.4 | 26,399 | 25.7 | 34,468 | 24.6 |
| TOTALS | 29,162 | 100.0 | 37,944 | 100.0 | 75,443 | 100.0 | 102,658 | 100.0 | 140,209 | 100.0 |

tually stationary, increasing by only two per cent between 1851
and 1891.  Even to maintain its position, however, it exhibited
substantial absolute growth, evidence of increasing domestic
investment opportunities in manufacturing.

    The faster growth rates of the tertiary sector are scarcely
surprising.  Thresholds for services are more likely to be reached

27

before those for manufactured goods. And, it is important to note, manufactured goods can be imported, but services must be performed within the regions. Hence, tertiary activity, which is essential to the successful performance of the export sector, will at first grow more rapidly than the secondary sector. The primary and tertiary sectors will grow together, contributing to the increase in domestic investment opportunities in manufacturing. It is to be remembered that the export sector cannot grow and flourish without the presence of an attendant service sector.

In summary it may be said that the changes of the period are perhaps more significant for their direction than for their magnitude. The small changes recorded were precursors of greater change to come. The structure of the economy had not dramatically changed. At the end of the period we still find the lopsided economic structure expected of a region growing due to the success of its primary export industries.


PRIMARY MANUFACTURING

Although the relative importance of the secondary sector changed scarcely at all, there was considerable absolute growth and, as shown by Table 2, structural changes were occurring. [1]

In view of the region's heavy dependence upon primary staple exports for its growth, the structure of manufacturing may seem rather curious. In 1851, for example, almost 60 per cent of manufacturing employment was in consumer goods. Forty years later consumer goods still accounted for almost 50 per cent of employment in manufacturing. Both primary manufacturing and producer goods grew in relative importance, but their growth was not sufficient to alter substantially the structure of manufacturing found at the beginning of the period.

Could the structure of manufacturing, as shown in Table 2, have been anticipated? A negative answer is unavoidable for it must be recognized that a potentially major segment of manufacturing, that is, primary manufacturing, is a random element. While there are good reasons for expecting final demand linkage and resultant consumer goods industries, there is much less

[1] The total employment in manufacturing in Table 2 is not the same as employment in the secondary sector in Table 1. The latter table accepts uncritically the census definition of manufacturing. Table 2 describes a more narrowly defined manufacturing sector which excludes activities that rightly belong to the tertiary sector, for example, clothiers, jewellers, and blacksmiths.

certainty about forward linkage and its effect -- primary manufacturing. Even if primary activity dominates the regional
economy there is no necessary reason why it should dominate
the manufacturing sector. Indeed, primary manufacturing as
understood for the purposes of this research, may never develop
in the region. The next few paragraphs provide some reasons
why this situation could arise.

The presence and amount of primary manufacturing seem to
rest largely on chance, dependent upon the interaction of many
unforseeable factors. The most obvious point of all is that developments in any region are dependent upon the resource base.
Each region has a distinctive resource base, and therein lies
much of the uncertainty about the role of primary manufacturing.
Products from different sets of resources may or may not have
to be processed before export. Related to this is the question of
what products are in demand in export markets. External demand
is just as unpredictable as the resource base.

The importance of primary manufacturing in the structure of
manufacturing may depend on the nature of the primary commodity
which a region finds it can produce and export. The state of technology and the nature of the commodity determine the weight loss
in the initial processing of any primary commodity. According
to Dales, only those commodities experiencing weight loss and
consequent reduction in transport costs incurred in reaching the
market region can give rise to primary manufacturing.[2] So
defined, primary manufacturing will only occur in the region
producing such commodities, for high costs forbid their transportation to another region for initial processing.

[2]According to Dales' classification of manufacturing, flour milling does not constitute
primary manufacturing because wheat is economically transportable over long distances.
His definition of primary manufacturing is as follows: "Primary manufacturing industries
are industries engaged in the processing of domestic natural products (including hydro
electricity as a natural product) up to the point where the output of the industry is
economically transportable over long distances. A corollary of this definition is that no
Primary Manufacturing industry processes a natural product that enters into inter-regional
or international trade in any significant volume." This is probably the most precise
definition of primary manufacturing so far attempted, but it obviously has weaknesses,
some of which are recognized by Dales. For example, he classifies pulp and paper, and
sawmilling as primary manufacturing industries. But he does note that "wood pulp is
traded internationally in sizeable volumes." It should also be remarked, however, that
certainly in the past, wood bolts for conversion into pulp moved from Canada to the United
States in sizeable quantities and that unmilled wood was the basis of the Canadian trade
with Britain for several decades. Also, Dales does not consider the fact that interregional
or international trade do not necessarily imply long distance haulage of primary commodities.
In fact, to quote just one example, international trade between Ontario and the United States
can involve much shorter transport distances than trade within Ontario. Where distances

With other products there may exist no particular advantages in processing before export; in fact, quite the opposite, for the end produce of processing may be a commodity which incurs higher transfer costs. By the definition accepted here, industries processing these commodities would not be considered as primary manufacturing industries.

The state of production and transportation technology also affects the relative importance of primary manufacturing within a region. Improvements in production technology widen the resource base, making possible the exploitation of previously untapped resources which provide the raw materials of new primary manufacturing industries.

Improvements in transportation technology reduce time spent in transit and diminish the importance of the perishability factor. Refrigeration techniques applied to transportation equipment have finally almost completely eliminated perishability as an important consideration. Regions consequently could add new primary manufacturing industries to the industrial sector, for example, butter production in New Zealand. Of course, technology could have the opposite effect -- elimination of primary manufacturing industries.

Due recognition must be paid to the availability of investment capital in the developing region, to its economic policy, and to the fiscal policies of the market nations. If a developing region is largely dependent upon its own resources to promote development, it may be a while before capital is available to develop primary manufacturing industries. Perhaps, only when perceptible profits have accrued to the primary sector will investment in primary manufacturing industries occur. Government policy may deliberately or accidentally precipitate or retard such a process.

It is hoped that the enumeration of the above few factors makes it clear why the appearance of primary manufacturing industries is not inevitable in a developing region. Such industries are, of course, desirable, because they provide employment outlets in a developing region and stimulate investment opportunities in other economic activities, accelerating the possibilities of thresholds being reached for the production of other goods and the pro-

---

involved in international trade are short there is no necessary reason why primary manufacturing should be located in the region producing the inputs of primary manufacturing. For these reasons some of the comments made in this section may seem at variance with Dales' definition of primary manufacturing. See J. H. Dales, "Estimates of Canadian Manufacturing Output by Markets, 1870-1915," Papers, Canadian Political Science Association, Conference on Statistics 1962 and 1963, p. 77.

vision of services.[3] Finally, the more materials that are processed before they leave the region, the greater are the region's export earnings. This can be very important in providing more funds for investment.

The closer we approach the first economic stirrings of the region, the greater the likelihood that the product of primary activity will be exported in an unprocessed form. In fact, during the early years of development, primary manufacturing may largely operate to supply domestic markets with such basic products as boards, staves, bricks, tiles, and the like. As economic opportunities are perceived, as the economic organization becomes more·sophisticated, and as development capital comes available, there will emerge a growing tendency to process export commodities before they leave the region, thereby raising the value added to the product and increasing export revenue.

The development of a transportation system may be crucially related to growth of primary manufacturing as well as to primary activity as a whole. Until costs of reaching export markets are reduced by means of improved transportation within the region, a primary activity and its associated manufacturing may be completely or partially excluded. In South Ontario the greatest growth rates in primary manufacturing occurred in the first twenty years of railway construction, i.e., 1851-1871. Most of this growth was associated with the sawmilling industry, the distribution of which changed substantially during the study period, suggesting that the railways permitted the exploitation of previously untapped areas. By far the greater part of the primary manufacturing represented in Table 2 was sawmilling. It was only in a few areas and mainly towards the end of the period that the processing of agricultural products for export assumed any importance.


CONSUMER AND PRODUCER GOODS

In a region developing on the basis of staple exports there are many grounds for expecting secondary manufacturing to be dominated by consumer goods industries. While a certain demand for producer goods will exist from the earliest days of settlement in a region such as Ontario, it is unlikely that until the export sector has manifested forward and final demand linkage effects

[3]See C. P. Kindleberger, Foreign Trade and the National Economy (New Haven and London: Yale University Press, 1962), pp. 196-205.

31

for some time that producer goods will grow to any significant extent. Economies gather momentum slowly, if at all. While income from the export sector will encourage indirectly some producer goods industries, it is more likely to first affect consumer goods, the growth of which will re-inforce the demand for producer goods. In secondary manufacturing the first thresholds will be found in consumer goods. Consequently, the greatest relative importance of consumer goods is expected in the early years. Through time, the relative importance of producer goods will grow as a result of absolute growth, especially if the export staples are instrumental in facilitating the growth of service centres, and demanding an improved transportation network. Thereafter, consumer and producer goods will grow together, with the unique circumstances of each region determining their absolute importance.

Even with staple exports growing it is likely that for some time the total income of the region will remain low with correspondingly low per capita incomes. Hence, the effective demand for goods will be weak, although strengthening. A second characteristic of the export-based region is that initial demand for producer and consumer goods is final demand. A few basic needs, for example, for food, clothing, shelter, fuels and utensils, will generate the first effective final demands. As Hirschman points out, industrialization can start only with industries that deliver to final demand, "...since ex hypothesis no market exists as yet for intermediate goods."[4] Small population, low population densities and low incomes prevent the attainment of thresholds for the production of many goods. In some cases, no doubt, thresholds are reached if the whole region is considered, but the cost of distributing from one establishment at smallest efficient size could be prohibitive. For many products domestic demand will be negligible.

The first secondary manufacturing to develop will, therefore, likely have the following characteristics. It will produce goods meeting simple basic needs. Products will require skill in their production and/or a lot of time. Without these conditions there is no reason why they cannot be made at home by those engaged in the primary sector unless technology necessitates production scales unattainable to the household. Raw materials will largely consist of domestic materials (flour, clay, leather, wool, etc.)

[4]Albert O. Hirschman, The Strategy of Economic Development (New Haven: Yale University Press, 1958), p.121.

and semi-manufactured products (cloth, iron and steel bars).
Production will be at a minimum scale of operation with each
production unit supported by a small number of people. Many
activities will, in fact, be represented by cottage industry, since
establishment of production requires little investment either in
buildings or equipment. The demand for most goods is widespread
throughout the populated area.

The distinguishing feature of the structure of a highly industrialized region is the importance of the producer goods group.
According to the estimates made by Dales, producer goods accounted
for 53 per cent of the value of output of primary and secondary
manufacturing in the United States in 1949 and 49 per cent in
Canada.[5] In 1870, the corresponding figure for Canada was 25
per cent. The most important contributor to this difference is
the unfinished producer goods group. In Canada, while investment goods moved from 8 per cent to 10.5 per cent in their share
of value of output of manufacturing between 1870 and 1949, unfinished
producer goods moved from 14.5 per cent to 31.5 per cent.[6] The
point is that it is weakness in unfinished producer goods that keeps
down the relative importance of producer goods and maintains the
supremacy of consumer goods during the early phases of development.

Unfinished producer goods become more important as the
division of labour in manufacturing increases. Revising a theorem
of Adam Smith, Stigler argues that the division of labour is limited
by the extent of the market.[7] As long as the market for manufactured goods is small and widespread, plants will be small and
widely distributed,[8] and a division of function between establish-

[5] See Table 4.

[6] Dales, "Estimates of Canadian Manufacturing Output by Markets, 1870-1915," p. 75.

[7] G. T. Stigler, "The Division of Labour is Limited by the Extent of the Market,"
Journal of Political Economy 59 (June 1951): 185-193.

[8] While similarities have been found between contemporary underdeveloped areas and
the areas which began their successful development in the 18th and 19th centuries, in
this matter the parallel ends. There have been many technological changes in recent
times, one result of which has been an increase in the minimum efficient scale of
production for many commodities. Normally, today's underdeveloped areas borrow
the latest technology when introducing the production of a good, so that often one or two
plants at minimum scales of production can absorb all the demand for any particular
product. For example, Guyana and Surinam are each adequately supplied by one modern
brewery. This is in striking contrast to the several score of breweries supplying South
Ontario in the 1860's. Consequently, there is less likelihood of a widespread distribution
of manufacturing compared to Ontario and other developing areas in the 18th and 19th
centuries.

ments will be inhibited. But as markets grow, establishments can relinquish the production of certain articles or parts to other establishments which can produce at lower costs at higher levels of output. Growth of intermediate goods production, however, is closely allied with agglomeration economies which cannot be realized to a significant extent until transfer costs are greatly reduced, and even then may only be slowly realized. While the market is limited, the possibilities of realizing agglomeration economies are restricted irrespective of transfer costs, for the low division of labour associated with a limited market eliminates many of the possibilities for the production of intermediate goods. Thus, the producer good element as a whole will be small, and will remain so until the chain of events precipitated by greatly reduced transportation costs associated with an enlarged market and with spatial concentration of manufacturing gets underway.

As Table 2 illustrates, the relative importance of consumer goods declined during the study period although there was a slight rise in the last decade. Conversely, producer goods grew in relative importance. Their rise, however, was relatively slight because primary manufacturing was rising at an even faster rate during part of the period, thereby keeping down the producer good share of total manufacturing. When primary and secondary manufacturing are separated and treated individually, the growth in importance of producer goods is more apparent. Table 3 shows the developments in the subdivisions of the major groups during the study period. Here, the contribution of primary manufacturing to the total manufacturing of the region is removed. The table shows a smaller relative decline in consumer goods and a greater relative increase in producer goods, developments to be expected as a region grows and diversifies its economy. Movement in the two groups was relatively smooth.

There is reason to believe that producer goods might take rather large leaps, breaking the evenness of slow, steady growth. The reason for this is simply that the minimum efficient scale of production for certain producer goods is large. A long time may elapse before the threshold for a plant at minimum scale of operation is reached; but once reached, a rapid increase in the relative importance of producer goods may be visible[9] particularly since a few "key" producer goods industries attract other producer

[9]This may be more apparent through a value of production index rather than by means of an employment measure, since certain industries for example, iron and steel, are capital intensive.

TABLE 3   STRUCTURE OF SECONDARY MANUFACTURING: 1851-1891 ABSOLUTE EMPLOYMENT

|  | 1851 | Per Cent | 1861 | Per Cent | 1871 | Per Cent | 1881 | Per Cent | 1891 | Per Cent |
|---|---|---|---|---|---|---|---|---|---|---|
| **Consumer** | | | | | | | | | | |
| Food, drink, tobacco | 2,124 | 8.6 | 2,728 | 9.2 | 6,373 | 4.6 | 8,247 | 10.8 | 10,357 | 9.8 |
| Sundries | 441 | 1.8 | 758 | 2.6 | 1,849 | 3.4 | 2,838 | 3.7 | 3,803 | 3.6 |
| Clothing and footwear | 10,487 | 42.4 | 11,770 | 39.8 | 14,743 | 27.9 | 20,498 | 26.9 | 29,892 | 28.3 |
| Household goods | 2,538 | 10.3 | 1,966 | 6.7 | 4,060 | 7.4 | 5,690 | 7.5 | 8,293 | 7.8 |
| Consumer durables | 1,807 | 7.3 | 2,553 | 8.6 | 7,717 | 14.1 | 9,384 | 12.3 | 13,803 | 18.1 |
| Total – consumer | 17,397 | 70.3 | 19,775 | 66.9 | 34,742 | 63.5 | 46,657 | 61.2 | 67,148 | 62.6 |
| **Producer** | | | | | | | | | | |
| Construction materials | 530 | 2.1 | 857 | 2.9 | 643 | 1.2 | 1,378 | 1.8 | 3,539 | 3.3 |
| Supplies to primary and tertiary | 379 | 1.5 | 150 | 0.5 | 979 | 1.8 | 953 | 1.3 | 1,266 | 1.2 |
| Investment goods | 2,624 | 10.6 | 3,945 | 13.4 | 9,383 | 17.1 | 12,287 | 16.1 | 15,563 | 14.7 |
| Total – finished producer | 3,583 | 14.3 | 4,952 | 16.8 | 11,005 | 20.1 | 14,618 | 19.2 | 20,368 | 19.3 |
| unfinished producer | 3,806 | 15.4 | 4,815 | 16.3 | 9,007 | 16.5 | 14,984 | 19.6 | 19,225 | 18.2 |
| Total – producer | 7,339 | 29.7 | 9,767 | 33.1 | 20,012 | 36.5 | 29,602 | 38.8 | 39,593 | 37.4 |
| Total – secondary manufacturing | 24,736 | 100.0 | 29,542 | 100.0 | 54,754 | 100.0 | 76,259 | 100.0 | 105,741 | 100.0 |

goods to them. The primary iron and steel industry is a good case in point.

The jump in the relative strength of producer goods expected with the establishment of an iron and steel plant did not occur during the study period but it quite easily could have done, for eight blast furnaces were established in Ontario between 1879 and 1914. The five set up before 1895 failed mainly because locations close to local ore supplies were chosen, rather than locations close to secondary market users and where easy access to substitute materials was available.[10] Had one succeeded the relative importance of producer goods in 1891 may well have been greater than it was.

Table 3 allows us to examine the structure of manufacturing in greater detail. Some aspects of it may seem surprising, such as the great relative importance of clothing and footwear. There are a number of reasons for expecting a different degree of development between the different types of manufacturing. During the period when settlement is still proceeding we expect a high self-sufficiency in food and drink products. A large proportion of the labour force is in agriculture and there is a strong probability that food will be the last side of home production to be totally relinquished by the farmer before he specializes completely on sending goods to the market, directing all his energies towards that end, and purchasing all his material requirements from specialists. But at the same time, even when the initial settlement is still going on and many people are still at the pioneer stage, service occupations will give some impetus to food industries. Some will appear very early notwithstanding a high self-sufficiency on the part of primary producers. Such industries will include flour and grist milling, distilling, brewing, and a few others. Their early establishment is explained by technical problems in home production, economies of scale and legislation, one or more of which take them out of the sphere of activities of farmers living at near-subsistence levels.

As regards the other consumer goods it is in fact unlikely that all farmers or other early settlers, except in the earliest migrations were even capable of fabricating their own consumer needs. Despite the limited range of their needs while establishing themselves in the new homes, and even allowing for a competence to produce articles with their own skill and labour, it is probable

[10] For the early history of iron and steel industry in Canada, see W. S. Donald, The Canadian Iron and Steel Industry (Boston: Houghton Mifflin, 1915).

that imports first satisfied many needs, and that specialists quickly appeared to satisfy consumer needs as farmers and others narrowed the range of their activities in the drive to produce primary exports. In his account of the development of the furniture industry in Ontario, Cooper describes the activities of one furniture maker whose experience must have been frequently repeated:

A typical story of the early 1860's tells of a young man who walked through the bush with his carpenter's kit from Waterloo County to the Queen's Bush. There he found work splitting rails for 50 cents per hundred. Then he bought some lumber from the local saw mill, and at night made articles of furniture which he sold to the farmers. In this way he obtained a little money as well as some farm produce which he sold to the local grocer. With the money he bought more lumber. He continued to do this until he had acquired enough capital to join others in starting a furniture factory. The firm that he and his partners formed progressed steadily; later some of the executive staff started their own plants nearby and so developed a furniture factory town. [11]

The emergence of different kinds of manufacturing reflects the changing priority and breadth of demands. Basic, widely distributed, and frequently felt needs will be answered first; accordingly, clothing and footwear are likely to have an early dominance. The cottage phases of these industries have very low thresholds and a relatively large number of people will be engaged in them.

Of the remaining elements of the consumer goods sector, consumer durables will most likely rank next to clothing and footwear in importance. At first, the range of consumers goods demanded by most of the population will be narrow and restricted. A number of factors account for this. In the 18th and 19th centuries the actual choice of available consumer goods was narrower than it is today. It is only in the last few decades that the range of consumer goods has greatly widened (T.V., radios, record players, washing machines, etc.). A wider range of consumer durable goods is to be associated with a higher standard of living than we expect to find amongst farmer settlers, even if they are prosperous. For some time most of the population would not have the income to spend on additional items once basic consumer durable expenditures had been made. Consumer durable needs would be largely restricted to furniture and stoves, although some of the wealthier members of the community would have a much wider range of demands.

[11]R. T. Cooper, "Furniture" in A Century of Industrial Development in Ontario, Studies in Selected Industries (Toronto: Ontario Department of Economics and Development, 1965), p. 53.

TABLE 4 VALUE OF OUTPUT OF CONSUMER AND PRODUCER GOODS INDUSTRIES
AS A PERCENTAGE OF TOTAL MANUFACTURING IN CANADA, 1870-1949

|  | 1870 | 1880 | 1890 | 1900 | 1910 | 1949 |
|---|---|---|---|---|---|---|
| Consumer goods | 55.0 | 51.0 | 47.5 | 43.0 | 39.0 | 34.5 |
| Producer goods | 25.0 | 29.0 | 31.5 | 33.5 | 42.5 | 48.5 |

SOURCE: J.H. Dales, "Estimates of Canadian Manufacturing Output by Markets,
1870-1915," Papers, Canadian Political Science Association, Conference
on Statistics, 1962 and 1963, p. 75.

Producer goods industries are likely to be dominated by
consumer goods industries for a considerable period of time.
According to Dales' estimates, producer goods were more important in the US as early as 1870, whereas, in Canada, their
dominance was not established until 1910. Table 4 shows the
movements of the two groups. It is necessary to make some
comments on this table and interesting to make some comparisons
with Table 2 (Absolute and Percentage Structure of Manufacturing
Employment by Major Groups, 1851-1891). Both tables show the
same thing, but in a different way. Table 2 shows the structure
of manufacturing by means of employment data while Table 4
does the same, utilizing value of output data. In view of the
different measures used it would scarcely be surprising if the
results were different, but it is striking how similar the tables
are for the three dates included in both tables (1871, 1881, and
1891). The closeness of results is remarkable not only because
different measures were used, but because Table 2 shows the
structure in Ontario, while Table 4 shows the structure for all
Canada. The difference between consumer goods results for
1871 and 1881 may partly stem from this fact.

Such similarity in results is encouraging, and strengthens
confidence in their validity, particularly in view of the elaborate
and partly intuitive processes by means of which the data were
derived. It is equally welcome to see that both tables show the
same trends in the relative positions of the two major groups.
The picture is one of continuous relative decline in consumer
goods and the converse in the case of producer, except, as shown
by Table 4, producer goods rose very swiftly between 1900 and
1910. In fact the relative increase of this period was greater

38

than the entire period from 1910 to 1949. The rapid rise at the beginning of the century coincides with the development of Canada's iron and steel industry which itself was closely tied to the settlement of the Prairies and extensive railway building there. The low producer goods figures at the beginning of the period show that it takes time for a considerable demand to develop for complex and/or costly equipment. At first, investment goods manufacturing will consist of simpler types of goods such as foundry products, agricultural tools, wagons, saddle and harness equipment, and other fairly "simple" goods. The "supplies to primary and tertiary sectors" will most likely develop in response to the rather more common and widespread needs of farmers and foresters for such goods as axes, dynamite, edge tools, etc.

Most complex capital goods, when needed, will be imported, because the skills and capital required for their production as well as the market will still largely be lacking. For reasons given earlier, unfinished producer goods will not be highly developed. Those present will mostly supply the more common consumer goods industries; for example, blockmaking and engraving will supply the printing industry; scouring and weaving will be related to dressmaking and tailoring; tanning related to boots, shoes, saddle and harness making and so on.

When Table 3 is examined in more detail, it is clear that while substantial absolute growth occurred in all types of manufacturing, there was no drastic change in structure. The most striking alteration was the relative decline in clothing and footwear. This largely occurred due to faster growth rates in other types of manufacturing. For example, while clothing and footwear grew approximately three times during the study period, consumer durables grew about seven times, investment goods six times, and unfinished producer goods about five. This suggests that thresholds were being reached for a wider range of goods, and that some import substitution was going on. In fact the results indicate a maturation of the industrial sector as a whole, but still slight compared to the changes that were to occur around the turn of the century. Relative decline in clothing and footwear was not matched by a corresponding large increase in another sub-group of manufacturing, rather it was matched by relatively small gains in most sub-groups.

CONCLUSION

The period under study was characterized by intermediacy, or
better, by its transitional character. By 1851 Ontario had known
several decades of growth. By that date and throughout the period,
the structure of manufacturing displayed a degree of maturity that
one would hesitate to identify with a simple pioneer economy.
But quite fundamental changes were still required before the
producer goods dominance of this century would appear. Nevertheless, the structure was changing and the industrial sector was
maturing, given that we associate maturity with a dominance of
producer goods.

# IV

# Spatial variation in the structure of manufacturing

Even the most casual observer could not fail to notice that in all regions certain activities cluster in a few localities. Such clustering differentiates structure through space, and means that aggregate structure depicts a situation that is unrepresentative of most parts of regions. In addition to this ubiquitous source of spatial variation in structure there are likely to be forces at work in export-based regions which have a far-reaching impact upon the location of economic activities, and therefore, also, upon spatial economic structure. This additional source of spatial structural variation is explainable with reference to the settlement process, the friction of distance, the locational requirements of different activities and many other factors. To explain structural variation is, however, a complex matter, and initially, no attempt is made here to provide a fully comprehensive explanation. Later chapters deal with the distribution of activities, and beyond that structure and distribution are considered jointly.

# SETTLEMENT PROCESS AND ECONOMIC STRUCTURE

Exponents of export-base theory have paid little or no attention to the spatial distribution of economic activities. Regions are normally regarded as uniform entities and no consideration is given to how and why the parts of a region differ in terms of growth. One of the major reasons for expecting variation in structure has already been mentioned, namely, all parts of a region are not settled simultaneously; rather, there is an out-ward movement from some point or area of initial settlement so that a few years, or several decades, could separate the date of first settlement in different areas of the region. This being so, one may hypothesize that the structure of manufacturing in any part of the region will reflect the age of settlement.

If a uniform plain assumption is made, settlement most probably would extend outwards evenly from the core area. Relaxation of this unrealistic assumption, and recognition of an uneven distribution of resources and natural transportation routes permits anticipation of irregularity in settlement and a diminished degree of concentricity in pattern. The circular pattern of sim-ilarly dated settlement implies a similar pattern would be found in the structure of the economy and in the structure of manufac-turing. If growth proceeds by means of a diversification process around the export sector, then the longer a part of the region has been settled, its resources exploited and some products exported, the greater the likelihood that the economy of that area has become diversified. In the total economy the primary sector will decline in relative importance as the export sector, through its linkage effects, stimulates the growth of tertiary and secondary activities.

If commencement of export activity varies with distance from the core, then the structure of the economy will also vary with distance. Even though the structure of the economy of the whole region will change if the region is successfully developing, the relationship between distance from the core and structure should continue to maintain itself simply because with increasing dis-tance from the core there has been a progressively diminishing time for the multiplier mechanism resting on the export sector to operate.

# TIME, DISTANCE AND THE STRUCTURE OF MANUFACTURING

It is not possible to be so positive about the structure of manufacturing because of the primary manufacturing component within it. Just as it is impossible to predict on the basis of general
principles what the relative importance of primary manufacturing
will be, so is it equally impossible to predict its locations and
spatial patterns. There is one exception. This is when we assume we have a resource which is ubiquitous, which alone would
give rise to primary manufacturing, which is exhaustible, and
which is in demand in world markets. Under such circumstances,
the structure of manufacturing in the sense of its division between
primary and secondary manufacturing could well exhibit a pattern
in its spatial and temporal variation. If the resource is exhaustible, as was timber in the American past, one could well expect
to see the major lumber areas moving outwards from the core
area in association with the extension of settlement. Each area
in turn would see primary manufacturing rise to its relative
peak and then decline again. With time the areas at their peak
would be further and further removed from the core, while conversely, primary manufacturing would decline with increasing
proximity to the core. Figure 1 attempts to provide an idealized
graphical representation of these ideas. Of course, as soon as
the resource is allowed to vary in quality, ease of exploitation,
etc., some unevenness and irregularity in the pattern would become manifest. But the essential outward movement of the areas
experiencing a relative peak in primary manufacturing would
still manifest itself. It should be noted that the diagram depicts
relative importance of primary manufacturing, because by allowing the quality of the resource and the cost of its exploitation,
etc., to vary, there are no reasons to expect regularity in pattern when dealing with absolute figures.

These statements are, of course, very hypothetical and are
only possible given the assumed conditions. In the absence of
these conditions it is quite impossible to generalize about likely
developments and nothing can be said about spatial and temporal
order in structure in the sense of division between primary and
secondary manufacturing.

With regard to secondary manufacturing the situation is less
unpredictable. While the magnitude of secondary manufacturing
could vary with the scale and success of primary activity and
primary manufacturing, reflecting the distribution of unique con-

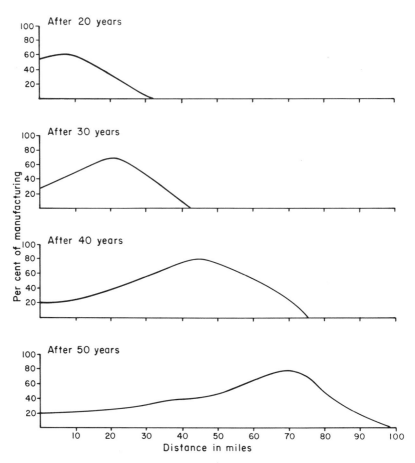

Figure 1.  Hypothetical variation in the relative importance of
primary manufacturing through time and space

ditions and characteristics in any particular region, there are
strong grounds for anticipating considerable order in the spatial
and temporal change in structure.  The first part of this chapter
pointed up reasons for anticipating a definite progression in the
development of secondary manufacturing.  It seems that the impact of the export sector will first express itself through final
demand linkage, that is, consumer goods.  And as examination
of aggregate structure shows, certain types of consumer goods
will be clearly dominant for a while.  With time, however, backward linkage will become more important, finding its expression
in the faster growth rates of producer goods, which may eventually become dominant.

44

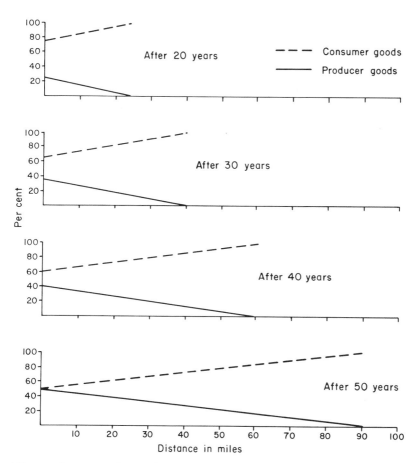

Figure 2. Hypothetical variation in the relative importance of consumer goods and producer goods industries through time and space (employment expressed as a percentage of total employment in secondary manufacturing)

If time and distance explain the spatial variation in the structure of manufacturing in the same way as it has been postulated they explain spatial variation in economic structure, the following developments should occur.

1. All areas at the same distance from the core will have much the same structure;
2. All areas at the same distance from the core will experience the same change in structure at the same time;
3. The further removed an area is from the core the greater

45

will be the consumer element in manufacturing and the lesser the producer element. This arises because the further an area is from the core, the less time there has been available for the operation of the processes that lead to the growth of producer goods.

Figure 2 attempts to show the hypothesized change in the relative importance of consumer and producer goods through time and space in a region where settlement has proceeded evenly outwards from an original nucleus of settlement. At ten-year intervals the relative positions of the two groups are shown by means of a graph. In each case the x axis represents distance along a line from the centre of the core and the y axis plots the percentages that consumer and producer goods each make up of total secondary manufacturing. This simply shows that the relative importance of each group changes as distance changes; that distance increases with time; that relative importance of each group changes as distance changes; that distance increases with time; that relative importance changes with time. For example, in the fourth decade the relative importance of consumer goods at forty miles from the centre of the core is the same as the relative importance of consumer goods at ten miles from the centre of the core in the second decade.

That many objections can be levelled at this simplistic representation of structural change is scarcely surprising. In the first place manufacturing cannot really be depicted as occurring along a continuous line through space. Manufacturing is a point phenomenon and such can only be approached through the aggregation of statistics pertaining to it for unit areas. The graphs aim at depiction of a concept, however, not at a true representation of the real phenomenon. In the second place much has been assumed and other considerations ignored, for example, whether settlement ever extends from only one core.

SETTLEMENT IN SOUTH ONTARIO

The assumptions of one settlement nucleus and regular extension of settlement from it, are quite unreal and it is doubtful it they have ever been produced in reality. The nature of settlement expansion obviously depends on the character of the physical environment and the interaction between this and the knowledge

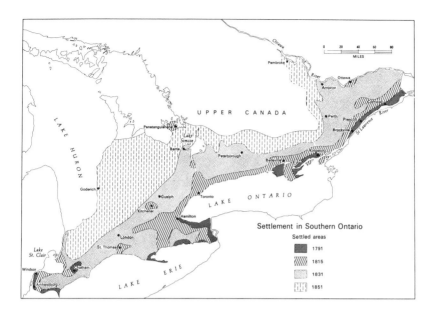

Map 2. Settlement in Southern Ontario

and technology of a group of settlers. In particular it depends
upon the period in history when settlement takes place, and on
the nature of the transportation system. In some parts of North
America, for example, railways preceded settlement and when
settlement subsequently got underway it created ribbons of agricultural land parallel to the tracks. The interstices were filled
at a later date. But perhaps this in only one example of many
possible variants from the theoretical ideal. The basic outlines
of concentricity of settlement related to time and distance may
still show through the seemingly unique and irregular patterns
of different parts of the world.

For Ontario, the idea of one original settlement core is certainly not relevant. Early settlement in Ontario, as in Quebec,
was greatly influenced by the accessibility provided by the Great
Lakes–St. Lawrence water system. Pioneer settlers took advantage of this natural routeway by first moving laterally. Inland
movement came later and it was by no means along a uniform
front. Map 2 shows that the first areas in Ontario to be settled
were widely separated along the shores of the Great Lakes and
the St. Lawrence River. Some of the areas conceivably could
be regarded as nodes or cores of settlement, but in eastern
Ontario there was a long narrow band of settlement that extended

47

from approximately Brockville to the border of Lower Canada. Succeeding settlement spread along the Lake Ontario shore and also penetrated inland from the head of Lake Ontario into the Grand River Valley and some distance beyond. In this a continuous settled area was created extending from a few miles east of present day London to the border with Lower Canada. For a time, for example in 1815, there were also several isolated areas of settlement which subsequently became part of a continuous band of settlement. Such settlement outliers included areas around the present day cities of Kitchener, Ottawa, and Penetanguishine. Thereafter, settlement moved outwards from a very broad front that extended more or less across the breadth of the province, moving away either from the shores of Lake Erie or the settled areas along Lake Ontario or the St. Lawrence River.

Map 1 may give the impression of a steady even extension of the settled area away from the lakes, whereas the settlement tended to move in a series of prongs following easy routeways into the interior. Rivers in particular were followed, with settlers moving inland away from the ports established at their mouths.[1] During the entire first half of the 19th century the settled area was extended away from the lakes and by 1851 most of South Ontario south of the Shield was settled in some form or another.

If systematic variation in structure is to be found, then it will be along lines representing the directions in which land was settled and its resources put to use to provide exportable commodities. Map 7 shows such lines imposed upon the areal units for which data were aggregated. It is obvious that the areal units are far from perfect for examining change in structure related to time and distance. In many cases, they contain areas settled at widely different dates. This is particularly the case in central and eastern Ontario where the areal units are large and elongated, sometimes embracing areas first settled over a sixty-year period. Interpretation of trends, therefore, must be tentative.

SPATIAL TRENDS IN ECONOMIC STRUCTURE

Before examining the structure of manufacturing it seems appropriate to examine spatial variation in the relative importance of

---

[1] Spelt describes many of these movements. See J. Spelt, The Urban Development in South Central Ontario (Assen: Van Gorcum, 1955).

the sectors of the economy because the variables of time and
distance should affect the economic structure and hence the relative importance of the secondary sector vis-à-vis the importance of the primary sector which theoretically is at first totally
dominant. The central question is whether or not the secondary
sector is equally important throughout the region; if not, is there
order in its variation?

When the region is subidvided it is clear that economic
structure varied through space and time. Examination shows
that there were very few areas in which the importance of the
primary sector was greater in 1881[2] than in 1851, and that at
every decade some areas exhibited a much greater dominance of
of this sector than was the case in others.

Maps 3, 4, 5, and 6 give the impression of some relationship between the relative importance of the primary sector and
distance from the first settled areas, although even on this vis-
usal basis it is clear that the relationship is not perfect. At
first glance Map 2 appears to show exactly the type of pattern
expected, for clearly the relative importance of the primary
sector is greater in the more recently settled areas. Equally
clear upon inspection, however, is the variation among the older
settled areas where the primary was generally less important.
The eastern areas had a greater dominance of the primary sector
than other areas settled at the same time or even later. In the
central part of the study region, York and Wentworth in particular
were much less dependent upon the primary sector. This suggests
that there may have been a strong inverse relationship between
population and the relative importance of the primary sector.
Recently settled areas with a high relative importance of the
primary sector would have a small population while older areas
with a lower relative imporatnce of the primary sector would
have a greater population. A correlation and regression analysis
reveals that there was a moderately strong linear relationship
between population and employment in the primary sector. A
correlation coefficient of -0.7 was obtained.

In the succeeding decades the strength of any apparent relationship between the importance of the primary sector and distance from the first areas of settlement seems to weaken. Some
areas experienced a rise, including areas along the Lake Ontario
shore, but much of this is probably attributable to the later exploitation of timber reserves in the inland parts of such areas.

[2]Organization of the 1891 census precluded the compilation of comparable data.

49

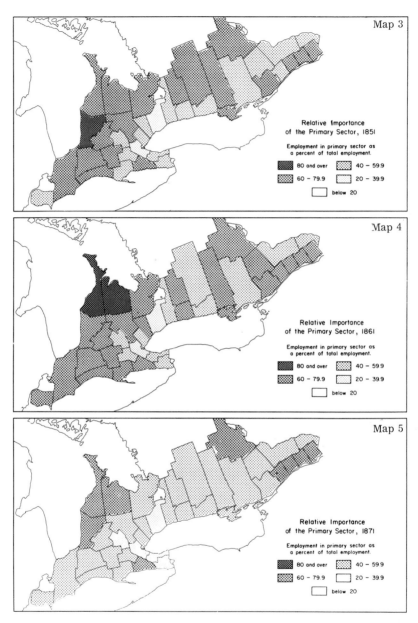

Map 3

Relative Importance
of the Primary Sector, 1851

Employment in primary sector as
a percent of total employment.

| | 80 and over | | 40 - 59.9 |
| | 60 - 79.9 | | 20 - 39.9 |
| | | below 20 |

Map 4

Relative Importance
of the Primary Sector, 1861

Employment in primary sector as
a percent of total employment.

| | 80 and over | | 40 - 59.9 |
| | 60 - 79.9 | | 20 - 39.9 |
| | | below 20 |

Map 5

Relative Importance
of the Primary Sector, 1871

Employment in primary sector as
a percent of total employment.

| | 80 and over | | 40 - 59.9 |
| | 60 - 79.9 | | 20 - 39.9 |
| | | below 20 |

By 1881 the picture was quite different. Most areas fell into
the same category with a primary sector between 40 and 60 per
cent of all activity, and the resulting pattern was one of high
uniformity. Even so, the most recently settled areas still had
the more important primary sectors, as for example, Bruce,

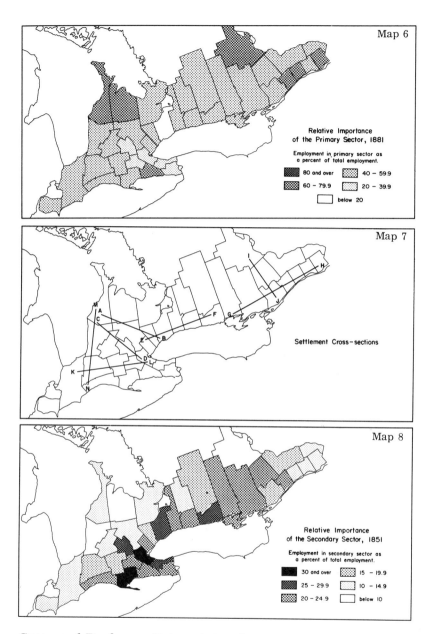

Map 6

Relative Importance
of the Primary Sector, 1881

Employment in primary sector as
a percent of total employment.

■ 80 and over ▨ 40 – 59.9
▨ 60 – 79.9 ▨ 20 – 39.9
□ below 20

Map 7

Settlement Cross–sections

Map 8

Relative Importance
of the Secondary Sector, 1851

Employment in secondary sector as
a percent of total employment.

■ 30 and over ▨ 15 – 19.9
▨ 25 – 29.9 ▨ 10 – 14.9
▨ 20 – 24.9 □ below 10

Grey, and Renfrew. But certain other areas settled at a much
earlier date than these also had primary sectors, the relative
importance of which was well above the mean, as for instance
Norfolk and Glengarry. The relationship with population was
weak. A correlation coefficient of only -0.36 was recorded.

51

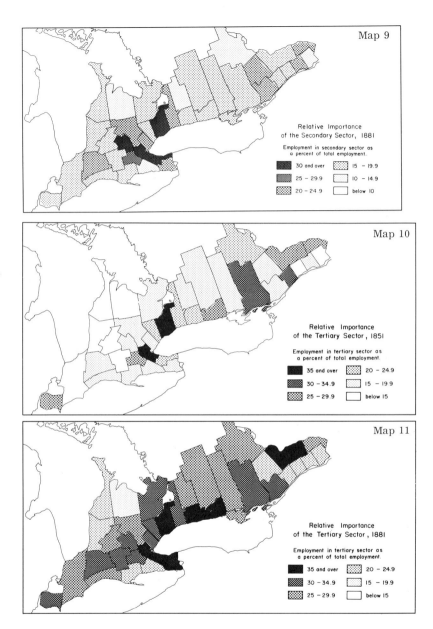

There appears to be no straightforward inter-connection between
date of settlement of an area and the relative importance of the
primary sector. Nevertheless, it can be said that these areas
where the primary sector was least important were all found
in the first settled areas.

While the maps are useful in illustrating a total regional pattern they are not ideal for showing a relationship between structure and distance because of the shapes of the areal units and because of the employment of grouped values that can obscure significant variation between similarly grouped areal units. A series of graphs was employed to circumvent this problem. In Figure 3 as in the following two diagrams, areal units have been arranged according to their position on one of several areal cross-sections depicted in Map 7. Shown in Figure 3 are the areal units along line A-B extending from Bruce to York, that is, from one of the last areas to be settled to one of the first areas to be settled. For each areal unit for each year the relative importance of the primary sector (percentage share of total labour force) was plotted on the vertical axis. These graphs show clearly the fall in the relative importance of the primary sector either from an 1850 or an 1860 peak. They also show that the relative importance of the primary sector at any time increased from the oldest to the youngest area, so that the relative positions of the counties were the same in 1881 as in 1851. Noteworthy is the progression in the decline of the primary sector from one area to the next until York is reached. Then the relative importance of the primary sector plummets. It seems almost as if an areal unit has been omitted between York and the neighbouring area.

Very similar results were obtained on all other lines extending through areas of progressively diminishing age (lines C-D, M-N, K-L, and I-J). For the purposes of allowing comparison with line A-B, graphs along line K-L are depicted (Figure 5). These show a fairly regular diminution in importance of the primary sector as time and distance increase. Middlesex is the major contributor to irregularity and appears to be playing a similar role to York on line A-B. It seems as if Middlesex and Oxford are in the wrong positions, for if regularity is to be obtained the positions of these two counties should be reversed.

In view of these results it is even more interesting to examine Figure 4, for in this case a line (E-F on Map 6) was run through several counties all of which were first settled at much the same time. A strikingly different pattern in obtained. Excepting York County, the relative importance of the primary sector in 1851 was between 45 and 55 per cent for all of them. And in 1881 they all lay between approximately 44 and 50 per

53

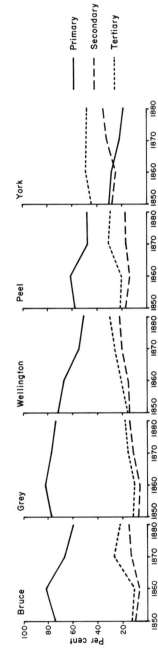

Figure 3.  Relative importance of the primary, secondary, and tertiary sectors in the areal units along line A–B (employment in each sector expressed as percentage of total employment)

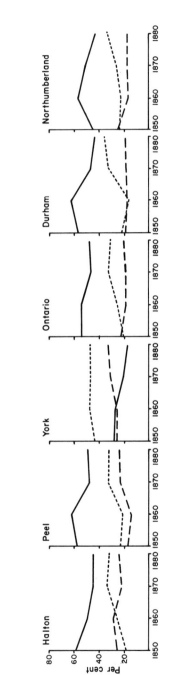

Figure 4.  Relative importance of the primary, secondary, and tertiary sectors in the areal units along line E–F (employment in each sector expressed as percentage of total employment)

cent. That is, they did not exhibit the gradation in values found along the lines passing through areas settled at progressively later dates. Although there was less uniformity, similar results were obtained along line G-H running through eastern Ontario.

If the relative importance of the primary sector is falling, it must be matched by movements in either the secondary and/ or tertiary sectors. In the region as a whole the secondary sector gained little ground during the study period, but this was certainly not the case for many subdivisions of the region. Maps 8 and 9 give some impression of the changes in the secondary sector from one area to another. It is difficult to see other than a very crude replication of the theoretical ideal of structure varying according to time and distance. But this is partly because the secondary sector contains primary manufacturing which is influenced by considerations other than time and distance. The emergent pattern is similar to that exhibited by the maps on the primary sector although the progression from high to low values is in the opposite direction. There is somewhat less uniformity among areas containing the oldest settlement but there is certainly no question that the areas consistently more important in the secondary sector were all among the first settled.

Figures 3 to 5 show the changes in the relative importance of the secondary sector. The same patterns repeat themselves except the trends are reversed. For instance, the graphs along line A-B from Bruce to York show quite distinctly that the secondary sector becomes more important through time in each area, and that the longer an area has been settled the more important the sector has become. Put another way, this means that the relative importance of the secondary sector diminishes with increasing distance from the earliest settled areas. The same trends are manifested along the other lines moving from recently settled to longer settled areas. As before, the lines running through Middlesex (e.g., line K-L), while showing a variation in the secondary sector with distance and date of settlement, suggest that Middlesex is misplaced. It seems as if it should be closer to the first settled areas.

As with the primary sector, line E-F is very interesting. Striking through areas of much the same date of original settlement its graphs show quite a different pattern. There is no progressive increase in the secondary sector from one area to an-

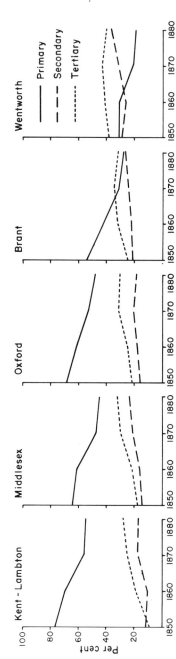

Figure 5. Relative importance of the primary, secondary, and tertiary sectors in the areal units along line K–L (employment in each sector expressed as percentage of total employment)

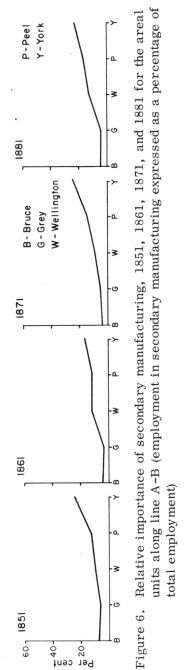

Figure 6. Relative importance of secondary manufacturing, 1851, 1861, 1871, and 1881 for the areal units along line A–B (employment in secondary manufacturing expressed as a percentage of total employment)

other. York is obviously in a category of its own with a much more important secondary sector than the other areas along the line. Between 1871 and 1881 the importance of the sector was remarkably uniform between them, and there seems to have been a levelling off during the same period. The other line parallel to Lake Ontario and the St. Lawrence River (line G-H) likewise produced no apparent pattern of movement in the secondary sector. While the secondary sector was more or less static in the region as a whole, the relative importance of the tertiary sector rose and that of the primary fell. As shown by Maps 10 and 11, almost every areal unit experienced a rise in the relative importance of this sector. Simultaneously settled areas, however, were neither uniform through space nor uniform in the change they experienced through time. Statements made about the two other sectors are equally applicable here. In both 1851 (Map 10) and 1881 (Map 11), while the earliest settled areas varied considerably between themselves, they nevertheless contained the areas with the greatest development of the tertiary sector.

Unlike the secondary sector there is little evidence of levelling out. The graphs record constant increases in this sector. For most areas at most times the tertiary sector was more important than the secondary sector. Where lines are drawn through areas of progressively more recent settlement the graphs show that the importance of the tertiary sector progressively declines and even though all areas along the line experienced an increase through time the progressive decline is maintained.

In summary, the following statements can be made:
1. There were considerable variations in structure within the region because, although most areas were passing through the same pattern of structural change, they were doing so at different times. All areas were moving towards maturity, that is, an increasing importance of the secondary and tertiary sectors, but some areas were more mature than others and more mature than the region as a whole. Throughout the period 1851 to 1881 two areas consistently stood out as being structurally more mature than the rest of the region. The first was York County standing on its own. The second was a line of counties running from the Niagara Peninsula through to the early settled inland counties on the Grand River Valley, namely, Brant and Waterloo. It will be apparent to some readers that these two areas are presently among the most industrialized in Ontario today.

2. Spatial variation in structure could by no means by described as haphazard. As a general rule the longer an area had been settled the more important were the tertiary and secondary sectors and the less important was the primary sector. The extension of settlement was not haphazard. It was first a lateral movement along the St. Lawrence-Great Lakes and then a vertical movement inland away from this axis.

3. In addition to time and distance, other factors were influencing the spatial variation in structure, for although early settled areas had the more mature structures, they themselves were not uniform, some being more mature than others. Also, there was no perfect uniformity among other simultaneously settled areas. It does seem that date of settlement and therefore distance are important in affecting spatial variation in sturcture. But this is not the whole story. Other factors must be considered.


SECONDARY MANUFACTURING

Secondary manufacturing grows in response to developments internal to the region. It develops as profitable opportunities are created, exploited, and realized. A widening range of profitable opportunities calls forth a widening range of industries. With time the opportunities for the introduction of each type will emerge, and accordingly, each type of manufacturing will grow. Hypothetically, industries will appear in a set pattern, emerging and growing as a reflection of the success of the region's export sector.

Elements of primary manufacturing are related to a completely different set of circumstances and conditions. These are external to the region, and do not directly stimulate secondary manufacturing. Some primary manufacturing industries develop when interaction between external demand conditions and internal supply conditions create profitable opportunities for their introduction. Naturally, some primary manufacturing is a response to internal conditions, and even export-orientated industries will supply a varying proportion of their output to the domestic market. Export-orientated primary manufacturing is one of the factors creating the conditions to which secondary manufacturing is a response. But it is not essential to the growth of secondary manufacturing. After all, primary manufacturing is an extension of the primary sector, and it is the primary sector which is essential for secondary sector development.

If an examination were made of the structure of manufacturing in the sense of a division between primary and secondary manufacturing, due regard would have to be given to their dissimilar growth conditions. Export-orientated primary manufacturing can wax or wane quickly according to variations in external demand conditions. It is locationally erratic and can appear and grow in any part of a region dependent upon the distribution, quality, and quantity of resources, and the profitability of exploiting these resources within the framework of contemporary technology. For this reason, the relative importance of secondary to primary manufacturing is likely to vary randomly through time and space. But this does not mean that the structure of secondary manufacturing will reveal a similar randomness.

Whether or not the primary sector has ancillary primary manufacturing is really unimportant for structural development, because both export-orientated primary industry and primary manufacturing have much the same effect in encouraging the diversification of the economy. Secondary manufacturing requires time to develop in quantity and structure. Irrespective of the importance of primary manufacturing in total manufacturing, the importance of secondary manufacturing will relate to the settlement process and the length of time an area has been settled. Export-orientated primary manufacturing can grow very quickly because it is supplying large external markets. Secondary manufacturing can only grow as fast as the region provides opportunities for expansion, and this requires time.

It is clear that the relative importance of secondary manufacturing in the total economy varied with distance, i.e., with date of settlement. Maps 12 and 13 (Relative Importance of Secondary Manufacturing in the Total Economy) show patterns very similar to those depicted by the maps showing the secondary sector as a percentage of the total economy. Graphs (Figure 6) drawn along line A-B (Map 7) show a striking increase in the relative importance of secondary manufacturing as the line moves from the "youngest" to the "oldest" areas. The graphs along line E-F (Figure 7) which passes through · similarly dated areas, do not show this progression.

59

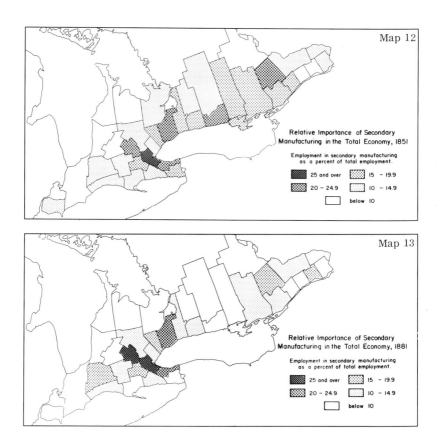

Map 12

Relative Importance of Secondary
Manufacturing in the Total Economy, 1851

Employment in secondary manufacturing
as a percent of total employment.

25 and over    15 - 19.9

20 - 24.9    10 - 14.9

below 10

Map 13

Relative Importance of Secondary
Manufacturing in the Total Economy, 1881

Employment in secondary manufacturing
as a percent of total employment.

25 and over    15 - 19.9

20 - 24.9    10 - 14.9

below 10

Between 1851 and 1891 the following developments occurred within secondary manufacturing. An overwhelming majority of the areal units experienced a relative increase in the producer good group and a corresponding decline in the relative importance of the consumer group. Thirty areal units out of a total of thirty-eight saw a relative increase in the producer good group. Hence it can be said that the greater part of the region was the scene of an increasing maturity in the manufacturing sector. Few areas saw a steady progressive decline in consumer goods. Rather the picture was one of variety, almost of chaotic confusion. The relative importance of each group rose and fell, sometimes quite sharply, with each areal unit providing quite distinctive patterns of movement. Figure 8 gives some impression of this diversity.

As a result of the variability expressed by sharp upward and downward movements in individual areal units there was very little spatial patterning in structural change at any time.

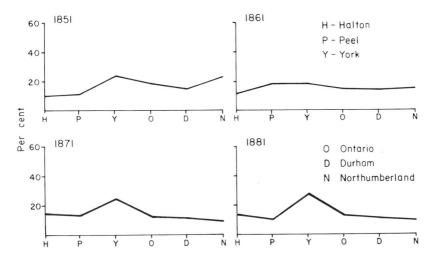

Figure 7. Relative importance of secondary manufacturing, 1851, 1861, 1871, and 1881 in the areal units along line E-F (employment in secondary manufacturing expressed as a percentage of total employment)

When areal units are arranged according to their positions on some of the lines on Map 7 and consumer goods expressed as a percentage of secondary manufacturing there is no manifestation of a progressive decline at any time (see Figure 9). Consumer goods declined throughout the period, but they did not fall in such a way as to exhibit a pattern that could be associated with time and distance.

Cartographic representation of the importance of the consumer goods group (Maps 14 and 15) no more reveals a spatial pattern than the other devices employed, although at the start of the period the pattern came quite close to what was expected. With the exception of Norfolk, which had the lowest consumer component, and Elgin, all the areas where consumer goods were of least relative importance were along the Ontario shore. Needless to say not all of the lakeshore areas can be included for Wentworth and Lennox-Addington-Frontenac were in the same category as many inland areas. The same can be said for the areas along the St. Lawrence River. But further evidence of the expected pattern is provided by the peripheral parts of the region. These, the last areas to be settled and exploited, had the highest consumer component.

61

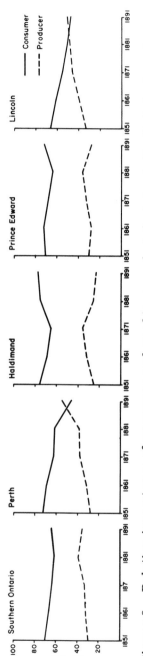

Figure 8. Relative importance of consumer and producer goods industries in South Ontario and selected areal units for 1851, 1861, 1871, 1881, and 1891 (employment in each group expressed as percentage of total employment in secondary manufacturing)

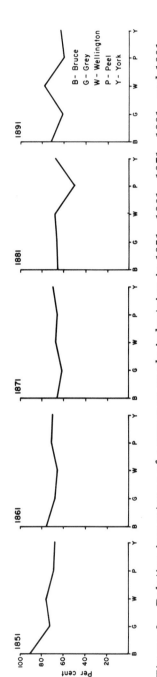

Figure 9. Relative importance of consumer goods industries in 1851, 1861, 1871, 1881, and 1891 in the areal units along line A–B (employment expressed as percentage of total employment in secondary manufacturing)

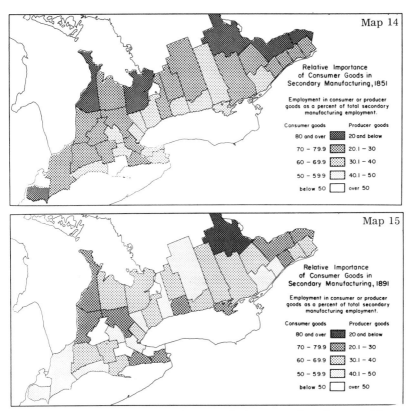

Map 14

Relative Importance
of Consumer Goods in
Secondary Manufacturing, 1851

Employment in consumer or producer
goods as a percent of total secondary
manufacturing employment.

| Consumer goods | | Producer goods |
|---|---|---|
| 80 and over | | 20 and below |
| 70 - 79.9 | | 20.1 - 30 |
| 60 - 69.9 | | 30.1 - 40 |
| 50 - 59.9 | | 40.1 - 50 |
| below 50 | | over 50 |

Map 15

Relative Importance
of Consumer Goods in
Secondary Manufacturing, 1891

Employment in consumer or producer
goods as a percent of total secondary
manufacturing employment.

| Consumer goods | | Producer goods |
|---|---|---|
| 80 and over | | 20 and below |
| 70 - 79.9 | | 20.1 - 30 |
| 60 - 69.9 | | 30.1 - 40 |
| 50 - 59.9 | | 40.1 - 50 |
| below 50 | | over 50 |

After 1851 there was a marked absence of pattern. The
relative importance of consumer and producer goods varied
erratically within and between countries, and the various subdivisions of the two groups exhibited a matching irregularity.
In short, the spatial distribution of structural change was
complex and confused. The various maps showing the relative
importance of selected subdivisions clearly point out the absence of spatial pattern in the structure of manufacturing. They
emphasize that there seems to be little or no relationship between the relative importance of a manufacturing group and the
time when an area is settled, and therefore, its distance from
first settled areas.

CONCLUSIONS

Economic Structure
The salient feature of the preceding analysis is that there was
no structural uniformity throughout the region while it was

63

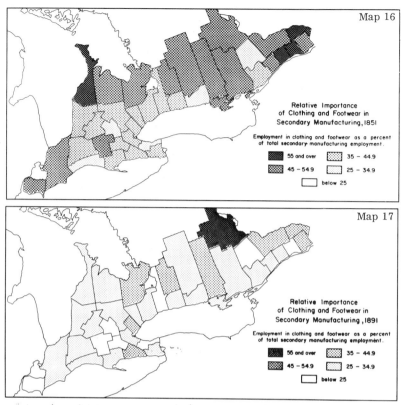

Map 16

Relative Importance
of Clothing and Footwear in
Secondary Manufacturing, 1851

Employment in clothing and footwear as a percent
of total secondary manufacturing employment.

55 and over    35 – 44.9

45 – 54.9    25 – 34.9

below 25

Map 17

Relative Importance
of Clothing and Footwear in
Secondary Manufacturing, 1891

Employment in clothing and footwear as a percent
of total secondary manufacturing employment.

55 and over    35 – 44.9

45 – 54.9    25 – 34.9

below 25

diversifying and maturing economically.

Dissimilarity in structure was to be anticipated for it is axiomatic that development cannot commence simultaneously in all parts of a newly developing region. The development process gets underway at progressively later dates as each part of the region is settled. The less time available to the development process the less mature the structure is likely to be. This raises the question of whether or not structural dissimilarity is simply a function of the length of time during which development processes have operated. If this were so we could anticipate a spatial regularity in structural variation that would reflect the way in which the region was settled. Of course, if settlement was spatially haphazard then so also would be the spatial distribution of structural patterns. But while the settlement of a region is most unlikely to extend outwards from a point or line in a perfectly even manner, it is no more likely to proceed in a completely haphazard manner. It must start somewhere and it must end somewhere and allowing for mod-

64

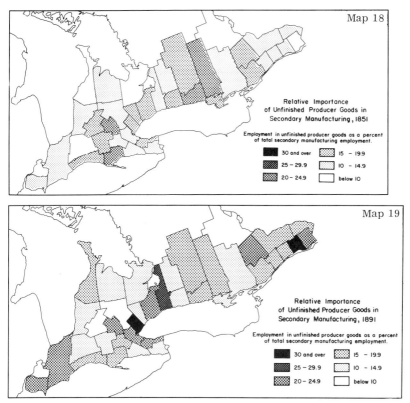

Map 18

Relative Importance
of Unfinished Producer Goods in
Secondary Manufacturing, 1851

Employment in unfinished producer goods as a percent
of total secondary manufacturing employment.

- 30 and over
- 25 – 29.9
- 20 – 24.9
- 15 – 19.9
- 10 – 14.9
- below 10

Map 19

Relative Importance
of Unfinished Producer Goods in
Secondary Manufacturing, 1891

Employment in unfinished producer goods as a percent
of total secondary manufacturing employment.

- 30 and over
- 25 – 29.9
- 20 – 24.9
- 15 – 19.9
- 10 – 14.9
- below 10

ifications arising from response to physical and human environmental factors, it will extend across space fairly evenly
from the beginning to the end of the process.

The structure of the economy and of manufacturing were
crudely examined in relation to this premise that structure
varies according to the time available for it to develop.

With regard to overall economic structure, it was found
that most parts of the region were exhibiting the same structural trends; that is, the primary sector was decreasing in
relative importance. In general, the longer an area had been
settled, the more important were the tertiary and secondary
sectors and the less important was the primary sector. To a
considerable extent the pattern of variation in structure matched
the way in which the region had been settled. Nevertheless the
spatial pattern had irregularities. Some areas were more
mature than other areas first settled at an earlier time. Such
irregularities suggest that while time is very important in explaining economic structure, it does not provide the total ex-

planation. The difference in structure found between eastern Ontario and the head of Lake Ontario, for example, the great difference in the importance of the secondary sector, obviously cannot be explained by a difference in time available to development processes, for these areas were settled at much the same time.

Several points should be considered here. First there are some methodological considerations. Could the data employed in the study cause unexplained variation? Census data are not entirely reliable and it is possible that some errors have been made in data transformation and other statistical manipulations. These could have been responsible for some minor variations in results, but it is most unlikely they would be responsible for the kind of difference that exists say, between York and Glengarry.

Part of the irregularity in variation may arise from the size and shape of the areal units used in the analysis. Such as they are, they can contain areas settled at widely separated dates so that calculations of structure could easily be unrepresentative of any of their particular parts. There is really no way around this problem, for even after exhaustive examination of settlement that resulted in the delineation of smaller areas of similarily dated settlement it would be impossible to fit the available economic data to the empirically derived areas.

Reality is always more complex than the simple models employed to investigate it. Every region has unique characteristics, physical and human, not encompassed by the parameters of a model. Of course, the model can be redesigned in many cases to accommodate them, or at least some of them. But it is doubtful if all unique circumstances and eventualities could be anticipated. At best, it may be possible to incorporate some of the more probable ones, predicting what effect they may have on structure if and when they occur within a region. One fails to see how this could be incorporated into a general model for when it is applied to a particular region there is no knowing where or when unique circumstances and events will occur in that region. They are "peculiarly unique" to the region.

In this matter thoughts are particularly directed towards unpredictable factors that can retard the development of a mature economic structure. Factors which facilitate it will be considered shortly. Two examples of possible retarding factors will be discussed.

If we return to the early explanatory remarks on export-base theory, it will be remembered that the theory is only applicable to regions with certain characteristics which "...have an absence of inhibiting traditions and have grown up within a framework of capitalist institutions responding to profit maximizing opportunities in which factors of production have been relatively mobile." While such conditions must be met by the greater part of the region it is perfectly feasible that there are pockets where they are lacking.

Then of course there is the already mentioned unique arrangement of resources in each region. These can cause irregularities in the expected pattern without totally disrupting it. The region will develop successfully if the export sector of the region as a whole is successful. It is quite understandable that the region may contain within itself areas which are not "pulling their weight." If these are too numerous the region may scarcely develop; but if they are the exception rather than the rule, the region in aggregate will advance in spite of them. They will, however, represent pockets of different structural development, perhaps areas with a permanently immature structure. The situation of eastern Ontario immediately comes to mind on this point.

It is axiomatic that just as some factors retard development others may facilitate it. A particularly industrious ethnic group, or a particularly favourable resource endowment, may enable some areas to develop a mature structure more quickly than others. These fall into the category of what are here regarded as unique factors. But above and beyond these particular features of particular regions, there are forces and factors so far not alluded to, which would be found in all regions, and which enable parts of a region to mature more quickly than others. These forces are more than likely to re-inforce the advantages certain areas have by being settled early. These are the forces affecting the distribution of manufacturing and services. Manufacturing, which is the central concern of this study, will distribute itself in such a way that the secondary sector develops faster in some areas than in others.

The structure of the economy was examined to realize the extent of spatial variation in the relative importance of the secondary sector. Although there were irregularities, there was a clear diminution in the importance of the sector as time available for its development decreased. Among the irregularities the most significant was the variation between similarily dated settlements. A similar variation was found in the tertiary sector. The conclusion is drawn that while the importance of the sectors varied with the time available for their development, they varied in a way which suggests that certain areas had more than the advantage of extra development time. The explanation of this is not found in export-base theory, but in that theory directed towards explanation of the location of economic activity.

## Structure of Manufacturing

The structure of manufacturing was considered in relation to time. There were no grounds for anticipating a spatial regularity in the ratio of primary to secondary manufacturing, but there were reasons to anticipate some spatial regularity in the structure of secondary manufacturing.

It was found that most areas repeated the trends manifested by the entire region. There was, however, very limited evidence of structure maturing according to the length of time available for development. Maturation, in the sense of an increase in the relative importance of producer goods, occurred in most areas. Some areas depicted a situation that was not reached by Canada as a whole until after the turn of the century, namely, a producer goods dominance in secondary manufacturing. In 1891 these areas were Lincoln, Brant, and Perth. Of the first two it could be expected, but there were other areas (for example, York, Halton, Durham, and Prince Edward Counties), where theoretically the likelihood of the development was just as great.

Examination of the sub-groups revealed no spatial regularities. Most areas showed the expected trends in structure but there was certainly no relationship between the relative importance of a group and the time an area had been developing.

The relative importance of industry groups in an areal unit depends upon the way in which industries are distributed through the region, that is, on the "quantities" or "amounts" of manufacturing found in different areas. Structural variation therefore arises out of the distribution patterns of different industries. In dealing with distribution we are dealing with absolutes. In South Ontario, industries, in an absolute sense, distributed themselves in such a way that there was no special regularity in the proportion each constituted of the total.

So far the question of distribution has not been considered. This is the next step of the analysis. The central question is what factors determine the distribution of manufacturing in a developing economy. The first stage is to examine some general principles and ideas that offer guide lines to a study of distribution. With the aid of these it is hoped to develop a hypothetical explanation of why manufacturing grows more strongly in some areas than in others and why its groups distribute themselves in such a way that structure varies in a patternless manner through space and time. Thereafter, the reality of distribution in South Ontario will be examined.

# V

# Distributional patterns of manufacturing: theoretical considerations

Parts of this chapter draw heavily on location theory in attempting to explain the spatial behaviour of manufacturing. However, a review of the developments in industrial location models over the last several decades, with their intricacies and deficiencies, cannot be provided here. At intervals, comprehensive reviews of the literature have been published. Several review articles have appeared lately, originating in a growing dissatisfaction with location theory, particularly with Weberian and neo-Weberian location theory. These point up the deficiencies of extant models and at times suggest new directions of attack. The fullest treatment of the literature is provided by Hamilton,[1] but articles by King[2] and Alonso[3] are also valuable. Of less recent origin is Isard's major contribution to location theory.[4] This is valuable not only for the ideas

[1] F. E. Ian Hamilton, "Models in Industrial Location" in Models in Geography, eds. R. J. Chorley and Peter Haggett (London: Methuen, 1967), pp. 361-424.

[2] L. J. King, "Approaches to Location Analysis," The East Lakes Geographer 2 (August, 1966): 1-16.

[3] William Alonso "Location Theory" in Regional Development and Planning, eds. John Friedmann and William Alonso (Cambridge, Mass.: The MIT Press, 1964), pp. 78-106.

[4] Walter Isard, Location and Space Economy (Cambridge, Mass.: The MIT Press, 1956).

expounded but also for its review of theoretical antecedents. In the sixties, Haggett[5] discussed aspects of industrial location models as well as many other types of models of relevance to problems in human geography.

Throughout the years many important modifications and additions have been made to the central works of location theory, [6] but almost without exception they have received coverage in the works of the above-mentioned authors.

To claim that this section adds conceptually or methodologically to industrial location models would be pretentious to an extreme. A contribution in that direction in not intended. Rather, the aim is to employ elements of industrial location theory as explanatory components in what is hoped is a fresh approach to a central geographic problem, namely the "temporal dynamics of spatial structure and spatial systems."[7] In particular the emphasis is placed upon spatial characteristics of manufacturing looked at within an economic development framework.

Pred states that "... industrialization and urbanization may be interpreted as interacting spatial processes by modifying traditional location theory and wedding it with concepts of contemporary origin."[8] Working at a more macro-scale of enquiry than Pred and subsuming urbanization, this study attempts to examine the causal relations between economic development and the distributional aspects of economic activity. Employment of certain elements of location theory in conjunction with other concepts, both old and new, from economics and economic geography, provides the conceptual and analytical bridge between economic growth and the spatially expressed components and products of it. In many ways current models inhibit essays at "explanation" of the evolution of industrial

---

[5] Peter Haggett, Locational Analysis in Human Geography (London: Edward Arnold Ltd., 1965).

[6] Alfred Weber, Theory of the Location of Industries (Chicago: University of Chicago Press, 1929), an English translation of Uber den Standort der Industrien, with introduction and notes by Carl J. Friedrich; and August Lösch, The Economics of Location (New Haven: Yale University Press, 1954). An English translation by William H. Woglom of Die Raumliche Ordnung der Wirtschaft.

[7] National Academy of Sciences, The Science of Geography, Report of the ad hoc Committee on Geography: Earth Sciences Division, NAS-NRC Publication 1277 (Washington, D. C.: National Academy of Science-National Research Council, 1965), p.4.

[8] Allan Pred, "Some Locational Relationships Between Industrial Inventions, Industrial Innovations, and Urban Growth," The East Lakes Geographer 2 (1966): 45.

patterns through time. Some elements of these models however can provide crucial links in an explanation that must also incorporate conceptual props from other disciplines which have applied them to problems of a non-geographic nature.

## THE MARKET AND A FINITE NUMBER OF LOCATIONS

While primary manufacturing is tied to raw material deposits, whether they be sporadic or ubiquitous, secondary manufacturing can theoretically supply any areal segment of the market from any point in the spatial continuum of the market. In practice, the number of potential production points for market-oriented industry is not infinite as soon as the economic growth process is initiated. The association of industrialism with urbanism provides the explanation for the reduction of points to finiteness. As a region grows, a matrix of non-agricultural population clusters is formed. While it is certainly not unalterable, this matrix endures with a high degree of persistence as a region develops. Differences develop as some clusters grow faster than others, developing into towns, or eventually cities, while other centres remain perpetually as villages. Manufacturing is a factor of very considerable importance in causing the selective growth of certain centres over others.

We can think of the distributional patterns of manufacturing industry as being arranged and re-arranged on a locational matrix of non-agricultural settlement clusters. The patterns at any time will depend on the manner in which industries are allocated to different nodes of the matrix. At one extreme, all establishments may be located in one city, and at the other extreme, is the virtually impossible likelihood that they are equally distributed among all the nodes. In reality we would expect the distributional pattern to lie between these two extremes, but with the tendency for manufacturing to move towards ever greater concentration in its distribution.

# SETTLEMENT, LOCATION, CONCENTRATION, AND WEBER'S ONE POINT MARKET

A useful approach to understanding the development of total industrial patterns within a region seems to be to start at the beginning of a region's economic development, when conditions presumably are at their simplest, and proceed from there, systematically incorporating the increasing complexity that develops with time.

Let it be assumed that settlement has been underway for some decades, with agriculture and other activities moving into the region, and that the export sector has successfully stimulated the economy such that a demand exists for some manufactured commodities with production thresholds attained. What factors control plant location within this environment? As a first step in answering this question attention is diverted to Weber's location model.

Industrial location models are based on the concept of economic man, and on the corollary that entrepreneurs seek to maximize profits. There are two main approaches: the Weberian, or least-cost approach, which abstracts from the reality of a spatial market and variability in sales through space; the Lösch or market-area approach, which abstracts from the reality of spatial variation in production costs.

Weberian theory has been designed to explain location given a set of assumptions describing rather atypical conditions. It was developed to handle a situation in which raw material point sources are known and likewise the one-point market place. Numerous assumptions are made; for example, demand is inelastic; transport rates are directly proportional to distance and vary only according to weight. With raw material and market points specified the locational problem becomes, first of all, one of determining that point where total transport distance is minimized. This is the least-cost location for supplying the specified market unless total costs can be lowered through deviation to a point offering labour and/or agglomeration economies. Deviation occurs only if the savings per unit output at the new location are equal to or greater than the extra transport costs per unit output incurred by moving the location away from the least-transport-cost point. Many features of Weberian theory have been criticized. Hamilton provides a summary of the major criticisms and points out that: "By disproving the reality of Weber's basic assumptions...critics have undermined the very essence of his model."[9] Nevertheless, there is a great deal in Weber's writings that is of real value in understanding the development of total distributional patterns. Some of his ideas are explored in subsequent paragraphs. In particular, it is interesting to relate his theory of the location of the individual plant to his concept of locational strata.

LOCATIONAL STRATA

In addressing himself to the likely sequence of events when a population enters an unoccupied area for the purpose of building up an isolated economic system, he conceived the idea of locational strata.[10] The first is the basic agricultural stratum that lays down the locational framework for subsequent economic development. This corresponds to the market area and is areally expansive through time, thus echoing Perloff's and Wingo's hinterland concept.[11] On this market area consumption nodes develop. In the Weberian system these reflect the distribution of the locational components of a primary industrial stratum. But Weber assumed a closed economy, and thus the antithesis of an export-based region. In an open economy there seems to be no need for primary industry to be a pre-condition for secondary industry. If agriculture is export oriented, a system of service centres connected by transport linkages inevitably develops to supply the services and organization essential to farmers and their commercial activities. The Weberian closed system requires the primary industrial stratum to provide the locational base for the next stratum, namely, the secondary industrial stratum; but in an open economy it is perfectly feasible for the agricultural stratum to be the locational base of a service stratum which then provides the nodal market points for secondary industrial activity.[12]

[9] F. E. Ian Hamilton, "Models in Industrial Location," p. 217.

[10] Alfred Weber, Theory of the Location of Industries, pp. 214-221.

[11] H. Perloff and L. Wingo, "Natural Resource Endowment and Regional Economic Growth," in Regional Development and Planning, eds. John Friedmann and William Alonso (Cambridge, Mass.: The MIT Press, 1964), p. 217.

[12] These remarks may be based on a mistaken interpretation of what Weber, or perhaps his translator, meant by the terms primary and secondary.

There are strong resemblances between Weber's locational structure and Friedmann's notice of regional structures.
The latter talks of the immature and mature regional structures. The first

...will be characterized by a low order of functional specialization, with
many small independent communities spread out fairly evenly over the land-
scape. Each little community will be the economic centre of a small agricultural production area....[13]

This kind of structure would characterize the export-based
region in its early decades of development. The small independent communities, whether associated with the primary
industrial stratum or tertiary activity, would represent the
loci for Weber's secondary industrial stratum.

It was also recognized by Weber that most secondary
industries do not supply a market that is co-extensive with the
total market area. For example, the market for machine
tools is composed of that group of establishments employing
machine tools in their production processes. In spatial form
this market is likely to be very different from the market of
the baking industry which is essentially the total regional
market area. Implicit in his work is a recognition of different
scales of production in different industries. Consequently, he
sees the third stratum as being composed of numerous substrata each of which "...is oriented to and is smaller than
the preceding one, the first substratum being the only one
directly oriented to the primary industrial stratum."[14]

Weber also introduced two strata that develop independent
of economic forces. The first is the central organizing stratum, while the other, the central dependent stratum, is related to it in the same way the secondary is related to the
primary stratum. Probably, Weber greatly underestimates
the significance of these. In the first place, it is doubtful if
they do develop completely independent of economic forces.
The capital of a region, for example, may be located in that
centre that is growing most rapidly, perhaps because of above-
average accessibility. The centre may then grow more
rapidly in view of its capital status. There is certainly no

[13] John Friedmann, "Locational Aspects of Economic Development," Land Economics
32 (1956): 219.

[14] Walter Isard, Location and Space Economy, p. 29. It is interesting to note the
resemblances between Weber's idea of substrata and Lösch's concept of nets of market
areas, with the mesh size changing according to different economic activities.

doubt that the organizational stratum can powerfully influence the spatial patterns of economic growth and thence the long-term forms of spatial structure. Selection of a centre as administrative capital may cause it to become the focus of regional transportation routes. This has many implications for spatial growth patterns, particularly through the initial advantage with which the centre is endowed.


LOCATIONAL STRATA AND THE SINGLE PLANT

These ideas on spatial structure were never clearly related by Weber to his theory of individual plant location. But he did provide enough conceptual stepping stones to permit the conjunction of the two sets of ideas. If we return to the settled area of the newly developing export-based region, we find this is co-extensive with the agricultural or primary stratum which represents the maximum market area. With time, and as an inevitability of economic development, population clusters develop. These represent the market nodes, and individually each is the market in the classical Weberian location problem. In this situation a market node or point, and one or more raw material sources[15] are designated. First of all, the least-cost, or optimal location is found on the basis of transportation costs alone. Almost invariably it will be found at the market or raw material source. In recognition of assumptions already made, primary manufacturing will always locate at the raw material, and as a corollary, secondary manufacturing will always locate at the market.

The question is -- which market? Weber never analyzed the question of which market location is chosen in the first place. The market location is always given in this theoretical approach. Weber's hypothetical entrepreneur never has to consider a choice between alternative market areas or between alternative market points. It must be assumed from Weber's conception of locational strata and his appreciation of the role of agglomeration in industrial location, that he visualized a situation in which numerous entrepreneurs first of all select a point market, and locate at the least-cost point to supply that market.

[15]Weber did not allow raw material sources to possess areal dimensions.

WEBER AND AGGLOMERATION

It is strange that even though so many of his ideas on individual plant location are based on faulty assumptions and evasion of vital locational considerations, his ideas on agglomeration and total orientation of industries come close to describing reality. Even if Weber had not considered locational deviation to low labour cost locations, and deviation arising from agglomeration economies, there is nothing in his theory to suggest that one market point would not be selected by several plants producing the same product, or that plants of several different industries would not locate at the same market point. He never attempts, however, to describe or predict resultant total regional patterns if this is occurring. But we can assume that the magnitude of manufacturing at any point will be greater, the larger the potential market at any market point. Weber discusses concentration of plants at one market point above and beyond concentration arising from the fact that several entrepreneurs happen to select their optimal locations with regard to a particular market point.

An entrepreneur can be attracted to a location other than the movement minimization one, if the savings in labour cost per unit of output are greater than the extra transport costs involved. Weber also argues that agglomeration economies can cause a location deviation from both the minimum transport and labour cost locations to a third and final optimal cost point. An agglomerative factor is defined as "...a cheapening of production or marketing which results from the fact that production is carried on to some considerable extent at one place... ."[16] Two sets of agglomerative forces are recognized. First, there are internal economies of scale, that is, production and organizational economies internal to the plant. Second, there are economies of association that include the development of technical equipment, labour organization, and marketing economies.

Although the location of the individual plant is uppermost in his mind, by considering agglomeration he is unavoidably moving from single locations to patterns of distribution, presenting a picture (albeit implicitly at times) of numerous plants of different industries finding their optimal locations to supply different point markets. Now, at no time does Weber employ

[16] Weber, Theory of the Location of Industries, p. 126.

77

the term "market area." In fact, the normal tendency is to associate him with the one-point market. Yet, careful reading of his chapter on agglomeration[17] indicates that his speculations about it only make sense if he permits of a conceptual switch from a one-point market to one with spatial dimensions. In the first instance Weber discusses the familiar economies of scale within the plant. If this type of concentration occurs, axiomatically, the centre where the larger plant is established must serve the markets of the small workshops which it displaces, thereby serving a market area. Agglomeration also occurs "...when local aggregation of several plants simply carries farther the advantages of the large plant."[18] If several plants of the same industry or different industries come together at one point, then this centre of agglomeration must serve the markets from which plants theoretically have been deviated in order to agglomerate.

Many allege that Weber's theory lacks dynamism. To a degree this is true. But there is no question that he understood agglomeration as an on-going process. Essentially, he saw manufacturing as always moving towards concentration, although absolute concentration would never be reached. Before examining this point in more detail let us see how these aspects of Weberian theory so far considered will affect the developing export-based region.

Individual plants or workshops are set up and located to supply market nodes. Establishments locate at the several market nodes in the settled parts of the region. There is every reason to expect that many market nodes are chosen by plants of several different industries, and quite possibly by two or more plants of the same industry. The bigger a market node the more industry one would expect to find located there. Due to the nature of the region's spatial development, there is an unavoidable and inevitable spatial inequality in consumption power. The longer an area has been settled, the greater consumption power is likely to be, and hence the more manufacturing likely to be found there. Consequently, even when we discount the operation of true agglomeration forces as understood by Weber, we can anticipate concentration of manufacturing in the earlier settled parts of the export-based

[17] Ibid., pp. 124-172.
[18] Ibid.

region. As argued earlier this means that concentration is built into the spatial structure of this type of economic region. It will be found even at the earliest stages of development. When agglomeration arising through economy is added, there is strong reason to anticipate continued concentration in those areas where industry is already concentrated, because it is such areas that provide the economies derived from agglomeration. Accidental and non-accidental agglomeration will therefore mutually re-inforce one another, and the earlier a part of a region is settled the greater the likelihood that it will feel the effect of these interacting forces.

In Weber's eyes pure agglomeration occurs if there is a function of economy for the plants involved, and develops where the critical isodapanes[19] of the plants overlap. He never explicitly stated that agglomeration must necessarily occur at an existing market node. But in the case of secondary manufacturing supplying the domestic market, a location not at a market node would be illogical, if only from considerations of labour supply. Furthermore, it would not make sense for the node where agglomeration occurs to be smaller than the nodes from which individual plants deviated, for implied in agglomeration is a greater level of production at the agglomeration than the total output of the individual units at their physically separated locations.

Agglomeration is a feature of most economic activities, and is not confined to specific types of regions. In general we can be more certain of its occurrence than about the location of its occurrence. In a previously uninhabited export-based region we can be more certain of its location than is generally the case, because when a region has been progressively settled through time, market nodes in the longest settled areas are likely to be larger, so that the probability of more and larger plants is greater. The larger the production units, or as Weber would say -- "the higher the units" -- the greater the likelihood of the overlap of critical isodapanes, so the possibilities of agglomeration will be correspondingly greater. The early start of parts of the region therefore allows the inauguration of a cumulative process which is virtually irreversible.

[19] An isodapane is a line connecting the locus of points of equal total transport costs. The critical isodapane is the line along which the savings from agglomeration exactly balance the extra transport cost resulting from deviation from the minimum transport cost location.

For any developing region it is to be anticipated that population densities will rise and transportation costs will decline. Such developments further encourage agglomeration. As transportation costs are lowered the possibilities of location deviation to take advantage of agglomeration economies are constantly improved. The larger markets necessary to larger units of production are created both by the increasing density of population and by spatial extension of the market. Again, such trends will favour the early as opposed to the recently settled areas. If manufacturing contains within itself concentrative tendencies, and some parts of a region are growing more successfully than others, it is only reasonable to expect the concentration to occur in these successful areas because they offer more profitable opportunities to a greater number of entrepreneurs.

Consideration of the region's organizational structure as understood by Weber is very relevant here. Unquestionably, the spatial administrative pattern has a powerful impact on spatial economic structure. At the least, it can serve to set the seal on the future development of spatial patterns. The capital city and major regional administrative centres will be the first centres to be linked up by an improved transportation system. This indubitably enhances their chances of developing strong manufacturing sectors. In Ontario, one decision above all others influenced the form of spatial structure as it has developed up to the present time. This was the decision to make Toronto the capital of the province. Several other centres in South Ontario could just as well have been chosen, for the site and situation of Toronto had few particular advantages. Kerr and Spelt state that "...an analysis of site and situation alone does not suffice to explain the birth and growth of the city."[20] But once the decision was made, the result was "...an indelible imprint on the geography of Ontario."[21]

Agglomeration, as Weber noted, is aided and abetted by many factors. For instance, as the value added through manufacture increases, the agglomeration potential of manufacturing also increases because transport costs become less and less important in total costs. Nor did he neglect division of labour in manufacturing. As production processes are

[20]Donald Kerr and Jacob Spelt, The Changing Face of Toronto, Memoir 11 (Ottawa: Geographical Branch, Mines and Technical Surveys, 1965), p. 31.

[21]Ibid., p. 35.

subdivided among plants in response to extension of the market in a growing region, the later stages of production tend to be oriented towards the consumption nodes; "...these remaining locations will almost always be situated at the place of consumption, due to advantages of the market."[22] The familiar notion of localization economies for industries related through their materials, or what Estall and Buchanan describe as the economies of vertically linked industries,[23] is introduced as another factor leading to agglomeration. "It is of importance for this agglomeration that the different processes be rooted in the same place and, therefore, lie near one another...."[24]

Although many of his assumptions are faulty, and others are quite unrealistic, and although he neglects certain aspects of agglomeration, Weber's theory in total creates a picture that comes close to reality. Entrepreneurs do not search for optimal locations. Each selects a location that is least cost for supplying a specific market. In so doing, they cluster at certain nodes which have advantages for capturing more manufacturing activity. Conjunction of agglomeration with Weber's concept of locational strata produces a pattern of high concentration in markets and production, and a continuous but weaker market and production area with more dispersed settlement, population, and manufacturing.

The coalescence and overlapping of market areas with each other and with the centres of areas of material supply would result, as in reality. Industries, therefore, will procure their inputs from, and distribute their outputs to, a point, many points, or most usually, an area or many areas which tend to adjoin or overlap.[25]


THE MAXIMUM PROFIT LOCATION

In Lösch, we find one of the most powerful critics of the Weberian approach. He argued that it is of no significance to find the point of lowest cost because the demand for most products is elastic and varies with price, so that the optimum

[22]Weber, Theory of the Location of Industries, p. 188.

[23]R. C. Estall and R. O. Buchanan, Industrial Activity and Economic Geography (London: Hutchinson University Library, 1961), p. 109.

[24]Weber, Theory of the Location of Industries, p. 205.

[25]Hamilton, "Models in Industrial Location," p. 375.

location as understood by Weber would shift with each change in price. The right location is that where maximum profits can be made at the optimal level of production. The gap between costs and revenue is the important factor, there being no necessity that the least-cost location should coincide with the greatest-profit location.

The optimum location of Lösch is in fact quite a different sort compared to the least-cost location of Weber. He conceived of the optimal as that out of all possible locations within a region where, at a given scale of production, supplying a market of a certain size, profits are greatest. He also recognized that any changes either in the supply or the demand side would change the position of the optimal location. Weber never considered the optimal location in this sense, and there is no indication that this was his intention. In many ways his approach stays closer to the real world than that of Lösch. These two men were not theorizing about the same kind of location. Once the market is selected, irrespective of the reasons, Weber asks how costs can be minimized in supplying it. This is much closer to the way in which entrepreneurs behave than the behaviour which would be necessary to find the Löschian optimal location. In this case the optimal location is the best out of all possible locations. Its discovery would involve consideration of all possible supply and demand considerations for every possible location and market area, at all possible levels of production. Lösch acknowledges that the optimal location in this sense cannot really be found because all points in a region could never be analyzed in the necessary manner, so that the entrepreneur could never be certain that unexamined or partially examined locations would not yield a higher return. Hence, he concluded: "There is no specific and unequivocal solution for the location of the individual firm, but only a practical one: the test of trial and error."[26]

From a theoretical standpoint Lösch's optimal location is more acceptable than that of Weber, but an entrepreneur is almost certainly going to behave more like an actor in the Weberian model than in the Löschian model. Lösch himself states that entrepreneurs can only proceed by trial and error, for it is impossible for them to possess the vast quantities of knowledge necessary to find the optimal location. Furthermore,

[26] Lösch, The Economics of Location, p. 31.

it is equally impossible for them to know or predict all of the possible changes in supply and demand considerations that would cause the optimal location to be increasingly changing. Looked at from a broad perspective both theories blend into one another. Entrepreneurs consciously seeking the optimal location could proceed to it only along a Weberian path. Of course, having selected a market they ought to take more factors into consideration than Weber suggested. Production costs, for instance, will vary according to the location selected, and labour migration could be an important factor.

## UNCERTAINTY AND THE LOCATION DECISION IN REALITY

Whichever theory is chosen as the basis of a study of the real world, clearly the actions of entrepreneurs will not stimulate its prescriptions. The knowledge required to find the Löschian optimal location or a modified Weberian least-cost location is well beyond the grasp and resources of real decision makers. In any case it is doubtful if entrepreneurs, or at least most of them, would ever consider trying to procure such knowledge. It is suggested that Weber provides a more useful approach in simply allowing the entrepreneur to choose a market location. The concept of the optimal location in the Löschian sense is not really helpful in understanding the locational decision in practice.

Rejecting the concept of the optimum location as having no applicability to location in reality, Tiebout questions the deterministic nature of location models, arguing for the sake of clarity that firms act in a random manner.[27]

The original inspiration of Tiebout's ideas stems from a paper by Armen Alchian that advocates a more deterministic approach to economic analysis. In this he suggests a modification of economic analysis to incorporate incomplete information and uncertain foresight as axioms, and dispenses with profit maximization. The functioning of the economic system may be likened to biological evolution and natural selection, behaving "...as an adoptive mechanism which chooses among explor-

[27] C. M. Tiebout, "Location Theory, Empirical Evidence and Economic Evolution," Papers and Proceedings of the Regional Science Association 3 (1957): 74.

atory actions generated by the adoptive pursuit of success or profits."[28] The word "exploratory" is an important one deriving its significance from lack of knowledge of the present and the uncertainty about the future that lies behind economic decisions, including location decisions. Imperfect foresight and human inability to solve complex problems involving numerous variables are two of the major sources of uncertainty. Realization of profits determines which firms survive or fail.

Adopting Alchian's main thesis, but suggesting that firms could conceivably be located in an optimizing pattern, Tiebout sees patterns slowly changing through an evolutionary selection process:

...all we need postulate is a sufficient number of firms starting out in various locations. Next, we let evolution and the economic system pick out the survivors. If enough firms start out and the economic system gets to pick and choose it would not be surprising if reality yields results consistent with optimal conditions. And all of this can take place without assuming that the firm can find the path (adapt to) the optimum location.[29]

Tiebout brings us much closer to reality than either Lösch or Weber. In the real world location decisions are made; in the process and in the subsequent management of the firms, mistakes and miscalculations are inevitable. Some firms fail; others succeed. Success implies attainment of conditions closer to the optimum. Greater proximity to the optimum arises through luck, but also in many cases through wise and shrewd decisions based on above-average experience and quality of information. Luck corresponds to the adoption concept of Alchian, but wise decisions relate to adaptation to the environment.

The fate of a particular plant is quite unpredictable. There are simply too many unknowns. At an economically ideal location the entrepreneur can make a series of errors that lead to the closure of the plant. On the other hand, skilful management and efficient use of resources can cause a plant to flourish at a less than ideal location. More assurance attaches to the fate of a particular location, with location understood as a market node such as a village, town, or city. Individual plants die and are born, but the locations persist. In dealing with

---

[28]Armen A. Alchian, "Uncertainty, Evolution and Economic Theory," Journal of Political Economy 58 (1950): 211.

[29]Tiebout, "Location Theory, Empirical Evidence and Economic Evolution," p. 84.

aggregate distribution patterns even greater certainty of events characterizes our knowledge. Haggett is right in his observation that while it is not possible for us to predict the outcome of individual events we are in a position to simulate the general locational pattern.[30]

Plants are neither perfectly adapted to an environment nor completely adopted. The locational process is neither completely random nor exactly the opposite. Every location decision is a coin-tossing situation in the sense that the entrepreneur makes it with uncertain knowledge of what the future may bring. No doubt individuals vary enormously in their ideas of how much information should be possessed before a decision is made. In general, however, it can be assumed that the entrepreneur marshals whatever knowledge he has for one, two, or perhaps several potential production points. The important thing is that he will think he can make a profit. The element of luck will always be present for it will always be the case that some plants are better suited to conditions, only some of which were anticipated or known. And during the post-decision years, either because of calculation on the basis of rational treatment of garnered knowledge, or simply by accident, some establishments will be more successful than others. The processes considered here are neither random events nor the procedures that would be followed by rational economic man in possession of perfect knowledge of the present and future. Morrill might describe them as "...random within fairly strong limits or conditions."[31]

The position arrived at may seem paradoxical. On the one hand there are the theoretical optimal locations as understood by Weber and Lösch. On the other hand there is the imperfectly understood behaviour of real people -- people most likely unaware of the concept of the optimal location and the theory behind it -- people who do not look for the optimal location and who could not find it even if they were searching. We must accept human fallibility and the uncertainty that decision makers face, and accept the variation in these factors that reflects the innate differences that exist between people.

[30] P. Haggett, "Changing Concepts in Economic Geography" in Frontiers in Geographical Teaching, eds. R. J. Chorley and Peter Haggett (London: Methuen and Co. Ltd., 1965), p. 112.

[31] Richard L. Morrill, "Simulation of Central Places Patterns Over Time," Proceedings of the IGU Symposium in Urban Geography: Lund, 1960, Lund Studies in Geography, Series B, Human Geography, No. 24 (Lund: C.W.K. Gleerup, 1962), p. 110.

## SURVIVAL OF THE PATTERN

But we have been talking of the individual plant. It is known that whatever the fate of the individual plant the same distributional patterns, both of individual industries and of industry as a whole (i.e., secondary manufacturing), survive over long periods of time. While the plant composition varies and changes incessantly, the "macro-situation" remains relatively undisturbed, changing with the force of long-term factors of which plant births, deaths, extensions, and product-mix changes are "micro-mechanisms." What is more, the same patterns tend to repeat themselves from one region to another, and the same distributional changes re-occur. In particular, the tendency towards concentration, with a larger and larger share of manufacturing found at one or a few of the finite number of market nodes found within a region, is universal.[32]

## THE INEVITABILITY OF CONCENTRATION

Secondary manufacturing always locates at the market. The question is, at which market. Entrepreneurs make location decisions within the framework of their own ambitions, abilities, and knowledge, causing plants to be established at all market nodes. But through time, manufacturing will become increasingly inequitably distributed among the market nodes. This absolute and relative inequality of distribution arises through (a) some market nodes acquiring more new establishments than others; (b) the more successful market nodes eliminating competitors located at the smaller market nodes.

If a uniform plain was studded with equidistant service centres of equal size, and completely sealed off from the rest of the world, there is no question that with time there would be inequality in growth of centres and in the amount of manufacturing contained within them.[33] It requires only one entrepreneur with foresight, initiative, and/or luck, to exploit an opportunity that permits an increase in his scale of production,

[32]This statement avoids reference to number of plants since economies of scale may lead to a reduction in plant numbers as the absolute amount of manufacturing measured according to some index such as value added or employment, increases.

[33]It should be noted that perfect equality of all centres cannot be postulated even for a uniform plain. Some centres will always have a peripheral location in relation to other centres, while some others will always be centrally placed.

market area, and profit, or leads him to introduce a new product, to disrupt any postulated equality. The result of such a development could be to create conditions that make further growth in this centre more likely than in other centres. Growth is cumulative in its effects. Just as there is a multiplier effect between an export base and the rest of the regional economy, so there is a multiplier within a town or city. Introduction of a new element or expansion of an old one creates tensions that may express themselves eventually in new investment opportunities.

With an export based region there is no need to postulate such an initial equality. It simply does not exist from the beginning because of the way in which the region comes into being. Partly through chance (creation of a capital city), and partly due to resource endowment, an area with an early start gains an initial advantage, subsequently becoming the focus of an increasing concentration of non-primary economic activity. Early start, initial advantage, and concentration have been related by many writers.[34]

DISPERSAL

At this juncture, rather than asking, how and why does manufacturing concentrate, it is more useful to ask how dispersed manufacturing can be. There must be a pattern of a greater or lesser degree of dispersal that becomes more concentrated (a stage of maximum dispersal or minimum concentration) -- a time at which it occurs and beyond which concentration within the fixed boundaries of a settled region becomes the dominant spatial trend.

The main factors involved are relatively simple and can be succinctly expressed in a hypothetical statement: the more recently a region has been completely settled, the more dispersed manufacturing is likely to be, both in an absolute sense and in relation to population. This postulate is reached by way

[34]Edward L. Ullman, "Regional Development and the Geography of Concentration," Papers and Proceedings of the Regional Science Association 4 (1958): 179-198; Gunner Myrdal, Economic Theory and Underdeveloped Regions (London: Methuen and Co. Ltd., University Paperbacks, 1963), pp. 23-33; Lösch, The Economics of Location, pp. 79-84. E. M. Hoover, Location Theory and the Shoe and Leather Industries, Harvard Economic Studies 55 (Cambridge, Mass.: Harvard University Press, 1937), pp. 98-99.

of a number of logical steps, some of which are axiomatic, and scarcely require empirical verification.

A. (1) The more recently a region has been settled, the smaller is the total population.

(2) The more recently a region has been settled, the smaller is the total regional income.

(3) The smaller the population and the lower the regional income, the lower will be the demand for manufactured goods.

(4) The lower the demand for manufactured goods the more dispersed manufacturing is likely to be. While the market is small and the manufacturing sector also small, the obstacles to concentration are considerable and the advantages slight. Low total demand creates difficulty in the achievement of internal economies of scale, localization, and urbanization because these are achieved only at higher levels of output that are beyond the absorptive capacity of the region.

B. (1) The more recently a region has been settled, the more dispersed is the population.

(2) The more recently a region has been settled, the more important is the primary sector.

(3) The greater the relative importance of the primary sector, the greater is the probability that the market is dispersed.

(4) The more dispersed the market, the greater is the cost of distributing to it.

(5) The greater the cost of reaching the market, the greater is the likelihood the plants are small and dispersed because economies of scale and agglomeration are inhibited.

C. (1) The more recently a region has been settled, the greater are transport costs per ton/mile likely to be.

(2) The greater transport costs are per ton/mile, the more dispersed manufacturing is likely to be, for the greater is the possibility that thresholds for the minimal-optimal scale of production are greater than the economic transport area.

These steps are now related to the possible developmental trends in an export-based region.

DISPERSAL IN THE EXPORT-BASED REGION

It has been shown that the dominant industrial group in an
export-based region for quite some time is consumer goods.
The consumer goods market is represented by the population
of the region so that population distribution determines the potential spatial extent of the market. During this early phase
of development, population distribution is not likely to be characterized by large concentrations. Rather, the picture is one
of small population nodes set amidst fairly evenly dispersed
rural population; that is, the market has few significant concentrations and is best described as scattered.[35] When a
dispersed market is associated with high transport costs per
ton/mile,[36] the effect on consumer goods industries is usually
sufficient to deter or render impossible supply of the market
from one or a small number of production points. There are
always, of course, exceptions to the rule.

Distributional patterns are also partly understood in relation to the character of the consumer product. For a variety
of reasons, including high portability cost due to weight, fragility, low value added and perishability, and need for person-
to-person contact, the economic transport area of many consumer products is small. Bakery products, furniture, beer,
mineral waters, bricks, tiles, newspapers, and job printing
fall into this category.

Raw materials reflect the variety of industrial products.
These are of a rather simple basic nature. Many materials
are ubiquities, and certainly widely distributed (for example,
wheat, wood, barley, tan-bark, hides and clay). But in any
area supplies may be limited. In such cases an increase in
output not only increases the total transfer costs on the prod-

[35]In 1851 only 14 per cent of the Ontario population was urban, with urban population
referring to incorporated cities, towns, and villages of 1000 population and over. In
1861, 18.5 per cent was urban; 1871--20.6 per cent; 1881--35.0 per cent. These
figures are taken from Leroy O. Stone, Urban Development in Canada, Census Monograph
(Ottawa: Dominion Bureau of Statistics, Census Division, 1967), p. 29. Toronto, the
largest city, accounted for only 3.3 per cent of the regional population in 1851 and 7.1
per cent in 1891. In 1851, the five largest cities, Toronto, Kingston, Hamilton, Ottawa,
and London, contained 7.6 per cent of the regional population. In 1891, they contained
13.4 per cent. For a detailed analysis of population development and movement, see Iain
C. Taylor, "Components of Population Change, Ontario, 1850-1940" (Unpublished Master's
dissertation, Dept. of Geography, University of Toronto, 1967).

[36]This is particularly the case before modern tranportation techniques are introduced.
In most areas this has meant the introduction of railroads. These remarks on dispersal
have greater force if railroads are lacking.

uct, but also transfer costs on the raw material supplies. These trends still operate for many industries at present.

In consumer goods industries, therefore, several factors are likely to be working against the utilization of internal economies of scale in production, and likewise against economies of agglomeration. First of all, the state of technology may not be conducive to large plants. Second, when the sources of materials and the markets are spatially scattered, total transport distances to the market, and costs of overcoming that distance, tend to be prohibitive of production scale increases. Even when material sources are not scattered, as is likely for industries not using agricultural and other local primary inputs, but relying on materials imported into the region (for example, metals), costs in reaching scattered markets may still inhibit concentrated production based on internal economies of scale or agglomeration. Last, during the early stages of development transfer costs per ton/mile are very high, while many of the goods produced are of relatively low value added. The lower the value added and the higher the transfer costs per ton/mile, the shorter the distances that goods will be transported. In any case the market is small to begin with and as Florence points out:

The effect of the dispersion of materials and markets and of cost of transport will be re-inforced if the total market demand or the total supply of materials is small for any particular industry, for the more limited the jam, the thinner it will have to be spread.[37]

Although these markets have been specifically directed towards consumer goods industries, their validity for producer goods industries is almost as great. Examination of industrial structure showed that producer goods are slower to develop than consumer goods and for some time are considerably less important. In the long run there are strong grounds for anticipating a much greater degree of concentration in producer goods, but until the total market is greater and until transport costs are reduced due to the introduction of railways, they are not, on the whole, expected to have a distributional pattern greatly different from that of consumer goods.

It is within such a set of circumstances that the location and operating decisions that shape the framework of the long-term distributional pattern are made. As previously explained

---

[37]P. Sargent Florence, Investment, Location and Size of Plant, National Institute of Economic and Social Research (Cambridge: Cambridge University Press, 1948), p. 46.

there is little point in visualizing entrepreneurs searching out optimal locations. Decisions are not made in a totally irrational, foolish manner, but they are made on the basis of imperfect knowledge, and at times, wishful thinking.


DISPERSAL AND EARLY LOCATION DECISIONS

In general, it is doubtful if pioneer manufacturers consider more than a few potential production points. Some studies of long-lived successful establishments and companies are available,[38] and they certainly give a strong impression of the uncertainty behind early location decisions and the strong element of luck that attended success. A reading of the history of the well-known Canadian brewing family of Molson suggests that no location other than Montreal was ever considered for the first Molson brewery. Factors considered in its establishment give some indication of the way in which entrepreneurs approached the locational decision.

Molson and Loid saw a golden opportunity and seized it. By 1782 new elements had entered the picture. The British had added considerably to Montreal's native population and no doubt were yearning audibly for English ale. Porter was being imported selling at six guineas the hogshead. Molson and Loid probably also had support from official circles, especially Sir Jon Jonson, the Superintendent of Indian Affairs who was bitterly opposed to the rum trade and would see in the production of ale and lesser brews a hopeful and blessed alternative.[39]

There is no doubt that the locational decision was made on a hit and miss basis; the entrepreneur believed that he could supply a product to a community, taking some factors into consideration, but leaving a lot to chance, and facing unknown risks that might bring about his failure. With regard to the first year of operation of the Molson brewery we learn that Molson was scouring the countryside in search of barley.[40] This certainly does not suggest that he located with sure knowledge of his transfer costs. He took risks.

In an export-based region manufacturing follows the distribution of the population coming into existence when farmers,

[38]For example, A history of the Molson familiy is provided by Merrill Denison, The Barley and the Stream (Toronto: McClelland & Stewart Ltd., 1955); E. D. McCafferty, Henry J. Heinz (privately published by the Heinz Company, 1923).

[39]Denison, The Barley and the Stream, p. 26.

[40]Ibid., p. 40.

woodcutters, merchants, administrators, and others seem to offer a reasonable market. Craftsmen and merchants perceive opportunities to make profits within the confines of their own small local areas. The chances of survival of the individual production unit were probably much the same as at present. Speaking of the United States in the 1930's Kaplan observed that the number of new business ventures each year was very rarely below 10 per cent of the total population of firms in operation, and that only one-sixth of new businesses survive more than five years.[41] In response to the scattered market demand each small population centre becomes the focal point of manufacturing in a small market area. Occasionally, manufacturing may provide the original reason for a concentration of settlement. The larger the centre, the more manufacturers that are likely to be found there. In some industries the size of plant may be above average in the larger centres. This could be attributable to economies of scale made possible by the spatial intensity of the market, or quite simply, by the larger local market.[42] In larger centres, particularly the ports, or other points of entry if the region is land-locked, the potential market offered by the townspeople themselves would frequently seem sufficiently enticing to launch manufacturing establishments. But in smaller centres the manufacturers would look to both the population concentration as well as the surrounding rural population for their market. It seems likely that the smaller centres with their small workshops, foundries, sawmills, etc., exhibit in miniature several features of the central city in Von Thunen's theoretical isolated state. Rather than a flow of goods to the consumer the converse would be the case, with the customer moving to the goods; indeed, in some cases moving the raw material to the processing unit and returning with processed material. While this may not have been true of all goods, it

[41]A. D. H. Kaplan, "The nfluence of Size of Firms on the Functioning of the Economy," American Economic Revie 40 (1930): 74-84.

[42]It is interesting to note the case of the brewing industry in London in the 18th and 19th centuries. Since the city constituted such a large market that was incessantly growing, and the industry was technologically suited for large-scale production within the single plant, there was no need to await steam power or railroads to exploit the market at a larger scale of production. The structure of the industry moved from a situation in 1700 when innumerable small producers mostly sold beer which they themselves had made, to one of oligopoly by 1830, when a few large producers, consciously leading prices, dominated the market. See Peter Mathias, "Industrial Revolution in Brewing," Explorations in Entrepreneurial History 5 (1953): 208-224.

was probably the case for many for some time.[43] Therefore, there is not only a parallel with Von Thunen's model but also a parallel with the one-point market model of Weber.

Quite possibly a majority of the manufacturers at this time never considered separating production point and market place. Seeing a market opportunity, the man of enterprise asked whether or not the product could be manufactured and sold profitably in the centre that attracted his attention. Many industries at their inaugural scale of production would have virtually no constraints on the choice of their location. They could locate almost anywhere because the raw materials and markets were ubiquitous. Most raw materials of the food and beverage industries, for example, would be ubiquitous. In such cases Weber's locational figure is reduced to a point. This is the place of consumption at which production must occur. There is no sense in a location outside the community or the area that is to be served, and it is of no importance if the production process produces a weight loss or gain.

Other secondary industries, while not using ubiquities would gain no economic advantage by deviating from their intended market centres. Because of necessity of contact with customers, or because the production process is weight-adding, costs are minimized or profits are maximized by a location at a market nodal point. Even if not weight-adding, distribution costs for a product because of its bulk, fragility, perishability, and because of dispersal of markets would deter deviation to another type of location. In any case, most industries which are not using localized materials are using pure materials that are either produced in the region or imported.

As regards consumer durables, most raw materials are pure and/or ubiquitous in the earlier phases of production, and in cases may be weight-adding or bulk-adding. Included in such industries we would expect to find boat building, cabinet and furniture making, carriage making, and foundry products. Some of these also produce for the producer goods sector. Again, none of these industries would substantially gain from being located at sources of materials even if these are local-

---

[43] Guillet discusses some of these movements in Upper Canada. See Edwin. C. Guillet, Pioneer Days in Upper Canada (Toronto: University of Toronto Press, Canadian University Paperbacks Edition, 1964). See also T. F. McIlwraith, "Accessibility and Rural Land Utilization in the Yonge Street Area of Upper Canada" (unpublished Master's thesis, Department of Geography, University of Toronto, 1966).

ized. Transport costs are important but so also are the other factors previously mentioned.

Exactly the same conditions would apply to investment goods, for example, boiler making, pump making, saddle and harness making and wagon building, and for a number of unsophisticated unfinished producer goods whose market is the evenly distributed consumer goods industries and service industries. One must hasten to add that there will always be a number of industries which are not expected to exhibit the characteristics of uniform distribution throughout the region. These are crucially important in understanding concentration and are duly considered. It is also to be remembered that not all industries will be found throughout the settled part of the region for the simple reason that it requires time for all the elements to appear. Hence, at any time, representation of all industries becomes less likely as distance from first settled areas increases.

DISPERSAL TO CONCENTRATION

If we can identify a concurrence of factors that is causative of spatial dispersal, then we can assume that reversal of factor characteristics would encourage spatial concentration. In fact, in any region we would expect economic conditions to increasingly favour concentration. For instance, it is expected that the spatial intensity of the market will increase with the result that total transport costs in reaching the same size of market will decrease. This alone is sufficient to give rise to concentration, but when decreased ton/mile costs are added, the opportunities for concentration are even greater. Reduction in production costs per unit of output also lead to the same end. However, in view of the prior analysis of the structure of the economy and of manufacturing, it is known that the reasons for concentration are not explained only in terms of production and transportation costs.

CONCENTRATION AND THE STRUCTURE OF
MANUFACTURING

Concentration is also related to the structure of manufacturing. It depends not only on costs but also on the proportions of

components in total manufacturing. With any individual industry, concentration is understood in relation to costs, but for
manufacturing as a whole it must also be related to the structure of manufacturing. Some industries can concentrate more
than others. Analysis of structure indicates that the industries
with a greater proclivity towards concentration become increasingly more important as time goes on. Hence, there are really
two movements: concentration in all industries and the increasing importance in the region of industries with a greater tendency to concentrate. The structural distinction made between
consumer and producer goods was an important one for distribution insofar as it is the nature of producer goods to become
more concentrated than consumer goods. Hence, secondary
manufacturing as a whole is expected to become more concentrated as the producer component becomes relatively more
important. It is obvious that the supplier to a market is always
more concentrated than the market supplied. Consumer goods
industries are always more concentrated than the population
they supply otherwise there would be one production unit per
person. When the market is the total population, industries
are much more likely to be widespread, although concentrating
through time. The ultimate market for producer goods is consumer goods industries and other producer goods industries,
resulting in progressive stages of concentration and returning
us to the Weberian idea of locational strata and Lösch's market nets. A distinction between concentration and agglomeration should be made here. In certain industries economies of
scale within the plant may be the chief force behind concentration. In other industries, the economies arising from juxtaposition with other plants in the same or other industries as
well as with the labour force and services of an urban area may
be of paramount importance in causing concentration. This
latter type of concentration is normally known as agglomeration. Although almost all industries may enjoy agglomeration
economies, industries which supply to a widespread consumer
market and benefit more from economies of scale than from
agglomeration economies, will concentrate at a few, but widely
distributed points. This could be described as non-agglomerative concentration. Producer goods are more likely to move
towards agglomeration.

## A RECAPITULATION

The arguments presented so far require summation. As a region is settled consumer goods are likely to dominate the small manufacturing sector. Conditions for concentration are not propitious; manufacturing of all types tends to be widespread in small production units. But, starting in the first settled areas or parts of them, the following on-going developments occur. The market intensifies so that transfer costs as a proportion of total costs fall if the market areas remains the same. Also, ton/mile costs fall and have the same effect. The result is reduction in the barriers to concentration, agglomerative and non-agglomerative. Industries, whether of long standing or newly introduced, whether widely dispersed or not, are likely to concentrate with the years. Long-established, widely distributed industries concentrate, while newly introduced industries do not exhibit the tendency to distribute themselves widely. As this process gathers momentum it is encouraged by changes in structure which are both cause and effect of the change. The necessary intensity of market and absolute demand for successive producer goods industries is reached. Their progressive introduction gradually reduces the relative importance of consumer goods. Since concentration of their market is a pre-condition of their entry, they add to the general concentration; and since they benefit in many cases from the economies of agglomeration, they accelerate the processes of concentration in all industries that were a pre-condition of their establishment.

It is not possible to predict just how dispersed manufacturing or any component industry will become or when that will occur. The particular regional economic history is crucial, but unpredictable. A great deal depends on the introduction of low-cost transportation media. The longer a region has been settled, and the more of it that has been settled without railways or canals, the more likely is any industry, or all manufacturing to be dispersed. It seems safer to simply examine what processes operate once the point of maximum dispersal of manufacturing as a whole is reached. [44] Prior

---

[44] In such discussion it is difficult to ignore the experience of particular areas. Since the study area was scarcely fully settled by 1850, at which date the first railway line was almost completed, one suspects that maximum dispersal occurs around 1850, that is, when initial settlement is almost complete and the railway is introduced with its powerful concentrative effects.

to this arbitrary point in time, the locational decisions have
been made shaping the extant pattern, and after it the pattern
evolves in response to the operating decisions of previously
established plants, and the locational and operational decisions of new establishments. Since it is impossible to handle
all potential patterns of individual industries, attention is
focused on certain types. Because consumer goods industries
are likely to exhibit the greatest dispersal both in the past and
at present, the concentrative processes of widely distributed
consumer goods industries are first examined.


CONSUMER GOODS AND THE ELIMINATION PROCESS

Sooner or later the majority of widespread consumer goods
industries can be expected to exhibit the following development: (1) some degree of spatial concentration occurs; (2)
the number of plants relative to population decreases (or market of plants increases); (3) the number of production sites
(towns) at which units of the industry are found diminishes.
The result of such trends is to cause consumer goods (and
other, previously widely distributed secondary industries) to
become concentrated in the early settled area, and more so,
in those areas with additional initial advantages. It is difficult
however, to be sure about the patterns of any particular industry, especially as industry divisions are made finer.
More than likely most industries concentrate in the areas of
initial advantage, but the following developmental patterns in
a single industry are possible: 1) increasing concentration
in the major city; 2) increasing concentration at one location
(not the major city but a city or town in the first settled areas);
3) concentration in part of the region with production units
found at several locations (most likely in the early settled
areas); 4) continuing wide distribution, but fewer production
points with concentration in early settled areas.
      While patterns from one industry to another may be dif-
ferent they are all the result of the interplay of a limited number of common factors. All industries change in essentially
the same way, subject to the same general forces. The patterns of once widely distributed industries do not change as
the result of unique forces and factors. They change in different ways because the internal characteristics of the indus-

tries themselves promote or hinder the operation of forces; that is, they encourage or discourage interactions between factors, but the forces and the factors are the same.

The realization of economies of scale within the plant and firm, agglomeration economies and reduction in transportation costs are the fundamental bases of concentration. These rest on the assumption of constantly decreasing unit cost of production as the result of economies of scale, and of distribution costs moving towards zero. Although costs move towards zero they will of course never reach it. As cost per unit of output falls the number of production units also tends to fall. If these are plotted on a time axis the result is an asymptotic curve.

The perpetual transition from dispersal to absolute concentration is here described as a dilution or elimination process.[45] This consists of the gradual elimination of production sites.[46] Historical investigations abound with evidence of this process. One of the most consistent trends in the history of brewing in England in the 19th century was the decline of the small brewers and the gradual concentration of beer output in the bigger breweries.[47]

[45]Dilution may not be experienced by dispersed industries that are growing to meet export markets.

[46]While production sites are reduced in number, new plants and firms can still appear, but they will be at existing production sites.

[47]Vaizey writes: "...enterprising men with capital took advantage of the economies of large scale revealed by technical change.... While beer output grew, the bigger breweries grew faster, and their growth was accelerated by improvements in transport, the growth of urban agglomerations, and the increasing mechanization of the brewing process.... By 1880, brewing, like other trades of the time, was undergoing a process of concentration on larger units.

Despite the large number of plants still existing, the number over the years has been rapidly reduced from 11,752 in 1903-4, to 567 in 1949-50." John Vaizey, The Brewing Industry, 1886-1951 (London: Sir Issac Pitman & Sons Ltd., 1960), pp. 3-4 and p. 56.

A geographic study of brewing is provided by R. G. Golledge, "The New Zealand Brewing Industry," The New Zealand Geographer 19 (1963): 7-24. Golledge concluded that the distribution pattern of brewing in New Zealand was shaped by the combined effect of distance, historical inertia, economies of large-scale production and entrepreneurial policy. The last factor--entrepreneurial policy--can be very important. For example, spatial concentration may occur long after economies of size in the plant or firm have been exhausted. In Canada, the number of production units in brewing fell rapidly between 1930 and 1960 largely through a series of mergers. There is no evidence to suggest that this arose through the superior efficiency of larger firms based on scale economies, or that significant real economies have been achieved through these mergers. See J.C.H. Jones, "Mergers and Competition: The Brewing Case," The Canadian Journal of Economics and Political Science 33 (1967): 551-568.

## ELIMINATION AND ECONOMIES OF SCALE

One of the major contributing factors to dilution is the continued achievement of economies of scale. This includes not only technological economies of scale, but also managerial, selling, financial, and other economies. The broad result is the continued reduction of production costs enabling firms which have achieved large-scale economies to have a competitive advantage over smaller firms which have not.

Large scale economies may lead to a general advantage of the bigger firm. The point is this; if certain economies are available for a certain size of plant, then only those firms which are big enough to afford the capital investment required for this plant will be able to make use of these economies; any smaller sized firm...will not be able to do so. On the other hand, if there are economies open to small plants--and a technological development may sometimes favour small scale equipment--then any bigger firm may make use of them.... From this asymmetry it follows that small firms can never (in the long run) earn higher rates of profit than big firms because some advantages open to them are not open to small firms. [48]

Theoretically, dilution can proceed under the force of economies of scale alone. In the past however, it has often been inseparable from the reduction in transport costs per ton/mile that occurred more or less simultaneously with the application of new production technology. In a perfect market all firms would have equal opportunities to move towards the same levels of efficiency. But the market is imperfect; consumer demand is unevenly distributed because population is unevenly distributed. The result is variation in the spatial intensity of demand. Further, demand varies quantitatively.

[48] Joseph Steindhl, Small and Big Business, Institute of Statistics, Monograph no. 1 (Oxford: Basil Blackwell, 1945) p. 10. It is assumed that production at a larger scale leads to greater efficiency expressed in lower costs per unit of output, and higher profits. In any industry however, there are limits at which economies of scale within the plant are exhausted, although there may be economies for the firm, single or multi-plant, at still greater scales. The question of economies of scale, efficiency, plant and firm survival, and economic concentration is a very complex one, as testified by a voluminous literature. For an insight into these and related matters the following are very useful. P. S. Florence, The Logic of British and American Industry (London: Routledge & Kegan Paul Ltd., 1953); Gideon Rosenbluth, Concentration in Canadian Manufacturing Industries, A study by the National Bureau of Economic Research, New York (Princeton: Princeton University Press, 1957); and J. S. Bain, Barriers to New Competition (Cambridge, Mass.: Harvard University Press, 1956),

To establish whether or not economies exist at larger scales of production is also a very complex matter. See Caleb A. Smith, "Survey of the Empirical Evidence on Economies of Scale" in Business Concentration and Price Policy, A report of the National Bureau of Economic Research, New York (Princeton: Princeton University Press, 1955), pp. 213-238; and Almarin Phillips, "Concentration, Scale and Technological Change in Manufacturing Industries, 1899-1939, " Journal of Industrial Economics 4 (1956): 179-193.

Two population groups of the same size and density may be quite dissimilar in total effective demand. If demand varies spatially some production sites will be more advantageous than others for entrepreneurs desirous of achieving lower costs through the introduction of large-scale production. Immediately, it is possible to see a relationship between economies of scale and the spatial development patterns of an export-based region. Population density, urban centres, per capita demand, and spatial concentration of demand are likely to be greater the longer an area has been settled and developed. If there has been initial advantage their scale is likely to be even greater. The obstacles in the way of realizing economies of scale in production will probably increase with distance away from the first settled area. Considered alone, a lower density of population goes a long way in explaining anticipated smaller sizes of plant as distance from first settled areas increases, and therefore why concentration occurs even in industries supplying the final consumer market. Florence writes:

Plants 'rooted' to areas of sparse supply or 'tied' to areas of dispersed markets would necessarily be small. It was possible to test this interpretation statistically as far as the dispersion of markets was concerned, for in many cases the market is the population and market dispersion can be measured by the population density. It was in fact true that within any one industry serving a local market, the larger plants tended to be found in the more densely populated regions such as London or the industrial districts. This tendency was called the density effect.[49]

It is postulated that the larger the population of the centre at which a plant is located, the fewer are the difficulties in the way of introducing the economies of large-scale production. The first plants to appear and then to achieve higher levels of production with economies of scale will be in the first settled areas. The larger the urban centre the more probable is this occurrence. With time, production units in larger centres will eventually eliminate establishments in the smaller urban centres since these latter face greater difficulties in the way of realizing large-scale economies.[50] Under ideal conditions

[49] Florence, _Investment, Location and Size of Plant_ p. 87. See also, Rosenbluth, _Concentration in Canadian Manufacturing Industries_, p. 39.

[50] Hoover provides graphic examples of how such processes operate. In fact, his work is probably the most useful in tying together economies of scale and agglomeration to spatial change in manufacturing. He elucidates, for example, the matter of plant elimination through economies of scale. "If two producing centres are so placed that their spatial margin lines are negatively inclined in the region of their intersection,

this would lead to elimination of plants around the larger cities
with finally all plants being eliminated except those in the
largest city. The plant which achieves scale economies is in
a position to substitute production inputs for transport inputs
(whatever the state of technology). The market area can
then be extended until it is

...bounded by the locus or band of overlapping points where the marginal
cost of product plus transport inputs equals market price, or the marginal
cost of product plus transport outlays of a competitor-- whether that competitor
be a small local producer, or a large-scale producer from an adjoining region
competing at the peripheries of the space economy.[51]

In this manner the market area can be enlarged resulting in
the elimination of small-scale industry, particularly of the
handicraft type serving small local markets.[52]


## UNCERTAINTY, ELIMINATION, AND CONCENTRATION

At this point the interrelatedness of several different ideas
and theories is becoming manifest. Entrepreneurs acting on
the basis of incomplete information and uncertain knowledge,
with different goals and ambitions, equipped with dissimilar
abilities and the experiences of varied backgrounds, make
locational decisions in a more or less rational manner. According to Tiebout's argument, the establishments of some
of these entrepreneurs are adopted by the economic system.
It seems fair, however, to argue that adoption is all the more
likely to occur if entrepreneurs have tried to minimize uncertainty, that is, adapt to the environment. Plants adopted,
either due to luck and/or adaptation can be regarded as moving
towards the optimal location in the Löschian sense. In many
consumer goods industries initial locational decisions cause
small plants to be widely dispersed. As the market grows
and technology in production and transportation is improved,

there is no equilibrium possible with a divided market. Whichever of the two centres
gets the start of the other ... will eventually absorb the entire market. This throws
light on the oft-cited localizing factor of the momentum of an early start," Hoover,
Location Theory and the Shoe and Leather Industries, p. 98.

[51]Allan Pred, The External Relations of Cities During 'Industrial Revolution',
Department of Geography Research Paper No. 76 (Chicago: Dept. of Geography,
University of Chicago, 1962), p. 22.

[52]Weber discusses such an elimination process stemming from reduced transportation
costs. Weber, Theory of the Location of Industries, pp. 119-122.

the number of plants and firms in an industry generally decreases.[53] Survival of a plant and a location is more likely, the greater the population of the production centre, because location in a larger centre provides decided advantages for the realization of economies of scale. Thus we can see the Alchian economic survival hypothesis brought to life, working itself out through the dilution or elimination process of which the mechanism is the market extension of more favourably located establishments, causing the envelopment of the market areas of less favourably located concerns.[54] Finally, a reminder of the spatial characteristics of population in an export-based region must be added. In this type of region the probability is high that the largest centres and the greatest market intensity will develop in the first settled areas. It is in these areas therefore that we would expect to find the earliest, and at all times, the greatest application of economies of scale.

## ELIMINATION AND THE OPTIMUM FIRMS

A number of ancillary ideas and concepts are helpful to a fuller understanding of statements about dilution and market area extension. The first concept to be considered is that of the optimum firm. At any time in any industry, there is an optimum firm. This is

[53] Kierstead describes this process more flamboyantly. "During a period when the firms in any industry are expanding lay-out with the accompanying technical changes characteristic of modern industry, competition will become unstable because of the declining unit costs over time experienced by the firms. Under such circumstances, an output "retreat" to a lower cost, higher demand equilibrium such as Marshall describes is not probable. Competition assumes the form of vicious price-cutting. Dog must eat dog until the remnant of the pack learns the wisdom of co-operation. Prices will then be stablized and monopolistic or unbalanced competition will result." B. S. Kierstead, The Theory of Economic Change (Toronto: The Macmillan Co. of Canada Ltd., 1948), pp. 261-262.

[54] Plants may well extend beyond their optimal size, as indeed may firms. Elimination, therefore, can proceed when economies of scale achieved through mechanization and mass-production are exhausted. Baldamus argues that once an industry has reached a certain stage of advanced mechanization further economies of plant expansion are obtained, not so much from technical progress as from special methods of plant re-organization designed to secure fuller utilization of existing capital equipment. W. Baldamus, "Mechanization, Utilization and Size of Plant," Economic Journal 63 (1953): 52. In some industries the small plant has advantages, as in the production of specialized articles. It has the advantages in areas in which "the demand is not large, steady or uniform" (See John M. Blair, "Technology and Size," The American Economic Review 38 [1948]: 121-152). He also points out that in some industries there are now technical developments which tend to promote a smaller, rather than a larger scale of operations (ibid.,p. 128).

...a firm operating at that scale at which in existing conditions of technique and organizing ability it has the lowest average cost of production per unit, when all these costs which must be covered in the long run are included.[55]

Whether or not a firm is in the position to reach the optimum depends on output at the optimum level and on the size of the market available to it. At any time a number of scale economies are available to a firm. If the population of the production site is small and the surrounding population thinly distributed it may not be possible to attain these economies because the extra cost of transporting goods to a more distant population will outweigh the cost reductions procured by stepping up the scale of production.

Whatever the state of technology, the firm in the larger centre always has an advantage over the firm in the smaller centre. One plant may have a potential market of 50,000 people within a five mile radius, while another may have only 10,000 in the same radius. If mechanization gives advantage to larger plants the size of the optimum plant increases. But if the new optimum level of production requires 30,000 people, then only the first plant can reach the optimum and supply its customers without greatly increasing its average transport costs per unit of product. In trying to reach the optimum the plant at the smaller centre would raise its transport costs to the point where expansion of production would be unprofitable. But if it cannot reach the optimum it is in danger of being eliminated at some future date.


ELIMINATION AND THE THRESHOLD

As dilution continues, the smaller plants of formerly wide-spread industries cease to exist at the production sites with the smaller populations. This is so because there is a minimum population necessary at each production site to hold a plant at that production site. Through time as plants grow larger as a result of technological, organizational, and other changes, the necessary minimum population is raised. Some towns do not grow rapidly enough to prevent the loss of their plant.

[55] E. A. G. Robinson, The Structure of Competitive Industry (Chicago: University of Chicago Press, 1958) p. 11.

This is a crude re-statement of the threshold concept derived from Central Place Theory and Löschian market area hypotheses.

A threshold is the minimum population or volume of sales required to support a new factory or an addition to existing facilities, and until the city attains this demand level, it must import the industry's product from a more complex centre. [56]

Pred uses it to aid in the understanding of the growth of towns. Those not attaining a certain population would not likely acquire a plant of a developing industry. It must be added that attainment of the requisite population would not guarantee a plant locating there, since entrepreneurship, historical accident, and a number of other factors must be allowed for. While Pred uses the concept to account for areal extension and addition to the plants of an industry, it can be employed conversely to account for diminution in the number of plants and areal contraction.

## ELIMINATION AND ECONOMIES OF GROWTH

Firms and plants, just like cities, once they reach a certain size are likely to continue in existence and grow for a considerable period of time. Increases in scale can only be achieved through growth of the plant or the firm. Penrose has examined the economies of growth as opposed to the economies of size. Since growth is a process, while size is a state, she argues a strong case that there are economies from the point of view of the efficient utilization of the resources of society, which relate to the processes, but which do not pertain to the state, that is, to the size that is the by-product of the process. [57]

Economies of size refer to the cost of production and organization before or after expansion. Economies of expansion, however, relate only to the cost of effecting an expansion. They do not refer to the cost of production after production has been established or enlarged. The cost of expansion includes the cost of establishing additional production on a

[56] Allan Pred, "Industrialization, Initial Advantage and American Metropolitan Growth," Geographical Review 55 (1965): 168.

[57] Edith Tilton Penrose, The Theory of the Growth of the Firm (Oxford: Basil Blackwell, 1959).

smoothly operating basis and enlarging or creating the market which will absorb the additional output. Beyond a certain point in the development of an industry the cost of growth becomes too great for the smaller firms. Hence the likelihood is that the larger plants and firms will get bigger, while the smaller concerns, unable to achieve greater levels of output at lower per unit costs, will gradually go out of business or change their production. From the point of view of this study the end result is the same -- the smaller producers are eliminated.


ELIMINATION AND STRUCTURAL CHANGE

The dilution process occurring due to the application of economies of scale and/or reduction in transportation costs, is well exemplified by industries that were widely distributed at an early date in the region's development. Dispersal was due to at least one of the following characteristics: emerged to meet the earliest, most basic, and therefore most widespread demands; appeared before the introduction of modern land transportation systems; required close contact with the customer; produced on a made-to-measure basis; had a cost structure such that transportation costs constituted a high proportion of total costs; derived little economic benefit from juxtaposition with other producers in the same or other industries.

Few industries of today reflect these characteristics and hence the small number of industries which in their distributional parallel that of population. Ice, ice-cream, and soft drink manufacturing, as well as brewing, are probably the best contemporary examples of industries that can still concentrate due to an elimination process. As the industrial structure of a region matures new industries are constantly introduced. More and more of these have characteristics quite different from those described above. Industries with high minimal optimal scales of production appear, as also do those with high value added, and others requiring close contact with other industries.

The elimination process has its greatest relevance to consumer goods industries, for these are more important in

the early stages of development. This is not to say that
producer goods industries which appear at an early date will
not in some cases (e.g., foundries) attain wide dispersal
followed by dilution that causes concentration. However, the
structural bias towards consumer goods is corrected slowly
through time as more and more producer goods industries
are introduced as an integral part of the region's development.
As the industrial balance changes so also do the spatial economic conditions, creating an environment more conducive to
agglomeration. There is consequently a lower probability of
producer goods becoming widely dispersed through the whole
region in a similar way to many consumer goods industries.
Nevertheless the probability of some producer goods industries
moving by means of a dilution process towards concentration
must not be discounted.


ELIMINATION AND ECONOMIES OF AGGLOMERATION

Among producer and consumer goods industries there are
those which benefit not only from economies of scale in the
individual plant, but also from the external economies of agglomeration. For many industries there are cost savings
arising from juxtaposition to other plants in the same industry, to plants in related industries, and/or from a location in
a large urban centre. Hoover considers that agglomeration
economies rest on the same basic principles as those for
large-scale operation, namely multiples, massing of reserves,
and bulk transactions.[58] Where many plants of the same or
different industries exist in close proximity it is due not only
to low transport costs in procurement and distribution, but
also to some other economy or set of economies.

The thesis of the efficiency of the localization of particular industries hinges
on the existence in a close localization of a fairly logical specialization and
linkages between the neighbouring plants. Just as a single large plant may
be more efficient if integrated to some degree, especially in its services,
so a large locality may derive economies by a local integration.[59]

[58] Edgar M. Hoover, The Location of Economic Activity, Paperback Edition (New York:
McGraw-Hill, 1963), p. 79.

[59] Florence, The Logic of British and American Industry, p. 86. See also, Estall and
Buchanan, Industrial Activity and Economic Geography, pp. 102-107.

The arguments which have been advanced with regard to the distributional significance of scale economies in the single plant can obviously be extended to cover agglomeration economies if a localization is regarded as really constituting one production site (location). Localization in a single industry represents the second stage of concentration where a number of firms operating in a limited area can share immobile external economies. This type of localization can take place only if transport costs are low in relation to total costs so that the place of production may be cheaply diverted. In fact, considerable lowering of transport costs may be a prerequisite.

Areal coincidence of several plants at one production site has essentially the same effect as the concentration that occurs when one large plant supplants several small scattered plants. The actual spatial repercussions can be exactly the same. We can visualize a situation in which the plants constituting the agglomeration constantly enlarge its market area thereby eliminating plants outside the agglomeration. Plants at the localization lower their production costs and thence are capable of expending more on transport costs. In Pred's terms:

...agglomeration induces longer hauls by reducing and eliminating production for local markets when there are cost advantages elsewhere, i.e., marginal production costs at the agglomeration site plus transport outlays from the agglomeration site to an alternative production site, or city, are lower than the marginal cost of production at the alternative site.[60]

A contribution to agglomeration and elimination occurring in this way is likely. But concentration of manufacturing as a whole in an export-based region is more likely to occur in a different way.


AGGLOMERATION WITHOUT PREVIOUS DISPERSAL

As a region develops new industries are forever being introduced. With the progression of time there is a constantly decreasing likelihood that they will ever become dispersed to achieve a distribution pattern analagous to that of some of the early consumer goods industries. The dispersal and elimination process will be arrested or completely short-circuited.

[60] Pred, "The External Relations of Cities," pp. 37-38.

As the structural balance between consumer goods and producer goods industries moves in favour of the latter there is a concomitant development of conditions increasingly inhibitive of dispersal. New industries may continue to disperse but not to the same extent as earlier in the region's development, and dispersal tendencies are quickly diminished in cogency. However, it is argued that this restricted dispersal is in no way comparable to the near ubiquitousness characteristic of early consumer goods industries. Finally, during this period when industries of restrictive dispersal are introduced there is also the appearance, on a constantly increasing scale, of industries which grow only at that point or few points where they were first introduced. Producer goods, especially the unfinished variety, show this tendency.

At some point in a region's development, if not all the time, patterns of distribution are changing due to three mechanisms. These are: (a) dilution of very widely dispersed industries; (b) mild dispersal and concentration partly through dilution of relatively new industries; and (c) concentration with no prior dispersal of new industries. Perhaps these forces are always in evidence, but in an export-based region these are most likely to all be in operation and evident with the introduction of a modern transportation system, for then the barriers to concentration are really down.

Mechanisms b and c are most likely therefore to apply in the case of South Ontario to industries introduced during the course of the study period. Table 5 provides a sample list of industries introduced into Ontario between 1850 and 1890. An industry is regarded as having been introduced when it first appears under a separate heading in the census. Some may have had prior existence but their significance is regarded as minimal until they are first separately listed in the census.


LOCATION AND NON-DISPERSING INDUSTRIES

Two salient questions should be asked about industries introduced into the region during the study period. Where does the first plant locate? And if the industry grows, what distribution patterns develop?

TABLE 5    SAMPLE OF INDUSTRIES INTRODUCED INTO ONTARIO
BETWEEN 1850 AND 1890

**Food, Drink, Tobacco**

baking powder
preserved fruit and jelly

**Sundries**

buttons
household chemicals
combs
fireworks
patent medicines

**Clothing and Footwear**

corset making
oil clothing
underwear factories

**Household goods**

celluloid goods
rubber goods
tent and awning factories
toys
umbrellas

**Consumer durables**

bicycles
billiard tables
carpets
floor oil cloth
invalid chairs
lanterns
mattress making

mirror making
spring bed factories
washing machine factories

**Investment goods**

electrical appliances and supplies
elevators
emery wheel factories
fire-proof safes
car and locomotive works
optical instruments
refrigerator factories
scale factories
show cases
street lamps
ventilators

**Unfinished producer goods**

galvanized iron
glass works
glue
glycerine
hubs and spokes
ink
nut and bolt factories
packing cases
paints and varnishes
paper bags and boxes
belt and hose
cork cutting
type founding

The answers are obvious. The first plant of any industry could locate anywhere in the region, yet is much more likely to locate in the successful parts of the early settled area, and within that area is much more likely to locate in the major city than anywhere else. With regard to patterns, the answer is that virtually any kind of distribution pattern could develop. It is likely, however, to vary between one of total concentration in one city to dispersal between a small number of centres within the most populous part of the region (early settled areas with initial advantages).

109

# THE THRESHOLD

Existing literature describes the processes and factors sub-sumed by these answers. It is necessary, however, to des-cribe these and show their relations with the special conditions in the export-based region.

The threshold concept is of great relevance. Different industries require different threshold conditions. These are most likely to be first reached in the largest city where the number of people and purchasing power is greatest. It is perfectly reasonable to expect the threshold for a piano fac-tory to be reached in Toronto before any other centre. Ir-respective of the scale of the threshold (that is, national, regional, or local), the first plant established in response to its achievement is more likely to be in the major city of the region than anywhere else. If the threshold can be at-tained in a city, then a city in the early settled area is most likely to first provide it. If the minimal optimal scale of production requires a threshold that can only be provided by a region or a nation, the major city followed by the other major centres of the early settled area, is the place with the greatest probability of being chosen as the location for the first plant. From the point of view of distributional change it is equally important to point out that chances of survival are likely to be greater in the major city. Threshold attain-ment is clearly a cumulative process. If conditions are reached for one industry, its establishment thereby contributes to growth which leads to the attainment of further thresholds and so on.


## TRANSPORT COSTS

Because the total regional market is spatially concentrated due to the decline of population densities towards the youngest areas, total transport costs for a local, regional, or national market are likely to be lowest in the major city since from here it is probable that the greatest number of people can be reached with the minimum distance travelled. This likelihood is heightened because the regional transportation systems focus on the major city giving it inestimable distributional advantages. Furthermore, costs per unit of distance are

likely to be below average since freight concessions are frequently offered to the major centres in the network. Transportation costs on "raw materials" for many new industries
are also likely to be lower than at alternative locations. Raw
materials are understood in the broadest sense to cover both
unprocessed and semi-processed materials, as well as finished
parts and goods. Increasingly, the last three types of materials become the inputs of new industries and, in view of the
spatially cumulative nature of industrial growth, will be found
where the greatest growth occurs, viz., the major city and
surrounding early settled areas.

Regardless of the cost structure of an industry -- whether
it be high or low value added, whether transport costs constitute a large or small proportion of total delivered cost per
unit of output to the customer -- transport cost advantages
accrue to the producer at the central location.


## AGGLOMERATION AND THE EARLY SETTLED AREA

This discussion is framed in terms of likelihoods. The major
city is the location most likely to be chosen for new industries.
Indeed, it may well be the undetectable optimal location. But
it is not the only location that is chosen for the first plants of
new industries and it is most unlikely to be the only location
where they can survive on the basis of reasonable profits. It
does not always require a location in the major city to permit
survival of a new industry. Drive and initiative of the entrepreneur can more than compensate for a less than optimal
location. But there is a limit, imperceptible although it may
be, beyond which it is impossible to make a profit and survive,
and before this a zone in which survival for any length of time
is improbable. The idea expounded here is that of the geographic limit of possible production as discussed by Rawstron
and Chisholm.[61] For any product there is a line enclosing
the area of profitable production; it represents the boundary
of the economic margin beyond which profitable operations
are not feasible. In South Ontario the first bicycle factory is
most likely to be located in Toronto, but Hamilton, Kitchener,
and several other centres are by no means improbable loca-

[61]Michael Chisholm, Geography and Economics (London: Bell & Sons Ltd., 1966), p. 47.

111

tions. Historical accident can never be regarded as inconsequential since an entrepreneur in a non-central market node may give that centre a head start in the manufacture of a particular product such that the lead can be moved to another centre only with great difficulty. There is nothing to prevent an entrepreneur choosing any location to go into business. The question is -- will his business survive? If the first bicycle factory were established in a small village 120 miles northwest of Toronto chances of survival would be slight. This line of argument can be succinctly stated. The larger the centre in which the first plant is established the greater is that plant's chance of survival, but the further this centre lies from the centre of gravity of population the poorer are its chances of survival.

## UNCERTAINTY, AGGLOMERATION AND THE FIRST SETTLED AREAS

So far only transport costs and distances have been called on to support this assertion. More and stronger support is provided by the other underlying economic props of agglomeration.

Uncertainty which has already played a prominent part in this long argument is employed again as an important explanatory variable. Like all plants, the first plant of any industry to be established in a region faces uncertainty of the present and the future, but probably faces greater uncertainty than will ever be the case in that industry again. While the entrepreneur may have experience of the industry in another region, he faces at the least, the uncertainty of operating it under a new set of untried conditions. Although economies of scale, production relationships, as well as other external economies are normally and rightly regarded as forming the main explanatory core of agglomeration, Tiebout suspects that uncertainty, especially with regard to factor inputs, may be an important variable. [62]

The entrepreneur of a proposed new plant must face up to the question of the availability of certain factors of production. Although import substitution may be possible [63]

[62] Tiebout, "Location Theory, Empirical Evidence and Economic Evolution," p. 85.

[63] Import substitution also increases concentration due to the fact that regional importing centres as well as major migrant reception centres are located in the first settled areas.

there are programming requirements normally limiting the use of this device. Without perfect knowledge of available inputs the firm must choose a location where there is a good margin for all needed inputs. The "safest" location is the largest location. It is here that unforseen inputs, including labour inputs, can be met with the least difficulty. One can see the overlap in the argument with Myrdal's idea of cumulative causation. The larger a city becomes, the greater and greater becomes the probability that it can supply unforseen inputs.

As consumer durables become relatively more important in the consumer goods group, and as producer goods rise towards their dominance over consumer goods, the uncertainty attaching to the introduction of each industry most probably increases -- a reflection of the increasing complexity of new industries as the structure of manufacturing matures. The region's earliest industries produce relatively simple products from one or a few raw materials that are unprocessed or semi-processed. With time, as structure matures, more complex industries appear: industries requiring many different materials, including semi-processed goods and finished parts; industries requiring specialist services in production, and perhaps in marketing; industries requiring a great variety of labour skills. All these are most likely to be found in the larger cities and towns of the early settled area. The conclusion to be drawn is that maturation of structure and agglomeration are but two sides of the same coin.

While discussing structure it was pointed up that maturation of structure is associated with division of labour, which in turn reflects increase in the size of the market. Consumer goods with lower thresholds than producer goods appear first. Only as the region develops are the successive thresholds for individual producer goods industries reached. Division of labour, especially when evidenced by unfinished producer goods, is not only a function of market size but also of market concentration. It owes part of its origin to concentration, yet simultaneously causes concentration. As industry concentrates in a restricted area the opportunities for division of labour and the economic advantages attaching to it are most likely to be first perceived in the concentration. It is there that the point is first reached when the production of particular parts of a finished product, or particular operations, are

established as new separate industries. In this way develop
the close linkages and relationships of the various industries
of an agglomeration. Such ties require, or at least function
better, with close juxtaposition of firms, and with ease of
inter-personal contact.

Once consumer and producer goods industries are established in close areal proximity to one another, joined by
production relationships as well as enjoying the external
economies of agglomeration, the economic disadvantages of
a location outside the agglomeration tend to increase. As a
result, the probability of new industries first being introduced
elsewhere tends to diminish with time. Many of the forces
creating new industries are produced by already existing industries in the cities. New industries are introduced when
new thresholds are reached, when technological disequilibria[64]
arise, and when manufacturers attempt to make better use of
their resources.[65] There is also great significance in the
fact that the capital necessary to the introduction and establishment of new business ventures is more readily available
in the larger cities.

Pred arrives at the obvious conclusion that industrial
innovations and inventions occur where manufacturing is
already developed, and contribute to different growth rates
of urban-industrial complexes. He also relates innovation
to uncertainty. Innovation is most likely to take place in an
urban environment where manufacturing is already concentrated. This substantiates the uncertainty argument because
observation of success presumably reduces uncertainty.[66]
In the case of South Ontario innovation would largely take the
form described by Pred as implementation and adoption by
imitation.[67]

[64]See Allan Pred, "Some Locational Relationships Between Industrial Inventions,
Industrial Innovations, and Urban Growth, " p. 54. See also, by the same author, The
Spatial Dynamics of U.S. Urban-Industrial Growth, 1800-1914: Interpretive and
Theoretical Essays (Cambridge: MIT Press, 1966).

[65]Florence writes: "The economy of intergration due to common costs boils down to
this: if a manufacturer has a certain unused capacity in equipment or in finance (or in
brains of himself and staff) it may pay to balance up by taking on as a side-line new
processes or products using that idle capacity, " Florence, The Logic of British and
American Industry, p. 76.

[66]Pred, "Some Locational Relationships Between Industrial Inventions, Industrial
Innovations, and Urban Growth, " p. 53.

[67]Ibid., p. 47. It is interesting to note that one of the most important inventions to
emanate from Ontario, namely, the telephone, was commercially introduced in Ontario

114

These are among the main reasons why the plants of a
new industry tend to favour the most industrialized areas
more than other parts of the region. To a considerable degree
they are also the reasons why new industries subsequently do
not become widely dispersed. Even as industries gain a firm
foothold the economic handicaps imposed by location outside
the major industrial concentrations continue to restrict the
spatial extent of production. Widely dispersed industries concentrate due to the continual achievement of economies of
scale, a process which is frequently related to technical innovation. Associated with concentration is an increase in the
minimal optimal scale of production. As this rises the number of plants and production sites falls.[68] Reduction of transportation costs has the same effect; and again, the competitive
position of the larger producers is strengthened. This is just
as much the case for new industries, particularly the producer
goods moving towards ascendency in the industrial structure.
The powerful concentrative tendencies, however, exist at the time
these industries are introduced to the region. The elimination process is greatly restricted in operation, or completely
by-passed if the first producers make it too difficult for other
production sites to be employed. In many cases the initial
minimal optimal scales of production are much higher than
those for the first industries to enter the region. Also,
technological improvements in production and transportation
tend to increase threshold levels. These trends can progress
until entry to an industry is effectively barred.[69]

As always, in order to parallel reality, some relaxation
of constraints must be considered, otherwise one is obliged
to visualize all new industries locating at a few large centres
and remaining there forever more. One may say that the
higher the threshold, and the greater the external economies
of agglomeration, the greater the likelihood of a large city
location for original location and subsequent growth. International, national, and regional markets are most likely to

only after its success had been proven elsewhere. See C. M. Johnston, Brant County:
A History, 1784-1945 (Toronto: Oxford University Press, 1967), pp. 110-113.

[68] The number of plants does not fall if the market is expanding at a faster rate than the
application of economies of scale. The number of production sites (towns), however,
would still go on decreasing.

[69] See J. S. Bain, Barriers to New Competition, and also, "Economies of Scale,
Concentration, and the Conditions of Entry in Twenty Manufacturing Industries,"
American Economic Review 44 (1954): 15-39.

be supplied from the industrial concentrations. When thresholds are provided by less than the total region and the economies of agglomeration are slight, the greater is the likelihood that centres outside the main concentration are chosen.

## DISTRIBUTION AND PATTERNLESS
## SPATIAL VARIATION IN STRUCTURE

The examination of the structure of secondary manufacturing failed to reveal any significant spatial patterns. An important conclusion was that there seemed to be no relationship between the relative importance of an industrial group and the length of time an area had been developing. It was assumed that industries distributed themselves in such a way that there was no spatial regularity in the proportion each constituted of the total in each areal unit. It now seems relatively easy to account for this.

If manufacturing concentrates, small areas of the total region account for a large absolute amount of the regional total. Conversely, most areas account for small amounts of the regional total. As the quantities involved become smaller, the greater becomes the probability that one decision, or one entrepreneur, can greatly alter the structure of manufacturing in an areal unit.

It must be accepted that any type of manufacturing can be established anywhere. Individual human actions do not obey spatial theories. Although we can be quite confident that manufacturing as a whole, its groups, and most of its individual industries will demonstrate continuing concentration in a small part of the region, we can never be certain about where an individual plant of any industry might locate. Herein lies one of the major reasons for the lack of pattern in structural variation through space. There is little doubt, for example, that unfinished producer goods will become more concentrated in a small part, or a few areas of the region. On the other hand there is always the possibility that an areal unit outside the industrial concentrations will show a high proportion of employment in unfinished producer goods such that it has a producer goods dominance. This type of development becomes all the more likely as the size of the areal units is reduced, and industry sub-divisions are

116

made finer. The smaller the total amount of manufacturing in an areal sub-division, the greater is the possibility that an entrepreneurial decision can produce a "deviant" structure. Within the main industrial areas substantial increases in employment in an industrial group may not be sufficient even to maintain the relative importance of the group. Whereas, a handful of men in a small factory in a rural area could turn the industrial structure upside down in that area.

The reasons why this may occur have been amply discussed. In many cases such structural "deviations" will be eliminated through time due to the competitive superiority of producers in larger centres. But again, this need not be the case; an early start, entrepreneurial initiative, oligopoly or monopoly, singly, or in combination, could perpetuate the situation.

There are also a number of special location factors that could cause variations in structural pattern. It has been constantly, and quite correctly assumed, that all secondary manufacturing is market oriented. Notwithstanding, an industry may develop in an area removed from the main population concentrations because of some particular feature of the area. The migration of skilled craftsmen to a largely rural locality could provide the basis for an industry. Or, an industry could be raw-material oriented, not in terms of transport costs on the material versus those on the product, but simply because the material was there and not anywhere else. A woollen industry, for example, may develop in those areas where sheep are raised, despite the fact that wool is not costly to transport. Power sources may also be the underlying cause of some location decisions relating to rural areas.

Industries that develop at non-central locations need not necessarily be eliminated. The areas in which they locate may be endowed with long-term advantages, particularly in the form of a skilled labour force, and immovable capital equipment that enables them to maintain a strong competitive position against producers in central areas. Some industries will exhibit the well-known condition of geographical inertia.

The last reason for structural variability through space is found in the unpredictable spatial behaviour of primary extractive industries, and ancillary primary manufacturing industries. Not all secondary manufacturing industries find their major market in the main population concentration, or

117

derive special economies from a central market location. Some industries, for example, may develop to supply goods and materials to the primary sector, forming a distribution pattern that reflects the distribution of their primary market. Fruit and vegetable production, for instance, may lead to local development of unfinished producer goods such as packing cases and boxes.

Compared to the distribution of all manufacturing, such irregularly distributed industries will generally be very insignificant. But, the point is, in the areas in which they locate, they can be very important, and thereby endow those areas with a structure quite different from surrounding areas.

CONCLUSION

The study of spatial concentration has been the major preoccupation of those interested in the distribution of manufacturing. Probably the best theoretical account of concentration is provided by Weber. When his ideas on agglomeration are combined with his concept of the locational stratum, we are given a fairly good replica of real distribution patterns, but he leaves our knowledge of the mechanisms of concentration very much wanting. The gap between location theory and the events of the real world is a wide one. In particular, not enough attention is paid to the irrationality of man and the uncertainty behind his actions.

In this chapter an attempt has been made to come closer to the real world than location theory in its present form allows. Useful in the approach adopted is consideration of the economic growth process. Theories of location pay no heed to the dynamics of development. Almost no consideration is given to the fact that the composition and nature of economic activities are constantly altering. Divorce of economic growth processes from the processes of distributional change leaves us with but partial answers to both development and distribution problems.

From a layman's perspective the spatial mechanisms of industrial development may seem more obvious and simple than close investigation suggests. Manufacturing is neither static nor monolithic and the environment with which it interacts is even more dynamic and varied in character. To ex-

118

plain the distribution of an unchanging phenomenon is so complex at the best of times, but becomes immeasurably more so when the compositions of the phenomenon and its environment are constantly changing.

In the special case of the export-based region, manufacturing follows in the wake of settlement. Predominantly consumer oriented, it spreads itself throughout the settled areas. Then gradually, with no perceptible spatial or temporal discontinuities, the composition of manufacturing in the region as a whole moves towards a producer goods dominance. Structural changes through space are observable, with different areas at different stages of structural development. Distributional change is the inseparable partner of structural change. As total regional structure matures, the region acquires more and more manufacturing activity, which in locating causes considerable distributional change. Growth does not proceed through proportionate increments in all areas. It becomes concentrated in the first settled areas, and in only an areally restricted portion of these. Such a concentration always exists, if only because of the time-lag involved in the settlement process. Once established it inexorably grows through one of those cumulative multiplier mechanisms so characteristic of economic growth. Growth of population and its purchasing power; increasing population density; technological improvements that lead to division of labour and economies of scale; cheapening of transport costs; are all major contributors to this concentration. These factors contribute to concentration in two ways. First, formerly widespread industries experience reduction in number of production sites, with an increasing proportion of remaining sites found in a restricted area of the region. Second, as new industries are introduced, testifying to successful development based on exports, they tend to favour the most industrialized parts of the region. Even when firmly established many of these industries gain little advantage from decentralization.

Concentration is increasingly encouraged by the fact that as manufacturing grows in total, its character changes. New industries, at larger scales, with more complex production processes, requiring a wide variety of production inputs, become major contributors to total manufacturing output. Many derive considerable benefit from concentration, and by their presence improve the attraction power of the concentration for more new industries. So the process continues.

Consequent upon the operation of such forces, most of the region becomes less and less significant for its contribution to manufacturing output. Also, most of the region is structurally less advanced than the most industrialized areas. This is likely to be a lasting condition, since the likelihood diminishes that the producer goods industries will spread equally among all areas of the region endowing them with a similar structure. In the same breath, however, we must recognize that because the distribution patterns of manufacturing industry are the product of countless locational and operation decisions, it is unlikely that structure at any time will exhibit perfect patterns of spatial variation. Stubbornness, stupidity, special environmental or human advantages, can cause plants to be located in such a way that spatial regularity in structural variation is destroyed. Such observable irregularities, however, should not by any means completely obscure the broad progression of events as described above.

# VI

# Spatial patterns in south Ontario: 1851-1891

## MAGNITUDE AND GROWTH OF SECONDARY MANUFACTURING

The salient features of the spatial developments in secondary manufacturing as a whole are represented in Maps 20, 21,[1] and 22. The depiction of the absolute employment values gives a clear visual impression of spatial concentration. In 1851 secondary manufacturing was to be found in all the areal units of the study region, but in most of them there was very little of it. Were it not for an obvious greater magnitude in York

---

[1] To facilitate comparisons between areal units for the same date, and more particularly, to enable immediate identification of the more important manufacturing areas, Maps 20 and 21, as well as several subsequent maps, employ a magnitude index in addition to the proportional circles representing absolute employment. Calculation of the index is in two stages. The first is to establish the "average magnitude" of manufacturing for the areas in which manufacturing exists in a specific year. The second stage is to calculate the "magnitude rating" for each area. This is the percentage of the "average magnitude" as calculated in stage one. By this method an area which has a magnitude exceeding the "average magnitude" has a rating above 100. Those areas with a rating greater than 100 have been identified on the maps.

The terms used in this explanation are borrowed from R. L. Patni, the originator of the specific indices. See "A New Method for Measuring Locational Changes in Manufacturing Industry," Economic Geography 44 (1968): 210-217. Patni acknowledges that his methods are based on suggestions by John H. Thompson, "A New Method of Measuring Manufacturing," Annals of the Association of American Geographers 45 (1955): 416-436.

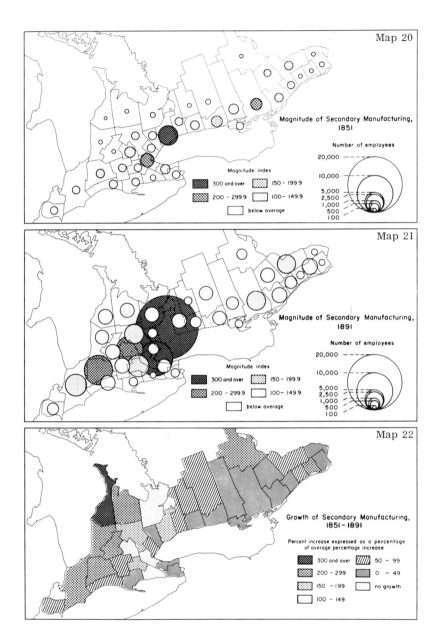

Map 20

Magnitude of Secondary Manufacturing,
1851

Number of employees

20,000 ----

10,000

5,000
2,500
1,000
500
100

Magnitude index

300 and over    150 - 199.9

200 - 299.9     100 - 149.9

below average

Map 21

Magnitude of Secondary Manufacturing,
1891

Number of employees

20,000 ----

10,000

5,000
2,500
1,000
500
100

Magnitude index

300 and over    150 - 199.9

200 - 299.9     100 - 149.9

below average

Map 22

Growth of Secondary Manufacturing,
1851 - 1891

Percent increase expressed as a percentage
of average percentage increase

300 and over    50 - 99

200 - 299       0 - 49

150 - 199       no growth

100 - 149

and Wentworth, one would not hesitate on the basis of this
visual information to describe the pattern as dispersed. The
other most important feature of this time is that the areas with
the greatest employment in manufacturing were mainly located
along the north shore of Lake Ontario, extending from Leeds

in the east to Lincoln at the US border. There was therefore a strong correspondence between the magnitude of manufacturing and the age of settlement.

By 1891 the situation was considerably changed. Most areas had more manufacturing, and some had shown a striking increase. The earlier slight lead of the Lake Ontario counties had been replaced by what appears as a considerable concentration around the western end of Lake Ontario, with extensions into the Grand River Valley and beyond to Middlesex. Some of the newly settled areas had improved their position, but had not risen above the average. Most of the Lake Ontario areas, however, had gone below average, so that their manufacturing was significantly less important that it had been at the beginning of the period. Map 22 (Growth of Secondary Manufacturing: 1851-1891) shows that except for some areas around the head of Lake Ontario, growth rates along the lake were below average for the region. The fastest growth rates were in the outer agricultural areas of southwest Ontario, such as Bruce, Grey, and Huron. This was to be expected of recently settled areas building on what was a very small base at the beginning of the study period (see Map 20). York, Wentworth, Waterloo, and Brant Counties, although not growing as fast as the above-mentioned areas, experienced above-average growth rates. Since they started with a considerably greater base, these rates were sufficient to make them the most important manufacturing areas.

The measures used in Maps 23, 24, and 25 give a simpler, but perhaps clearer picture of the major trends of the period. In 1850 it required a line of units extending from Middlesex along Lake Ontario as far as Leeds to account for 50 per cent of all secondary manufacturing in the region. In 1891 this important alignment of concentration was gone. Six areas in central and western Ontario accounted for the first 50 per cent and the same general area accounted for most of the next 25 per cent as well. The map of distribution of growth share (Map 25) shows that growth was more localized than the manufacturing to which it was an increment. Four units, three of them around the west end of Lake Ontario accounted for the first 50 per cent of growth, and most of the remaining growth was in western Ontario. As this occurred, most other parts of the region received comparatively little new manufacturing,

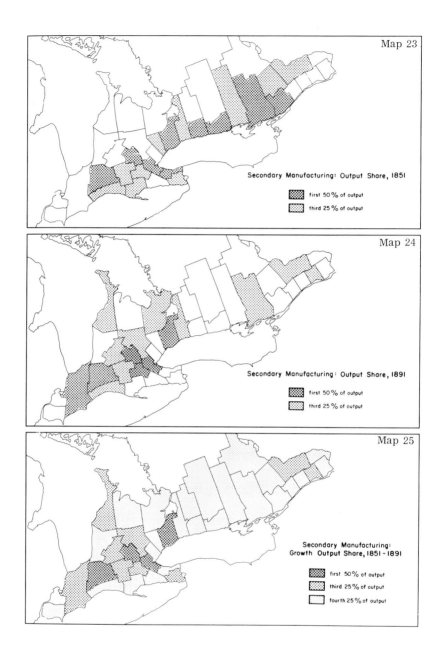

Map 23

Secondary Manufacturing: Output Share, 1851

▨ first 50% of output
▦ third 25% of output

Map 24

Secondary Manufacturing: Output Share, 1891

▨ first 50% of output
▦ third 25% of output

Map 25

Secondary Manufacturing:
Growth Output Share, 1851-1891

▨ first 50% of output
▦ third 25% of output
☐ fourth 25% of output

thus standing in sharp contrast to York which received approximately 27 per cent of the regional increase in employment,
and saw its total share of regional employment in manufacturing rise from 14 per cent to 24 per cent.

124

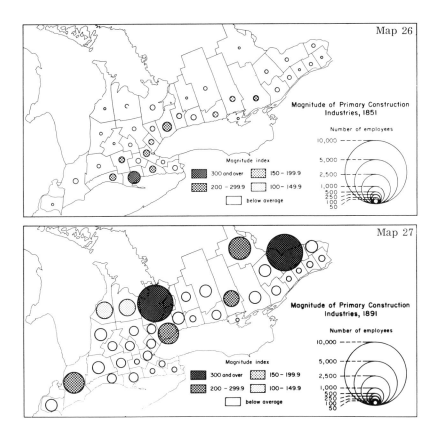

Map 26

Magnitude of Primary Construction
Industries, 1851

Number of employees

10,000
5,000
2,500
1,000
500
250
100
50

Magnitude index

300 and over    150 - 199.9
200 - 299.9     100 - 149.9
below average

Map 27

Magnitude of Primary Construction
Industries, 1891

Number of employees

10,000
5,000
2,500
1,000
500
250
100
50

Magnitude index

300 and over    150 - 199.9
200 - 299.9     100 - 149.9
below average

## PRIMARY MANUFACTURING

In view of what has been said about primary manufacturing, it
should be quite clear that although it is a component of secondary manufacturing their distributional patterns need not be
the same.  Furthermore, because of the different locational
patterns of the raw materials of the various primary manufacturing industries, and also because of the operation of both
external and domestic forces on them, there is no reason why
they should be characterized by one type of pattern or trend.
The primary construction industries have been selected to
prove the point.  As a group these behaved in exactly the
opposite way from secondary manufacturing as a whole (Maps
26 and 27).  At the beginning of the study period they were most
strongly represented in the early settled areas, but by 1891
they were clearly most important in the peripheral parts of

125

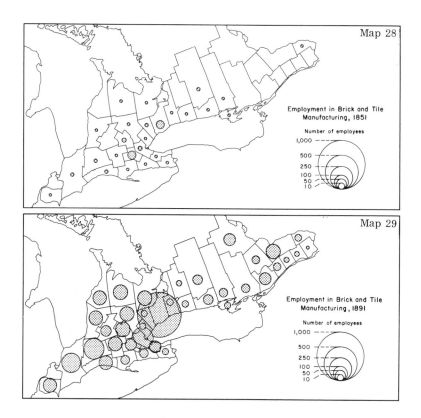

Map 28

Employment in Brick and Tile
Manufacturing, 1851

Number of employees

1,000
500
250
100
50
10

Map 29

Employment in Brick and Tile
Manufacturing, 1891

Number of employees

1,000
500
250
100
50
10

the region. However, when the group is disaggregated, and
two sub-groups -- brick and tile making, and sawmilling -- are
examined, the differences that can exist within the group are
distinctly shown.

The brick and tile industry moved in a way similar to
secondary manufacturing as a whole. Growth consolidated
what was a slight concentration in 1851 (Maps 28 and 29).
Although a primary industry, its raw materials were virtually
ubiquitous and its market was domestic, a combination which
permitted its distribution to reflect the distribution of market
demand. Sawmilling, on the other hand, was an industry
supplying both the home and foreign markets. In 1851 and 1891
its distribution was much the same as the primary construction
industries as a whole (Maps 30 and 31). The most important
areas in 1851 were along the shores of Lakes Erie and Ontario,
particularly the former, in the units of Elgin, Norfolk, and
Haldimand. Forty years later the industry had a substantially
greater employment and the most important production areas

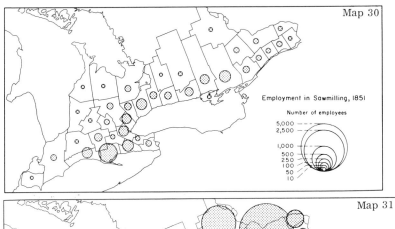

Map 30

Employment in Sawmilling, 1851

Number of employees

5,000
2,500

1,000
500
250
100
50
10

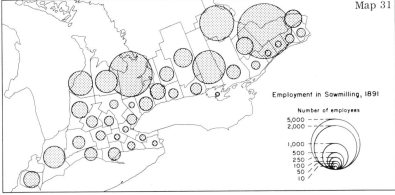

Map 31

Employment in Sawmilling, 1891

Number of employees

5,000
2,000

1,000
500
250
100
50
10

were at the peripheries of the region. The areas in which secondary manufacturing were most important were the least important in sawmilling. The major production areas of the industry had moved across the region, a development to be expected with a widespread but exhaustible resource.

While secondary manufacturing was agglomerating, the various primary manufacturing industries were exhibiting a variety of trends. Sawmilling and brick and tile making show two distinctly different trends. Other industries with localized raw material sources exhibited a wide variety of distributional patterns.

## CONSUMER AND PRODUCER GOODS

With the aid of magnitude and growth maps (Maps 32 to 37 inclusive) it is very plain to see that both the consumer and producer goods groups concentrated during the study period.

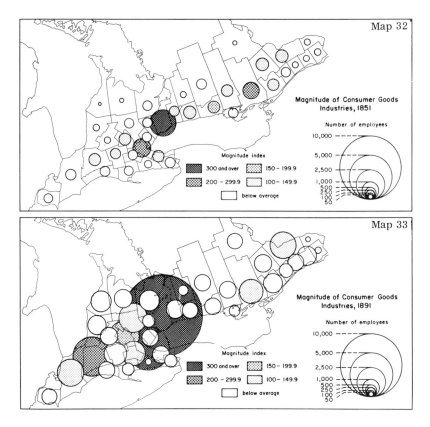

In the case of consumer goods the early alignment of localization along Lake Ontario, around the Niagara Peninsula, and
across to Middlesex, emerges once again.  As before, the
areas containing the largest urban units showed the greatest
localization.  By 1891 concentration was more marked, with
York and Wentworth emerging well above average magnitude.
Most of the early settled areas along Lake Ontario had not
managed to maintain their previous positions.  More recently
settled areas in the northwest, for example, Bruce and Grey,
had experienced considerable growth, indeed, above-average
growth, but were not the scene of any significant localization.
There was once again evidence of concentration in the Grand
River Valley, for example, Brant and Waterloo, and in
Middlesex -- all areas which had been settled by 1830.  Developments in the producer goods industries were similar.

    Just as with secondary manufacturing as a whole, these
two major groups grew most rapidly in the outlying parts of

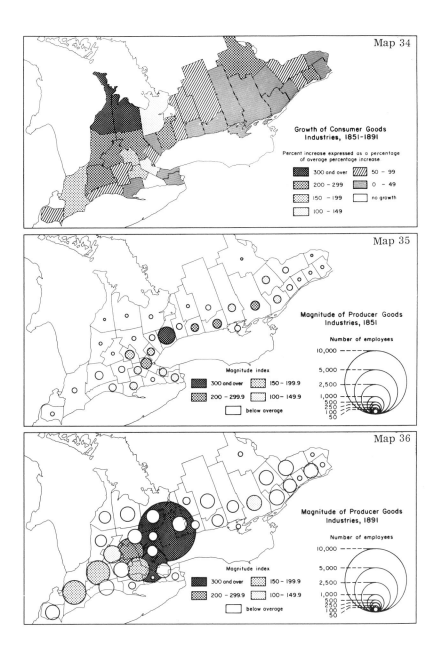

Map 34

**Growth of Consumer Goods
Industries, 1851-1891**

Percent increase expressed as a percentage
of average percentage increase

- 300 and over
- 200 - 299
- 150 - 199
- 100 - 149
- 50 - 99
- 0 - 49
- no growth

Map 35

**Magnitude of Producer Goods
Industries, 1851**

Number of employees

10,000
5,000
2,500
1,000
500
250
100
50

Magnitude index

- 300 and over
- 200 - 299.9
- 150 - 199.9
- 100 - 149.9
- below average

Map 36

**Magnitude of Producer Goods
Industries, 1891**

Number of employees

10,000
5,000
2,500
1,000
500
250
100
50

Magnitude index

- 300 and over
- 200 - 299.9
- 150 - 199.9
- 100 - 149.9
- below average

the region, particularly in the southwest. However, this rapid
growth was not enough to arrest the localization of manufacturing around the head of Lake Ontario despite the lower rates
in this area.

129

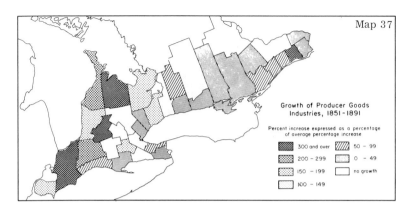

Map 37

Growth of Producer Goods
Industries, 1851-1891

Percent increase expressed as a percentage
of average percentage increase

- 300 and over
- 200 - 299
- 150 - 199
- 100 - 149
- 50 - 99
- 0 - 49
- no growth

## RELATIVE CONCENTRATION

The question that immediately arises is whether or not the concentration across southwest Ontario in its early settled parts,
is one that simply reflects the distribution of population. After
all, there can be concentration in an absolute sense coincident
with perfect dispersal, if dispersal is taken to mean perfect
correlation with some base magnitude, such as population.
Was there much manufacturing in York simply because it had
a large population? Did the above-average growth in Kent-
Lambton allow manufacturing to keep pace with population
growth, and development in other sectors of the economy? If
previously made theoretical speculations are correct, manufacturing in York would be greater than its population would lead
us to expect, while in Kent-Lambton it would be less. For the
region as a whole the following developments were anticipated.
Secondary manufacturing would become increasingly concentrated
relative to population. Hence, greatest dispersal would occur
at the beginning of the period, and least dispersal or greatest
concentration would occur at the end. Major groups, excepting
primary manufacturing, which is a special case, and all subdivisions of these, were expected to behave in a similar way.
They were not, however, expected to concentrate to the same
extent. It was argued that at the beginning of the study period
consumer goods would be more dispersed than producer goods;
that both groups and their subdivisions would become less dispersed, but the difference between them would be maintained
if not widened. With regard to primary manufacturing no certainty attached to its broad movements. Dispersal was just
as likely as concentration.

The first device employed to test these postulates was the coefficient of localization. This is a measure of the relative concentration of any given industry or group of industries compared to some total regional magnitude such as population or income. In essence it is a comparison of the percentage distribution by areal subdivision of employment in the given industry, with the percentage distribution by areal subdivision of the base magnitude. The coefficient is calculated in the following manner. For each subdivision, the percentage share of total employment in the given industrial group is subtracted from its percentage share of total regional population. All positive, or all negative differences are summed and divided by one hundred. The limits to the value of the coefficient are 0 and 1. If the given industry is distributed exactly the same as is population, the value will be zero. On the other hand, if the industrial group is concentrated in one areal unit, the value will approach unity. [2] This is a measure of relative concentration as opposed to absolute concentration. Like all measures of spatial concentration it has deficiencies. For example, if an activity and population are both highly concentrated in space and distributed in much the same way the coefficient of localization will be low. On the other hand, an activity which is less spatially concentrated than the first activity but distributed in a different way from population will have a high coefficient. Additionally it should be pointed out that this coefficient takes no heed of the location or nature of the concentration. Concentration in three contiguous units or in three widely separated units would give rise to the same coefficient value. Accordingly, results must be treated with caution. Indeed, it is advisable that they be supplemented by at least one other measure of concentration.

The coefficients of Tables 6 and 7 show that at no time during the study period was there a high degree of concentration in secondary manufacturing relative to population. Yet, concentrative tendencies were nevertheless evident. York, the most important manufacturing area had 14 per cent of the total employment with 8 per cent of the population in 1851. Forty years later the corresponding figures were 24 per cent and 12 per cent, showing that manufacturing had concentrated more than population.

[2] For a fuller discussion of the coefficient of localization see Walter Isard, Methods of Regional Analysis: An Introduction to Regional Science (Cambridge, Mass.: The MIT Press, 1960), pp. 251-254.

131

TABLE 6    MAJOR MANUFACTURING GROUPS:  COEFFICIENTS OF LOCALIZATION

| Group | 1851 | 1861 | 1871 | 1881 | 1891 |
|---|---|---|---|---|---|
| Consumer | 0.13 | 0.13 | 0.23 | 0.25 | 0.24 |
| Producer | 0.20 | 0.20 | 0.23 | 0.27 | 0.27 |
| All Secondary | 0.16 | 0.15 | 0.23 | 0.23 | 0.24 |
| Primary | 0.25 | 0.39 | 0.21 | 0.25 | 0.24 |

TABLE 7    MANUFACTURING SUBGROUPS:  COEFFICIENTS OF LOCALIZATION

| Group | Coefficient Value | | | | |
|---|---|---|---|---|---|
| | 1851 | 1861 | 1871 | 1881 | 1891 |
| Consumer goods | | | | | |
| food, drink, tobacco | 0.22 | 0.22 | 0.26 | 0.26 | 0.26 |
| clothing, footwear | 0.12 | 0.15 | 0.27 | 0.24 | 0.23 |
| household goods | 0.20 | 0.25 | 0.42 | 0.40 | 0.41 |
| consumer durables | 0.14 | 0.16 | 0.20 | 0.22 | 0.27 |
| Producer goods | | | | | |
| investment goods | 0.22 | 0.19 | 0.28 | 0.27 | 0.28 |
| all finished producer | 0.24 | 0.21 | 0.28 | 0.27 | 0.29 |
| unfinished producer | 0.20 | 0.20 | 0.26 | 0.29 | 0.31 |
| Primary | | | | | |
| food | – | – | 0.43 | 0.39 | 0.39 |
| construction | 0.30 | 0.41 | 0.22 | 0.25 | 0.30 |
| unfinished producer | 0.35 | 0.72 | 0.44 | 0.61 | 0.60 |

This relative concentration did not occur in an even progression. The decade 1861-1871 in particular, recorded most of the increase in concentration. Excepting primary manufacturing, the major groups behaved similarly. However, not all expectations were realized. Both at the beginning and at the end of the period, producer goods were more concentrated than consumer goods, but the difference narrowed. Indeed, in 1871 both recorded the same coefficient.

132

Primary manufacturing exhibited no trend. It concentrated markedly between 1851 and 1861, only to disperse again during the remaining thirty years. One suspects that the construction of the first railway lines made possible a greatly accelerated exploitation of a few areas well placed in relation to them, causing the industry as a whole to rapidly become more concentrated. When more railway lines were constructed and as demand continued to increase, the industry grew in other areas, thus causing a relative dispersal.

The subdivisions of the major groups exhibited trends that for the most part simulated those that were anticipated. In secondary manufacturing the greatest deviation from the distribution of population at the beginning was not in unfinished producer goods, but in investment goods. At the end, it was the distribution of employment in household goods that most differed from that of population. While all groups behaved much as expected, this development in household goods was surprising. In 1851 the coefficients were low, and clothing and footwear, as anticipated, came closest to paralleling the distribution of population. At the end of the period results were not quite as anticipated but they were not disturbingly different. Clothing and footwear, which had a higher coefficient than unfinished producer goods by the mid-point of the study period had decentralized relative to population, showing the greatest relative dispersal by 1891. In view of the arguments presented in the previous chapter, it would be regarded as very significant if the unfinished producer group had the highest coefficient. If it had not, one must question the validity of the theoretical arguments. From 1861, unfinished producer goods showed an increasing coefficient, overtaking the other producer goods groups, and by 1891 had the highest coefficient with the surprising exceptions of household goods.

Several inferences can be drawn from this development. The theoretical discussion has not adequately recognized the possibility that the introduction of mass-production techniques in a consumer good group could endow it with a high localization in all of the several senses in which localization or concentration can be understood. There could be a strong parallel with contemporary underdeveloped countries. If a domestic market develops for goods that can be factory made at large minimal-optimal scales of production, so that a few large central factories supply the total market, a high localization is likely, if

TABLE 8   COTTON MILLS IN SOUTH ONTARIO, 1891

| Subdivision | Number of Establishments | Employees |
|---|---|---|
| Brant | 2 | 280 |
| Stormont | 2 | 1,191 |
| Wentworth | 2 | 534 |
| Lennox-Add-Frontenac | 1 | 210 |
| Lincoln | 2 | 280 |
| | Total: | 2,495 |

SOURCE: Census of Canada, 1891.

not inevitable. The above-average localization in household goods was largely attributable to the textile industries. It was in the cotton industry in particular, that mass-production techniques were introduced, causing considerable change in the distribution pattern of the whole group to which the industry is classified. Without the development of large-scale production in textiles it is doubtful if the household goods group would have registered such a high coefficient value. Table 8 shows the scale and location of cotton mills in 1891.

Another important point regarding the high coefficient value of the household group and this method of measuring concentration in general is that no cognizance is paid to the size of the groups or industries being compared. When groups have a small total employment there is a greater likelihood that one or two large plants can greatly affect the spatial pattern, compared to a group with a comparatively large employment. The addition of the cotton mills industry to the much larger unfinished producers group would not have produced such a high coefficient value.

The third inference can be related to the differences between the producer and consumer goods groups. If theory is to be vindicated, the distribution of producer goods should differ from the distribution of population to a greater extent than the distribution of consumer goods. Now, in fact, the coefficients indicate that this was not the case. It might seem as if the theoretical arguments require revision in the light of the

134

facts. The results, however, do not necessarily spell disaster to the predictions that were made, because of the nature of this method of measuring localization. The coefficient values measure relative concentration per se,· that is, the distribution of manufacturing relative to the distribution of population. It does not measure or indicate the location of concentration. This is very important. Two groups or industries may have exactly the same coefficient value, but quite different distribution patterns. If an industry localizes in the most populated areas, then considerable magnitudes are required to produce a high coefficient value. The most important feature of producer goods is not simply that they localize but that they do so in the most populated areas. It will be shown shortly that when this is taken into consideration, producer goods were more highly localized than other groups.

Most of the movements in the coefficients of localization between decades must remain unexplained. Detailed studies beyond the scope and aims of this work would be required to do that. What is important is the general trend, which was certainly towards localization.[3]

While the coefficient of localization describes the deviation between the distribution of population and an economic activity for the region as a whole, it gives no indication of which areas are responsible for the deviation. It could be a few areas or many and it could be the least or the most populous areas. In view of the questions being investigated in this study, deviations in the populous areas are of the greatest significance. The device employed to examine the spatial variation in the relationship of population to employment in manufacturing is the familiar and often criticized location quotient.[4] This is a method for comparing a unit's percentage share of a particular activity with its percentage share of some base magnitude. In this case employment in manufacturing, or an industrial group, was compared to population. When the location quotient is unity it is normally said that an area has its proportionate share of the particular activity being investigated. When it is less than unity the area has less than its proportionate share, and when

[3] Coefficient of localization values have been calculated for different grouping of industries in 1870, 1880, and 1890. See E. J. Chambers and G. W. Bertram, "Localization and Specialization in Manufacturing in Central Canada, 1870-1890," Paper delivered at 1964 Canadian Political Science Meeting, Conference on Statistics, Charlottetown, P.E.I., Table 5, p. 20.

[4] W. Isard, Methods of Regional Analysis, p. 125.

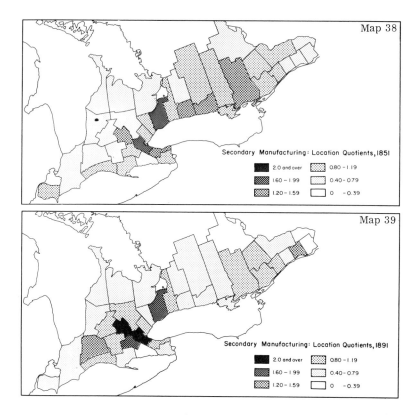

Secondary Manufacturing: Location Quotients, 1851

| | |
|---|---|
| ■ 2.0 and over | ▨ 0.80 – 1.19 |
| ▨ 1.60 – 1.99 | ▨ 0.40 – 0.79 |
| ▨ 1.20 – 1.59 | ☐ 0 – 0.39 |

Map 38

Secondary Manufacturing: Location Quotients, 1891

| | |
|---|---|
| ■ 2.0 and over | ▨ 0.80 – 1.19 |
| ▨ 1.60 – 1.99 | ▨ 0.40 – 0.79 |
| ▨ 1.20 – 1.59 | ☐ 0 – 0.39 |

Map 39

it is greater than unity the area has more than its proportionate share. For instance, if an areal unit accounts for 20 per cent of all employment in sawmilling in the region, but has only 5 per cent of the total population, the area's location quotient for sawmilling would be 4. Although this measure can be meaningless, and untenable inferences can be drawn from the results of its application, it can be of value when considered in conjunction with other concentration indices.

Maps of location quotients were drawn for all the industrial groups, but only those of secondary manufacturing (Maps 38 and 39) and consumer and producer goods (Maps 40, 41, 42, and 43) have been included. In the first place, the patterns that emerge largely speak for themselves, and in the second, the same patterns, with minor variations, are repeated from one grouping to the next. The two maps on secondary manufacturing set the scene, showing the broad patterns that characterized all groups. Were it not for the unfortunately elongated shape of some of the areal units, in 1851 there would have been a

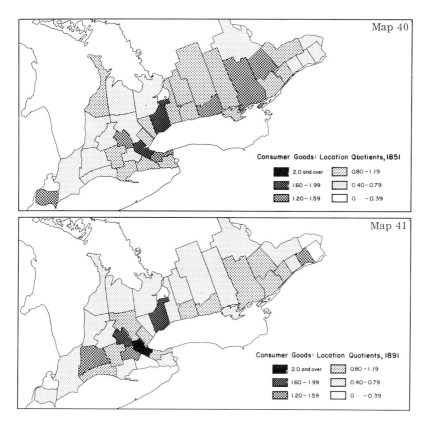

Consumer Goods: Location Quotients, 1851

| | |
|---|---|
| 2.0 and over | 0.80 - 1.19 |
| 1.60 - 1.99 | 0.40 - 0.79 |
| 1.20 - 1.59 | 0 - 0.39 |

Map 40

Consumer Goods: Location Quotients, 1891

| | |
|---|---|
| 2.0 and over | 0.80 - 1.19 |
| 1.60 - 1.99 | 0.40 - 0.79 |
| 1.20 - 1.59 | 0 - 0.39 |

Map 41

high correspondence between the areas which had more than
their proportionate share of manufacturing and the area that
was settled by 1831. The major exception to this statement,
as it has been to many other general statements, was the eastern-
most part of the region. Although settled very early, it had
much less manufacturing than would be anticipated on the basis
of its population. The same was true for most other areas settled after 1831, but in this case the result was expected, since
population will always grow faster than manufacturing in the
earliest phases of growth.

The salient feature in 1851 was the band of concentration
extending east-west across the region. The greatest development was found along the north shore of Lake Ontario and in
the Grand River Valley, viz., early settled areas with ports
and route junctions that acted as intermediaries between the
newly settled hinterlands and the outside world. York and
Wentworth showed the greatest development. Five other areas

137

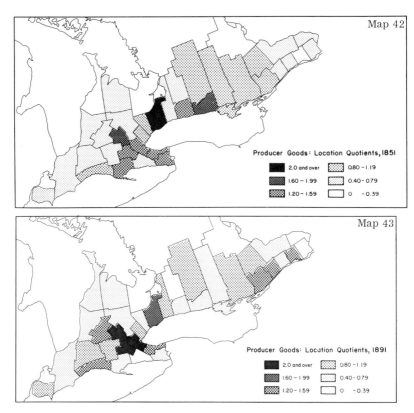

Producer Goods: Location Quotients, 1851

| | | | |
|---|---|---|---|
| ■ | 2.0 and over | ▨ | 0.80 – 1.19 |
| ▨ | 1.60 – 1.99 | ▨ | 0.40 – 0.79 |
| ▨ | 1.20 – 1.59 | ☐ | 0 – 0.39 |

Map 42

Producer Goods: Location Quotients, 1891

| | | | |
|---|---|---|---|
| ■ | 2.0 and over | ▨ | 0.80 – 1.19 |
| ▨ | 1.60 – 1.99 | ▨ | 0.40 – 0.79 |
| ▨ | 1.20 – 1.59 | ☐ | 0 – 0.39 |

Map 43

had well above their proportionate share. The other areas in this east-west band were only slightly above or below what would be expected on the basis of population size.

In 1891 most areas had less manufacturing than population would lead one to expect. Six areas had much more than their proportionate share. Once again these were York, Wentworth, Middlesex, and the Grand River Valley areas. Stormont, isolated by distance from other high-ranking areas, had a disproportionately high share. In southwestern Ontario a number of areas had experienced growth to the point where manufacturing was more or less proportional to population. There was another block of such units in east central Ontario.

The maps of consumer and producer goods illustrate variations on the same theme. In every case there is a decided east to west orientation of high-ranking units, which is replaced at the end by an areal concentration of high-ranking units around the head of Lake Ontario, and extending into southwestern Ontario. With a few exceptions, it was always the units that

138

ranked highest in 1851 that also ranked highest in 1891. These units increased their manufacturing share more than their population share -- a good indication of concentration. The biggest locational changes occurred in the moderately high-ranking units. In 1851 they were found along Lake Ontario, whereas in 1891, southwestern Ontario was the location of such units.

The distribution patterns that emerge show that the location quotient, like all concentration measures, has disadvantages for detecting concentration. In the first place it is difficult to draw meaningful conclusions when the quotients of different industries and groups are compared. It is also of limited value to compare magnitude (absolute concentration) with location quotient. It would be most surprising if the real concentration did not occur within the areas with high quotients, but the quotients themselves offer no guides to which combination of high-ranking units forms the real concentration. The problem is that areas with a high quotient may be insignificant relative to the total size of the industry. In the case of household goods in 1891, for example, Northumberland had a higher location quotient than York, yet, in every other sense, and especially in relation to household goods in the region as a whole, York was far more important. Put another way, household goods were more important to Northumberland than they were to York, but the household goods in York were of greater significance to the total region than those in Northumberland.

When we turn to the magnitude maps, problems of a like nature arise. Without question the area of real concentration lies within the units of above-average magnitude, but which units? Some of those which are above average may have a small amount relative to population. One could scarcely consider these as the areas of real concentration. If the magnitude maps and location quotient maps are compared, it is obvious some units with high magnitude have a low quotient, and that the opposite also obtained. Significantly, however, certain areas at the beginning and at the end of the study period had both a high magnitude and a high location quotient. The logical step would be to combine the two measures to determine the area of real concentration. This would be an area with large quantities of manufacturing, as well as much manufacturing relative to population. The latter fact might suggest that this is an area with a surplus of goods for export to the rest of the region. This was probably true, but it cannot be established

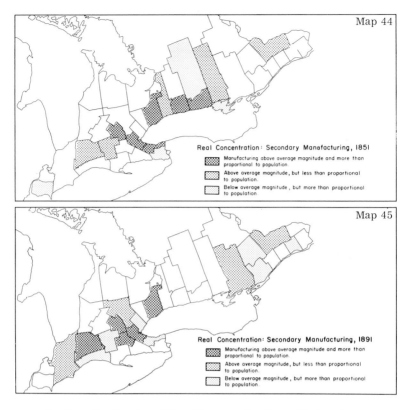

Real Concentration: Secondary Manufacturing, 1851

Manufacturing above average magnitude and more than proportional to population.

Above average magnitude, but less than proportional to population.

Below average magnitude, but more than proportional to population.

Real Concentration: Secondary Manufacturing, 1891

Manufacturing above average magnitude and more than proportional to population.

Above average magnitude, but less than proportional to population.

Below average magnitude, but more than proportional to population.

as a fact on the basis of location quotients. High values may reflect only the anticipated higher purchasing power of the first settled areas.

Maps 43 and 53 represent examples of the results of considering magnitude and location quotient jointly. For want of a better phrase they are described as representing real concentration. In every case, the east-west orientation of concentration in 1851 is quite manifest. In 1891 there was in all cases a decided contraction in the areal extent of concentration, but concentration in the various groups showed a variety of spatial forms. Household goods, which scored the highest coefficient of localization can be compared to unfinished producer goods which unexpectedly ranked second in the localization coefficient and not first. The former in concentrating, did so in a number of widely separated units that extended right across the region. The latter concentrated in a much more compact area around the western end of Lake Ontario, with one separate outlier. This difference raises the question of how

140

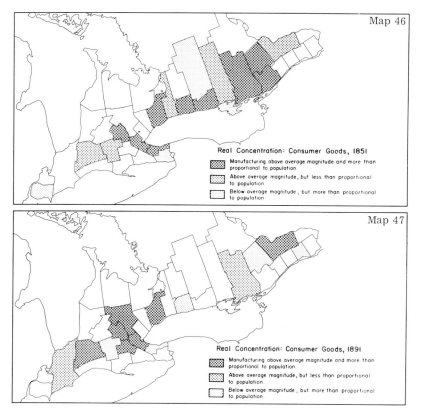

Real Concentration: Consumer Goods, 1851

Manufacturing above average magnitude and more than proportional to population

Above average magnitude, but less than proportional to population

Below average magnitude, but more than proportional to population

Map 46

Real Concentration: Consumer Goods, 1891

Manufacturing above average magnitude and more than proportional to population

Above average magnitude, but less than proportional to population

Below average magnitude, but more than proportional to population

Map 47

meaningful is the coefficient of localization, for in a real sense, unfinished producer goods were more concentrated than house-hold goods.

When all the groups are examined for 1891, it is found that real concentration in all groups occurred in only three units -- York, Wentworth, and Waterloo. Two areas -- Brant and Middlesex -- experienced real concentration in all but one of the groups tested. Other units experiencing real concentration did so in one, or at most, two groups. The area of real con-centration, therefore, contained a considerable proportion of the present manufacturing belt of Ontario. Since Lincoln, Halton, and Peel are now important manufacturing areas, they were joined with York, Waterloo, Wentworth, and Brant to form an area designated as the zone of real concentration in 1891. Both Brant and Middlesex had the same status in concen-tration, but the contiguity of Brant with Waterloo and Wentworth justifies its inclusion as part of the zone of concentration. The

141

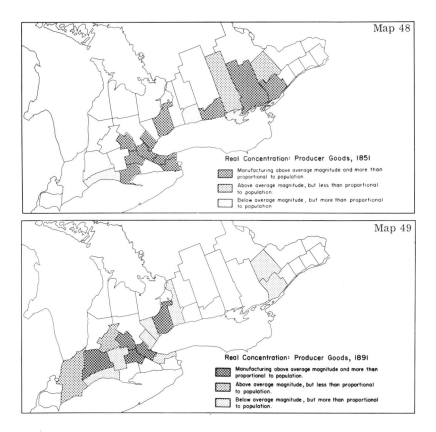

Real Concentration: Producer Goods, 1851

Manufacturing above average magnitude and more than proportional to population

Above average magnitude, but less than proportional to population.

Below average magnitude, but more than proportional to population

Map 49

Real Concentration: Producer Goods, 1891

Manufacturing above average magnitude and more than proportional to population.

Above average magnitude, but less than proportional to population.

Below average magnitude, but more than proportional to population.

physical separation of Middlesex justifies its exclusion. It can be regarded as an important secondary node of localization in 1891. Significantly, the group in which it did not experience concentration was that to which the greatest significance has been attached -- unfinished producer goods. The inclusion of Halton is a valid step on two counts. In the first place, it occupied a position between the most important manufacturing areas, York and Wentworth. Second, although it was not the scene of real concentration, in all groups but one, it experienced relative concentration. Lincoln in view of its contiguity and frequent relative concentration, was also included.

With this zone of concentration, or manufacturing belt delimited, it is informative to examine its share of manufacturing vis-à-vis the rest of the region. Table 9 provides the comparison.

In secondary manufacturing and all major groups and their subgroups, this zone increased its share of total regional man-

TABLE 9    SHARE OF EMPLOYMENT AND POPULATION IN THE "MANUFACTURING BELT" (York, Peel, Halton, Wentworth, Lincoln, Brant and Waterloo) AND THE REST OF SOUTH ONTARIO, 1851 AND 1891

|  | Manufacturing Belt | | The Rest | |
|---|---|---|---|---|
|  | 1851 | 1891 | 1851 | 1891 |
| food, drink, tobacco | 34.9 | 39.7 | 65.1 | 60.3 |
| clothing and footwear | 32.0 | 43.7 | 68.0 | 56.3 |
| household goods | 27.6 | 38.0 | 72.4 | 62.0 |
| consumer durables | 27.6 | 36.8 | 72.4 | 63.2 |
| all consumer | 33.1 | 42.9 | 66.9 | 57.1 |
| investment goods | 38.3 | 41.0 | 61.7 | 59.0 |
| all finished producer | 41.9 | 44.8 | 58.1 | 55.2 |
| unfinished producer | 36.6 | 51.7 | 63.4 | 48.3 |
| all producer | 38.4 | 47.1 | 61.6 | 52.9 |
| all secondary | 34.9 | 44.8 | 65.1 | 55.2 |
| primary construction | 25.9 | 12.4 | 74.1 | 87.6 |
| primary unfinished producer | 17.4 | 11.4 | 82.6 | 88.6 |
| population | 25.0 | 24.0 | 75.0 | 76.0 |

ufacturing between 1851 and 1891.  This took place while absolute growth was occurring everywhere except Haldimand.  Primary manufacturing behaved in an opposite manner.  There
was no concentration of primary manufacturing in the zone,
and its share fell considerably during the study period.

The summary picture presented by Table 9 supports several
of the hypotheses relating to the distribution of manufacturing.
On the other hand, some of the results do not support certain
of the theoretical speculations.  These will be examined in turn.

Secondary manufacturing had concentrated as was anticipated.  Both at the beginning and at the end of the period, the
area that was to emerge as the manufacturing belt had a greater
share of the producer goods industries than of the consumer
goods industries.  It was regarded as a distinct possibility that
the gap between the two groups might be widened, with producer
goods concentrating more rapidly in the core area of the early
settled districts.  In fact, however, consumer goods closed the
gap a little, concentrating more than was expected.  The distribution of employment in the clothing and footwear industries
seems to have been important in this development.  It appears
that large-scale economies and factory production supplanting
imports and widely distributed small tailor shops, made a sub-

143

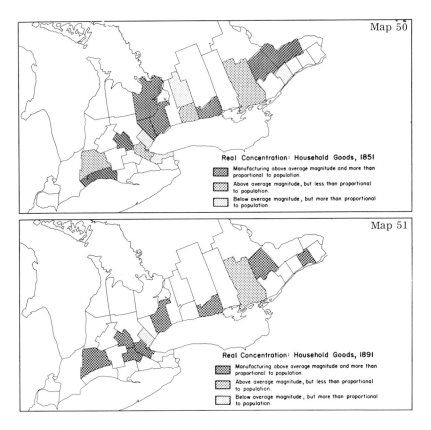

Map 50

Real Concentration: Household Goods, 1851

Manufacturing above average magnitude and more than proportional to population.

Above average magnitude, but less than proportional to population.

Below average magnitude , but more than proportional to population.

Map 51

Real Concentration: Household Goods, 1891

Manufacturing above average magnitude and more than proportional to population.

Above average magnitude, but less than proportional to population.

Below average magnitude , but more than proportional to population.

stantial contribution to localization in consumer goods as a whole. Possibly, the existence of large-scale economies and technological innovation have been underestimated in relation to consumer goods, while these and the importance of production relationships and external economies in producer goods have been overestimated.

Consumer durables, which were expected to exhibit the greatest concentration among the various consumer groups, failed to do so. A tentative explanation is that import substitution and large-scale localized production in consumer goods is most likely to occur with the production of those goods most in demand, and for which production processes, while on a large scale, are relatively simple. Clothing and footwear are likely to meet these conditions before consumer durables.

On the positive side was the behaviour of the unfinished producer goods group. No other group became so strongly concentrated in the manufacturing belt. The zone increased its

144

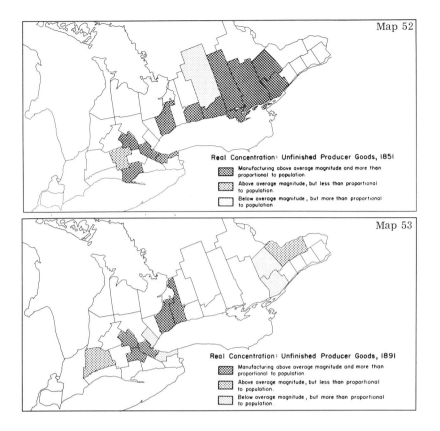

Real Concentration: Unfinished Producer Goods, 1851

Manufacturing above average magnitude and more than proportional to population.

Above average magnitude, but less than proportional to population.

Below average magnitude, but more than proportional to population.

Real Concentration: Unfinished Producer Goods, 1891

Manufacturing above average magnitude and more than proportional to population.

Above average magnitude, but less than proportional to population.

Below average magnitude, but more than proportional to population.

share of this group by some 15 per cent. Since unfinished producer goods have been regarded throughout as the key group,
this is of the utmost significance. Without their development
there can be no true industrialization. They are expected in
the long-run to show the greatest concentration, acting as the
key-stone in the cumulative growth-concentration process that
characterizes secondary activity. Where manufacturing as a
whole concentrates, so will unfinished producer goods, thereby
fixing the area or areas of localization, attracting development
of other groups around them, then responding with further
growth themselves.

The high localization of this group indicates that the changes
in the structure of manufacturing as a whole in the region
depended heavily on the developments in one small area. By
1891 over half of all the employment in this group was in the
manufacturing belt. Had the unfinished producer good group
not grown, secondary manufacturing would not have been so

concentrated by the end of the study period. One cannot say that unfinished producer goods themselves would have been less concentrated, for concentration may occur even if there is relatively little absolute growth. But one can certainly say that without growth in unfinished producer goods, as indicated by the analysis of structure, producer goods would not have been so localized and the differences between producer and consumer goods would have been much less.

The concentration of unfinished producer goods is all the more remarkable when it is recalled that the group's greatest period of growth, starting with basic iron and steel production in Wentworth, was yet to come. It certainly suggests that the basic distributional patterns within a region (not within a nation) take form at an early stage in a region's development. The period of most rapid Canadian growth which was associated with Prairie development and the First World War changed the scale of pattern form, rather than changed the form itself.[5] Admittedly there have been significant distributional changes since 1891. The greatest change was the growth of manufacturing in two border areas, namely, Essex and Lincoln. The latter, in any case, is included in the manufacturing belt. These two areas had particular advantages for the American branch plants which became numerous in the twentieth century.[6] Since the Second World War, however, the manufacturing belt has been strongly asserting its dominance and continues to capture a larger and larger share of total manufacturing.[7]

Analysis of structure showed that the manufacturing belt had more significant producer, and in particular, unfinished producer goods elements. This did not mean, however, that there was a simultaneous spatial concentration of these groups in the same area. Structural analysis simply gave an indication of relative importance within separate areal units. Analysis of distribution shows that one of the major elements of structural

[5] In 1961 the manufacturing belt contained 57.5 per cent of all manufacturing (measured by selling value of factory shipments) in the study region. Calculation based on data obtained from Canada, DBS, The Manufacturing Industries of Canada, 1961, Section G, Geographical Distribution (Ottawa: Queen's Printer, 1964).

[6] The location of American Branch plants in South Ontario has been investigated by D. Michael Ray in Market Potential and Economic Shadow, Department of Geography Research Paper No. 101 (Chicago: Department of Geography, University of Chicago, 1965).

[7] For recent distributional developments, consult The Economic Atlas of Ontario, ed. W. G. Dean (Toronto: University of Toronto Press for the Government of Ontario, 1969).

146

variation through space was the result of spatial concentration in both a relative and an absolute sense in one of the earliest settled parts of Ontario.

Likewise, although consumer goods were found to be relatively less important in the manufacturing belt, this did not mean that they were failing to grow in the manufacturing belt. In fact, they could have been concentrating more rapidly than producer goods without structural patterns indicating any change. As it was, the area that was most important for producer goods was also in an absolute sense very important for consumer goods. Structural differences were arising from variation in spatial concentration. All groups, excepting the primary, were concentrating in the manufacturing belt while growing at different rates. In all cases, there was concentration not just in the core, but in one, two, or several additional areas that were thus endowed with a "deviant" structure. The distributive tendencies of the household goods group provides an interesting example. This group was highly localized, but not in the main manufacturing core alone. It grew rapidly in several widely separated areas, thereby contributing to the irregularity in spatial variation in structure.

STRUCTURE AND DISTRIBUTION

Certain salient points emerge from this analysis of distribution. These are briefly summarized, then related to spatial patterns of structure.

Secondary manufacturing concentrated during the study period but primary manufacturing showed no similar distributive tendency. Within secondary manufacturing, the various subgroups, although concentrating, displayed variety in their distributional forms. The subgroups of primary manufacturing also displayed a heterogeneity of distribution patterns, but were not united by a common distributional tendency. The primary construction group experienced very far-reaching distributional changes, the end result of which was a pattern of distribution very different from that of secondary manufacturing. There was strong localization in the lightly populated, peripheral parts of the region. The other two primary groups were the most highly localized of all the groups used in the study but showed no definite distributional tendencies.

147

The secondary manufacturing industries possessed a consistency in distributional pattern that was lacking in primary industries. It was still, however, far from being a perfect consistency. In an absolute sense there was considerable redistribution. For the most part, the areas along the north shore of Lake Ontario except York County saw much less growth in both absolute and relative terms than southwestern Ontario. This distributional swing, however, was far from sufficient to undermine the lead in manufacturing activity enjoyed by the area around the head of Lake Ontario and the Grand River Valley at the beginning of the study period. Secondary manufacturing as a whole, and all its subgroups experienced more absolute growth in this area than in others. This was sufficient to increase its relative share vis-à-vis the rest of the region. But absolute growth was occurring in almost all other parts of the region as well. The nature of this growth engendered the patternless spatial variation encountered in the analysis of structure in chapter iv.

Two points must be clearly understood. Concentration also occurred outside the manufacturing belt. Middlesex increased its share of manufacturing to become an important localization in almost all secondary subgroups. In addition, outside both the manufacturing belt and Middlesex, the subgroups distributed themselves unequally among the areal units. In one, investment goods showed considerable growth, while in another household goods developed strongly. In some units all subgroups were poorly represented, and it required but slight growth in one to completely alter the structure of manufacturing in that area. Small changes, just as much as large, could lead to great structural variety among units. Although the events producing these structures were frequently unimportant relative to events and developments in the region as a whole, they were sufficient to cause variation within individual units that seems unrelated to time and distance. The second point is that such structural variation is just as likely to occur within the manufacturing belt as without.

Such developments are probable when analysis is forced to deal with different-size units, different-size groups, and the unpredictable behaviour of the individual entrepreneur. But these reasons must be joined with a more fundamental cause of structural variability. It is no paradox to say that the smaller the amount of manufacturing found in a unit, and the longer the region and the unit have been settled, the less predictable becomes the structure of the individual areal unit. As a corollary, the likelihood of identifiable spatial patterns in structure diminishes with time. This likelihood is further diminished if the region successfully industrializes. The more recently a unit has been settled, the greater is the probability of a consumer goods dominance in secondary manufacturing, for the range of domestic investment opportunities is at first limited in other directions. With time, even in those parts of the region that are not particularly successful, the range of apparent and real opportunities widens. The construction of a transportation network no doubt widens the range of apparent opportunities. The entrepreneur widens his vision, previously focused on his own small local area, to wider areas with consumer and producer good demands outnumbering those of the small local area. Particularly when a unit has not succeeded in developing much manufacturing, one or two entrepreneurial decisions can drastically alter its structure of manufacturing. In chapter v great pains were taken to explain why entrepreneurs may choose to locate plants in the most backward, undesirable, and marginal areas.

The economic growth theory, from which this work's concept of structure was derived, is, like many economic growth theories, applicable only to the aggregate economy -- in this case, the aggregate economy of the region. It is therefore when we are dealing with aggregates that we are in the best position to predict events (provided our theory is well-founded). There is, however, no spatial equivalent of the aggregate economy. When we deal with the space economy as a whole we have eliminated space, and when we recognize space, we have fragmented the aggregate. To examine space it is necessary to subdivide it into units of space or points in space. The less significant a point or unit becomes in contributing to the aggregate, the most potentially erratic can become distribution patterns because virtually all decisions have noticeable and immediate effect in the local area.

We can be sure of the occurrence of the concentration process in manufacturing. On empirical and theoretical grounds we know it will occur. Concentration produces spatial cumulation of aggregate share; a larger and larger proportion of the aggregate becomes restricted in a small area. As share of total increases, predictability increases. As concentration proceeds the greater part of the region has less and less of the aggregate; so predictability decreases. Provided one is dealing with reasonably large groups (dependent upon the detail of one's classification) it requires many decisions to produce structural change in the manufacturing belt. When many decisions produce a noticeable change what we have is a series of tied events that is recognizable as a major trend. When one decision can change significantly, what we have is an historical event that was no more likely than other potential historical events that did not occur.

It seems a reasonable conclusion that the absence of spatial pattern in structure and structural change of manufacturing outside the manufacturing belt is the product of its increasing insignificance. And this is the inevitable effect of the concentration process which is the mark and a condition of successful economic growth. It is quite certain that a core of concentration will form; and there is good reason to expect it to be part of the first settled areas. Thus indeed it was in South Ontario. As the concentration grows it more and more fulfills the expectations we have of the region as a whole, while the rest of the region follows a variety of courses as reflected in the structural variability. This in turn reflects the fact that success, if it is there at all, is based on development in one direction.

These thoughts are verified by the preceding analyses of structure and distribution. The above argument leads to the statement that the more recently a region has been settled, and hence, the more equitably distributed are the shares which in sum constitute the aggregate, the more likely we are to find spatial pattern in structure. The maps of chapter iv confirm this point. In several cases there was a clear gradient in structural change through space that paralleled in time and direction the settlement process of the region. With time, however, this pattern disintegrated and there was an absence of spatial patterning. From the above arguments it also follows that the fewer subdivisions we make of an aggregate, structurally, spatially, or both together, the more likely we are to find quite distinct spatial patterns that maintain themselves through time. This was clearly brought out in dealing with economic structure in chapter iii. The total economy was divided into only three sectors each of which was very large. None of these exhibited erratic behaviour like the subgroups of manufacturing.

150

It is salutory to review realized expectations. Our hopes
for the economy as a whole, divorced from spatial considerations, were realized. The same was true of total manufacturing. Our expectations for the structure of secondary manufacturing were also realized. Speculations regarding the broad
spatial tendencies of the economic sectors of manufacturing,
of its groups and subgroups, were fulfilled. By broad tendencies is meant concentration. As concentration gathered force,
the favoured area increased its share of aggregate manufacturing. It is mainly for this reason, allied with the fact that different groups concentrated to different degrees, that our expectations of the structure of manufacturing in the manufacturing
belt were realized. It is for the same reason that we must
expect a diminution in the spatial regularity of structure and
distribution outside the manufacturing belt.

Clearly, concentration and maturation are two aspects of
the same process. The more manufacturing concentrates, the
more mature becomes the structure of the core and therefore
of the region. And the more mature the structure of the core
and the region, the greater is the likelihood of continuing concentration.

Referring back to the analysis of structure it was found
that throughout the period two areas were consistently prominent by being structurally more mature than the rest of the
region. The first was York, standing on its own. The second
was a line of units extending from the Niagara Peninsula through
to the early settled inland units on the Grand River Valley,
namely, Brant and Waterloo. It was also oberved that Middlesex
was more mature than surrounding areas. Real concentration,
maturity in the structure of the economy and maturity in the
structure of manufacturing are spatially coincident. The structure of secondary manufacturing was not uniform among the
units within the zone of concentration. This is the inevitable
product of small area subdivisions and small industrial groups,
associated with the irrational and unpredictable locational and
operational decisions of the individual entrepreneur, and with
historical accident.

## CONCLUSION

It seems that a simple distance-time explanation of variation in structure fits the facts decreasingly well as development proceeds. The closer we approach the beginnings of the region, the stronger appears the relationship between date of settlement (time and distance), and structure of manufacturing. Or, we may say that from the beginning the tie between the structure of manufacturing and distance from first settled areas is a weakening relationship.

The mere passage of time gives way to concentrative tendencies as the main dynamic of structural change. Yet, perhaps it never surrenders completely, and it is next to impossible to determine the exact role that each plays. It seems that time available for development remains important but becomes divorced from its relationship of distance from first settled areas. Any area through time, even though it is becoming less and less important in the region, is likely to become more mature. But each unit proceeds at its own pace.

Predictable maturation coincides with the area where secondary manufacturing concentrates. Maturation of structure outside the concentration becomes more and more a chance process with regard to any particular unit. Inside the concentration it is a necessary process otherwise concentration would be retarded.

The structure of manufacturing was greatly influenced by the way in which activities distributed themselves. If there is no concentration growth opportunities will be restricted, so that structure will be more uniform and in any area will likely reflect the time available for development.

# VII
# Process in selected industries

This chapter examines changes in the characteristics and distribution of four secondary manufacturing industries. Between them they represent a cross-section of the classification as well as of the developments underlying the broader distributional movements so far examined. Each gives evidence of some of the processes which, when summed for all the industries in the study area, produce the total pattern changes.

For the most part, analysis is for the period 1871 to 1891. Examination of changes over the entire study period would have been more satisfactory, but regrettably, statistical data pertaining to establishments are not normally available until the Census of 1871. The data for prior times that are available for a few industries are incomplete and inconsistent. As such, they have little value for comparative purposes. The time period examined, however, is of sufficient duration to permit observation and recognition of long-term trends.

THE BREWING INDUSTRY

Brewing was among the first industries to be introduced to South Ontario. By virtue of its consumer market and its early start, it was widely distributed throughout the settled areas before the rail-

TABLE 10    BREWING INDUSTRY CHARACTERISTICS:  1851-1891

| Year | Establishments | Capital ($) | Value of Raw Materials ($) | Employment | Value of Output ($) |
|------|----------------|-------------|----------------------------|------------|---------------------|
| 1871 | 105 | 849,640 | 532,137 | 536 | 1,198,919 |
| 1881 | 106 | 2,663,340 | 1,556,790 | 935 | 3,372,408 |
| 1891 | 82 | 5,305,405 | 1,596,104 | 1,047 | 3,578,874 |

ways were developed.  The peak number of establishments in a
census year was reached in 1881.  Between 1871 and 1881, however, the number rose only by one.  In brewing, we are dealing
with an industry in which the distribution pattern has changed by
the dilution process.  Plants were eliminated as the growing industry (see Table 10) concentrated in a decreasing number of production centres.

   An underlying assumption of the postulates on the dilution process was that the demand for the product of the diluting industry
is as widely distributed as the total population.  Available fragmentary evidence does strongly suggest that the demand for alcoholic beverages was ubiquitous in South Ontario.  There are no
sales or consumption figures by area units, but data exist on the
distribution of liquor licenses during part of the study period.
The outlets for the purchase of beer and other alcoholic beverages
were numerous and widespread.  In 1874, for example, the Province
of Ontario issued 6185 liquor licenses.  These included tavern,
shop, and wholesale licenses.  No urban centres or populated townships were without licensed premises of some sort.  Over the
years the number of licenses declined.  Yet there was no evidence
of disproportionate decline in any area.  The 3414 licenses granted
in 1891 were very widely distributed.[1]

   Knowledge that license holders were dispersed throughout the
study area does not, of course, guarantee that the demand for beer
was a function of population size and distribution.  Guillet is confident that there was an ubiquitous demand for alcoholic beverages,
noting that ubiquitous profligacy, intemperance, and drunkenness
were more common than temperance, piety, and prohibition.

[1] Data obtained from "the Report upon the Inspection of Liquor Licenses for the year
1902," presented to the Ontario Legislature 21 March 1903, Sessional Papers vol.35,
Part IX, Sessional Paper 44, First session, 10th Legislature of the Province of Ontario,
Session 1903.

Taverns, saloons, hotels, and inns were found wherever settlement existed.[2] Within the region, however, taste may have had some effect on the distribution of demand for beer. In eastern Ontario, for example, there was no shortage of liquor licenses, yet at all times there were few breweries in this area compared to other parts of Ontario. Some areal units in this area have never had a brewery. This paucity may have reflected the predominance of local taste, just as the many breweries in those counties with settlers of German origin reflected a strong local preference for beer over other drinks.

During the study period, breweries were widely distributed throughout South Ontario. Even in 1891, only ten areal units out of a total of 38 were without a brewery. In the 1870's, when the number of brewing centres was at its peak, breweries were found in almost all major urban centres. With smaller centres the probability of a brewery being found was considerably less. In fact, as far as distribution between centres within a county was concerned, chance seems to have played an important role. Available records indicate that breweries were sometimes located in settlements with less than 200 people, while larger centres with 2000 to 4000 inhabitants were not production centres of this industry. The critical level seems to have been 4000 population. Above this population size all centres had at least one brewery in the 1870's. There is no evidence to suggest that temperance or local prohibition or taste influenced the choice of production centres. Here we are dealing with an industry that was predictably widespread throughout the region, but in which random factors affected its distribution between small urban centres.

It is not possible with census data to establish the number of production centres of the industry. Also, it is impossible to tell whether or not the same establishments and companies are being described from one census to the next. The only distributional information provided by the census is the number of establishments located within a census subdivision. We are left in ignorance of where, within the division, plants are located, and of whether or not relocations occur within the subdivisions between censuses.

Some information about production centres can be obtained from the 1850's onwards. Perusal of five directories[3] reveals a

[2]Edwin C. Guillet, Pioneer Inns and Taverns, 4 vols. (Toronto: Ontario Publishing Co. Ltd., vols. 1 and 2, 1956; vols. 3 and 4, 1958).

[3]The directories used were: The Canada Directory, by Robert W. S. Mackay (Montreal: John Lovell, 1852); The Province of Ontario Gazetteer and Directory (Toronto: Robertson

maximum total of 118 production centres in the study area. Not all of these were in operation at the same time. Although the directories are not very reliable, they do serve to indicate the general trends. The greatest number of production centres at one time was recorded in 1869 when there were 78. In 1882 the count was 61, while in 1895 there were only 45 production centres. Discrepancies between the number of production centres and number of establishments is accounted for by the clustering of establishments in certain production centres. In 1891, for example, nine breweries were found in Toronto, four in Hamilton, and three in London. Even though the directories are not totally reliable, there seems little doubt that production was being concentrated at a smaller number of production centres in an apparently less than perfect example of the elimination process. The directory information would seem to indicate that considerable elimination of production centres occurred, but it was not perfect, insofar as smaller producers at smaller centres survived when some of the larger producers in larger centres did not. Twenty towns were brewing centres continuously from 1851 to 1895. Without exception, these were the major port cities and inland regional centres.[4] Several larger or similar sized centres, also had breweries in 1895, but production had started at a later date than 1851.[5] While many of the smaller production centres were eliminated, sometimes after a productive life of only 10 to 20 years, some continued in production with remarkable persistence, causing the elimination process to work not quite in the theoretical way. In 1895, production was still continuing at such small, relatively unknown centres as Bamberg and Baden in Waterloo County, Formosa in Bruce County, and Hornby in Halton. At the same date, much larger centres, such as Chatham, Berlin (Kitchener), Galt, and Simcoe were no longer production centres of the industry.

Although the establishments of the industry were scattered across the study area during the entire study period, and production was found in some really small centres, beer production was

& Cook, 1869): Canadian Dominion Directory (Montreal: John Lovell, 1871); Lovell's Business and Professional Directory of the Province of Ontario for 1882 (Montreal: John Lovell & Son, 1882); Province of Ontario Gazetteer and Directory (Toronto: The Might Directory Company of Toronto Ltd., 1895).

[4] The centres were Barrie, Belleville, Brantford, Coburg, Hamilton, Kingston, Lindsay, London, Ottawa, Owen Sound, Perth, Peterborough, Port Hope, Prescott, Preston, St. Catharines, St. Thomas, Stratford, Toronto, and Goderich.

[5] These were Brockville, Guelph, Listowell, Orillia, Port Colborne, Sarnia, Strathroy, Tillsonburg, Trenton, Waterloo, Windsor, and Woodstock.

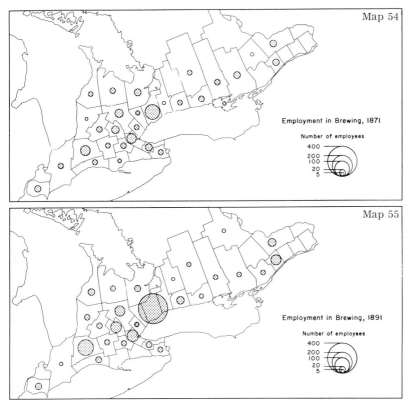

Map 54

Employment in Brewing, 1871

Number of employees
400
200
100
20
5

Map 55

Employment in Brewing, 1891

Number of employees
400
200
100
20
5

quite highly concentrated. Maps 54 and 55 show the distribution
of the industry in the years 1871 and 1891. Clearly, the industry
was widely distributed throughout the study area in both years,
but there was a somewhat higher magnitude in certain areas. In
1871, York, Wentworth, and Middlesex were the most important
producing areas. By 1891, despite the widespread nature of the
demand, the major production areas were concentrated in the
central and southwestern areas of the region, and several were
found in the manufacturing belt.

Between 1871 and 1891, most areal units and most production
centres and units were contributing a decreasing proportion of
total output (see Maps 56 and 57). In 1871, four areal units
accounted for the first 50 per cent of output by value, and another
five units for the third quarter of total production. By 1891, six
areal units were the source of the first 75 per cent of total industry output by value. Two areal units were responsible for over
half of the industry's production. Put another way, two production centres (Toronto and London) with 14 plants out of the indus-

157

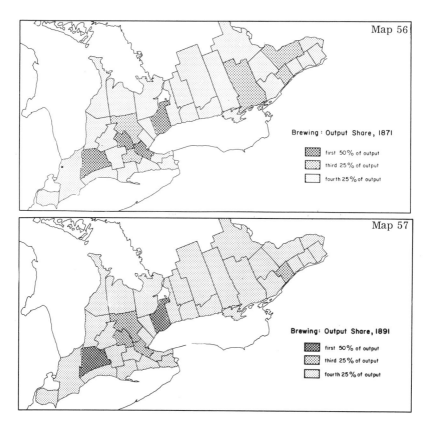

Map 56

Brewing : Output Share, 1871

first 50% of output
third 25% of output
fourth 25% of output

Map 57

Brewing: Output Share, 1891

first 50% of output
third 25% of output
fourth 25% of output

try total of 82, produced well over 50 per cent of all the beer by value in South Ontario.

Such striking concentration was happening at the same time as the number of establishments and production centres was falling, but as the output of the industry was rising. A majority of the areal units with establishments experienced a reduction in their number. This included the areal units in which the greatest growth occurred (see Map 59, Brewing: Changes in Manufacturing Employment, 1871–1891). A few areas received new establishments. Four of these areas were at the periphery of the region; areas which were settled late and still feeling local final demand linkage effects from the growth of the primary sector. The new plants were small, and as Map 59 shows, they produced but slight growth in the areal units in which they were located. Most areas lost plants. If the information of the directories can be relied upon, then it was the smaller plants in the smaller production areas which constituted the majority of those eliminated. Result-

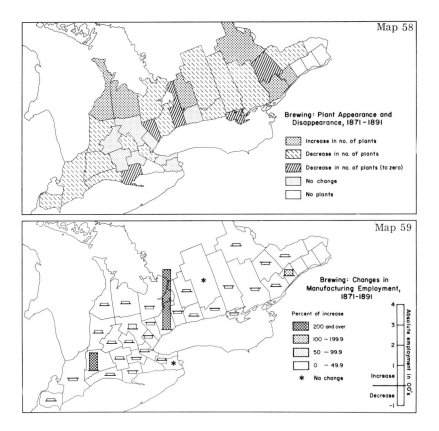

**Map 58**

Brewing: Plant Appearance and
Disappearance, 1871–1891

Increase in no. of plants

Decrease in no. of plants

Decrease in no. of plants (to zero)

No change

No plants

**Map 59**

Brewing: Changes in
Manufacturing Employment,
1871-1891

Percent of increase

200 and over

100 – 199.9

50 – 99.9

0 – 49.9

* No change

Increase

Decrease

Absolute employment in 00's

ing from this process was a dilution in the density of the pattern
formed by the establishments of the industry, with remaining
establishments still spatially widespread.

An interesting development was the total elimination of plants
in the two areal units either side of York (Toronto), suggesting
the attractive hypothesis that the competition from the large centre
was just too powerful for the small producers closest to the city.

As is evident from Map 59 many areal units experienced no
growth, while expansion in most of the rest was well below average. York and Middlesex grew so much that growth in other
centres was slight by comparison. Only one other areal unit
showed above average growth -- this was Grenville in eastern
Ontario. Separated by a long distance from Toronto, the nearest
growth centre, Grenville may have functioned as the centre of concentration for the industry in the east, just as Toronto and London
did in the west. One suspects, however, that the strong competitive power of Montreal would diminish hopes of a long-lived growth.

TABLE 11   ESTIMATES OF THE MARKET OF SELECTED BREWING CENTRES:  1881

| Centre | Value of production ($) | Estimated local centre consumption ($) | Estimated non-local consumption (basic) ($) | Local market as per cent of Ontario market | Basic market as per cent of Ontario market | Total market of centres as per cent of Ontario market |
|---|---|---|---|---|---|---|
| Toronto | 1,077,500 | 163,414 | 914,086 | 5.0 | 27.9 | 32.9 |
| Hamilton | 162,500 | 61,132 | 101,368 | 1.9 | 3.1 | 5.0 |
| Ottawa | 11,350 | 53,222 | – | 1.6 | – | 1.6 |
| London | 718,000 | 44,652 | 673,338 | 1.4 | 20.6 | 22.0 |
| Kingston | 72,600 | 23,955 | 48,645 | 0.7 | 1.5 | 2.2 |
| Brockville | 20,000 | 12,935 | 7,065 | 0.4 | 0.3 | 0.7 |

Method of calculation:  The average per capita consumption of beer in Ontario was calculated by dividing the total value of production of brewing by total population. With this figure, the value of consumption (non-basic) in each producing centre was calculated by multiplying the population of each centre against it. Value of non-basic consumption in each centre was subtracted from total value of production in each centre. The residue, basic consumption, was divided by the value of average per capita consumption to obtain an estimation of the number of people in the basic market.

With Toronto and London becoming so important in the industry, a large proportion of the total market must have been supplied by their establishments. Tables 11 and 12 represent the result of efforts to estimate the size of market in terms of population supplied from these centres and some second-rank centres. Both major brewing centres were producing far more than could be absorbed by their own populations. In both cases the basic market was considerably larger than the non-basic market. This was particularly the case with London. With both, the basic market grew faster than the non-basic market during the study period. Most of the smaller production centres examined were also producing more beer than their own local populations could absorb. In their case, however, the ratio of the basic market to the non-basic market was about unity or less than unity, not several times unity as was the case with Toronto and London.

It follows as a corollary from these findings that the often-employed theoretical concept of plants as spatial monopolists with-

160

TABLE 12   ESTIMATES OF THE MARKET OF SELECTED BREWING CENTRES: 1891

| Centre | Value of produc- tion ($) | Estimated local centre consump- tion ($) | Estimated non local consump- tion (basic) ($) | Local market as per cent of Ontario market | Basic market as per cent of Ontario market | Total market of centres as per cent of Ontario market |
|--------|------|-----------|----------|-------|-------|--------|
| Toronto | 1,395,403 | 308,074 | 1,087,329 | 8.6 | 30.2 | 38.8 |
| Hamilton | 225,800 | 83,266 | 142,534 | 2.3 | 3.9 | 6.2 |
| Ottawa | 20,000 | 32,749 | - | 0.9 | - | 0.9 |
| London | 533,000 | 54,361 | 478,639 | 1.5 | 13.3 | 14.8 |
| Kingston | 15,000 | 32,749 | - | 0.9 | - | 0.9 |
| Brockville | 60,000 | 14,948 | 45,052 | 0.4 | 1.2 | 1.6 |

in their own market areas, is highly doubtful. It is possible that small producers at a certain distance from the large centres had a small spatial monopoly, surrounded by the market area of the more distant large producer. There is certainly no doubt that if Toronto or London had had continuous spatial monopolies extending outwards from their centres until their estimated markets were reached, then many areal units for some distance around them would have contained no production units. But this was not the case.

A much more likely development is a variant on the first contingency. This is a situation in which the small producers have small local market areas in which almost all their sales are made. These market areas, however, most likely would not be spatial monopolies, but the scene of vigorous competition between small and large producers. This may not have been simple price competition with similar products. It must be recognized that there could have been considerable product differences within the industry. The biggest difference at the present and in the 19th century was that between draft and bottled beer. Another important product difference was between lager beer and ale, the former reflecting the German influences in North American brewing. Since draft beer does not travel well, it is likely that as distance from the larger plants increased they were competing against the small breweries with a different product. The small breweries would survive by concentrating on the least competitive product of the large breweries, viz., draft beer, while the larger breweries penetrated their market area with the more competitive bottled beer. Closer to the large breweries, competition in both draft and bottled beer would be great. Consequently, there was the likelihood of small breweries closer to large production centres being eliminated at an early date. Such developments occurred in the UK.[6] There is no reason why they should not be repeated in Canada.

There is very little evidence on the nature of market areas in the 19th century. The Royal Commission on the Liquor Traffic in the 1890's provides a few clues.[7] Several Ontario breweries came before the commission to give evidence on their activities and interests. Occasionally they were asked general questions about their sales areas. Some answers partly substantiate expectations about market areas.

Henry Calcott, a brewer in Ashburnham, a village very close to Peterborough, had a beer production that ranged from 144,375 gallons in 1888 to 67,800 gallons in 1891. His brewery, therefore, was a relatively small one for the area. He made two helpful observations. He noted that his output was sold principally in the County of Peterborough and that breweries from outside Peterborough were selling beer in that county.[8]

Mr. Alexander, an Inland Revenue officer of London provides further clues.

Question: "Have you any means of knowing whether the malt liquor made in these years (80's) was sent out of the district or consumed in it?"

Answer : "It was consumed in the district. Of course, breweries like Carling and Labatt (large London breweries) shipped a great deal away from here to Montreal, Hamilton, Ottawa, and Toronto, but with the other breweries it is mostly local consumption" (i.e., breweries in Elgin, Middlesex and Lambton Counties). [9]

[6] J. Vaizey, The Brewing Industry, 1886-1951 (London: Sir Issac Pitman & Sons Ltd., 1960).

[7] Royal Commission on the Liquor Traffic, "Minutes of Evidence taken in the Province of Ontario," Sessional Papers vol. 15, Sessional Paper 21 (2 parts), Fourth Session of the 7th Parliament of the Dominion of Canada, Session 1894.

[8] Ibid., Paper 21, pp. 66-68.

[9] Ibid., p. 359. Comments in brackets are inserted by author to facilitate comprehension.

TABLE 13    SCALE INCREASES IN BREWING: 1871-1891

| Year | Average Employment Per Establishment | Average Capital Investment Per Establishment in $ |
|------|------|------|
| 1871 | 5. 2 | 8, 044 |
| 1881 | 8. 8 | 25, 144 |
| 1891 | 12. 8 | 64, 700 |

From a traveller for the Carling Brewing and Malting Company of London we learn that among other centres he visited Port Stanley, St. Thomas, Strathroy, Ingersoll, Woodstock, and St. Mary's, several of which had their own local breweries at the time. [10]

Eugene O'Keefe, a Toronto brewer, owned one of the largest breweries in Ontario. In 1890-91, his brewery produced approximately 800,000 gallons of ale, porter, and lager beer, which it was claimed in his evidence, was sent all over Ontario and to Montreal. [11] Another Toronto brewer, Robert Davies, of the Dominion Brewing Company claimed that this company was selling beer from Vancouver to Quebec. With an output of 1,200,000 gallons in 1891, this was a large brewery by the standards of Ontario at that time. It is interesting to note that in the 1880's, this brewery commenced the production of bottled beer, in which it was competitively successful. [12]

With the industry growing, with the large breweries competing against the small breweries and each other, and with plants being eliminated, one would expect the average size of a production unit in the industry to rise. Table 13 shows that the average size of establishments did increase in the industry as a whole between 1871 and 1891. These figures, however, mask the substantially greater scale increases achieved by a few of the producers.

From Table 14 we learn that the first 50 per cent of output by value emanated from 14 establishments, the average size of which was more than 6 times greater than the average size of the 45 establishments in the areal units producing the last 25 per cent of output. Clearly, a few plants in the larger centres were organ-

[10] Ibid., p. 357. All these centres are within a distance of twenty miles from London.

[11] Ibid., p. 729.

[12] Ibid., p. 713.

|  | Number of Establishments | Average Employment Per Establishment |
|---|---|---|
| First 50 per cent of output value | 14 | 38.4 |
| Third 25 per cent of output value | 23 | 10.0 |
| Last 25 per cent of output value | 45 | 6.2 |

ized on a considerably larger scale than the majority of plants
which were scattered across the study area, located in smaller
towns and villages.

It was hypothesized earlier that as the result of economies of
scale, the larger plants would be more efficient. With growth,
they would increasingly be able to eliminate the smaller, less
efficient producers. While available data are not reliable enough
to conclusively prove that all larger establishments were more
efficient, they do seem to suggest that the larger establishments
were getting a higher return on each unit of labour and capital input. This conclusion is reached through an examination of what
are called output-labour share ratios and output-capital share
ratios. The first ratio was calculated in the following manner.
Each area's shares of the total regional output by value and total
labour force were calculated. When an area's share of both was
the same, that area recorded a ratio of one. This was regarded
as normality. A ratio of less than one indicated that unit was
getting an output less than proportional to its labour force, while
a ratio of greater than unity indicated an output more than proportional to labour force. The latter situation is indicative of greater
efficiency. The output-capital share ratio was calculated in exactly
the same way.

The output-labour share ratios show considerable differences
between the important and the insignificant production areas. In
1891, for example, the fourteen establishments producing the first
50 per cent of total output were getting a 30 per cent higher return
per unit of labour than the 45 establishments producing the last
25 per cent of output.

However, several cautionary notes should be observed. Census data are presented in such a way that when more than one

164

TABLE 15 OUTPUT-LABOUR SHARE RATIOS BY OUTPUT SHARE OF AREAL
UNITS: 1871 AND 1891

| | Number of Establishments | | Output-Labour Share Ratio | |
| | 1871 | 1891 | 1871 | 1891 |
| --- | --- | --- | --- | --- |
| First 50 per cent of output | 42 | 14 | 1.17 | 1.12 |
| Third 25 per cent of output | 18 | 23 | 1.16 | 1.02 |
| Fourth 25 per cent of output | 55 | 45 | 0.70 | 0.81 |

TABLE 16 OUTPUT-CAPITAL SHARE RATIOS BY OUTPUT SHARE OF AREAL
UNITS: 1891

| | Number of Establishments | Output-Capital Share Ratio |
| --- | --- | --- |
| First 50 per cent of output | 14 | 1.03 |
| Third 25 per cent of output | 23 | 0.82 |
| Fourth 25 per cent of output | 45 | 1.00 |

establishment is located in an areal unit it is impossible to isolate
the individual establishment. It was towards separate establishments that statements about process were directed. It is prefer-
able to isolate output shares by plant and not by areas as has been
done here. The reason for this is that the areal units responsible
for the first 50 per cent of output contain several small plants,
while the areal units producing the third 25 per cent of output contained some moderately large plants. Calculations aimed at establishing variation in efficiency will consequently be reduced in
validity when not made for individual establishments.

These tables, however, do have value, for plants tend to become smaller as output shares by unit areas decrease. With some
confidence it can be said that larger plants were getting a higher
return per unit of labour.

The output-capital share ratios do not show a similar variation between output groups. The surprise element is the last
group -- the last 25 per cent of output. Composed mainly of small
plants, this group had a ratio value greater than the third 25 per

TABLE 17 BREWING: RELATIVE DISTRIBUTION. MANUFACTURING BELT VERSUS THE REST OF THE REGION (All figures are percentages of regional totals)

| Magnitude Characteristics | Manufacturing Belt | | | Rest of the Region | | |
| | 1871 | 1881 | 1891 | 1871 | 1881 | 1891 |
| --- | --- | --- | --- | --- | --- | --- |
| Establishments | 39 | 39 | 33 | 61 | 61 | 67 |
| Employees | 43 | 42 | 53 | 57 | 58 | 47 |
| Salaries and Wages | 47 | 45 | 54 | 53 | 55 | 46 |
| Value of Raw Materials | 47 | 49 | 60 | 53 | 51 | 40 |
| Value of Output | 52 | 50 | 53 | 48 | 50 | 47 |

cent of output, and almost as great as the first 50 per cent of output. It was found that many of the smaller plants (one-man businesses or only one or two employees) were getting a high return per unit of capital (measured in relation to plant and machinery only). Such establishments had so little capital that it was virtually impossible for their share of output to be less than their share of capital. Otherwise they would not have been viable enterprises even for a year. Such establishments were operating with the absolute minimum of equipment. When we compare these to the larger establishments, it is suspected that we are comparing two different technologies, and hence the failure of the ratios to fall. The third 25 per cent group have a low figure because they are comparable to the first 50 per cent, but not getting the economies of scale of this group.

In chapter v, it was argued that the dilution process would most frequently apply to widespread consumer goods industry. The result of its operation would be to engender a variety of changes in pattern forms. One variant was "continuing wide distribution, but fewer production points, with concentration in early settled areas." Brewing did not exactly simulate this description, but it came fairly close. There were no particularly cogent reasons why this industry should become strongly concentrated in one town or area, especially since neither its markets nor its raw materials were highly localized. By 1871, the industry was strongly concentrated in York (Toronto), and as such, was concentrated in the manufacturing belt. York was but the major centre of concentration, the other two lay outside the manufacturing belt. Between

166

TABLE 18   AVERAGE EMPLOYMENT PER ESTABLISHMENT

|                     | 1871 | 1881 | 1891  |
|---------------------|------|------|-------|
| Manufacturing Belt  | 5.63 | 7.74 | 20.63 |
| Rest of Ontario     | 4.76 | 8.31 | 8.91  |

1871 and 1891, while Toronto became even more important in brewing, the manufacturing belt did not substantially increase its share of the industry.

One of the most interesting differences between the manufacturing belt and the rest of the region was that the former maintained its magnitude share with a proportionately smaller number of establishments, while the latter experienced a proportionate rise in number of establishments (see Table 17). This meant that plant size was increasing faster in the manufacturing belt than elsewhere. Tables 18 and 19 give illustrations of this point. These changes were largely due to developments in Toronto, and not in the manufacturing belt as a whole. Most establishments in this area, like most elsewhere, were in relative decline.

In the case of brewing, we are not really encountering increasing scale and efficiency in the manufacturing belt, but in a few large centres, particularly London and Toronto. From these, over 50 per cent of the total market was supplied. Within the manufacturing belt, the smaller producers were following the same trends as small producers everywhere. In fact, trends were moving faster than in the rest of the region. Although the manufacturing belt was maintaining its output share with a smaller number of establishments, its output relative to labour was declining (Table 17). This suggests that small plants in the manufacturing belt were even less  efficient than small plants elsewhere. The very stiff competition from Toronto may have discouraged any improvements in efficiency in the small plants of the manufacturing belt, thus causing them to fall behind the small plants in the rest of the region operating in a more favourable market environment. From Table 20 it can be seen that most areas in the manufacturing belt were contributing a smaller proportion of total output. This situation was paralleled in the rest of the region. As the breweries in Middlesex and Grenville grew and supplied larger markets, the other breweries declined in relative importance, or went out of production.

167

TABLE  19    BREWING:  AVERAGE VALUE OF OUTPUT PER ESTABLISHMENT
(Dollars)

|  | 1871 | 1881 | 1891 |
|---|---|---|---|
| Manufacturing Belt | 15,241 | 41,227 | 70,118 |
| Rest of Ontario | 8,969 | 25,846 | 30,649 |

TABLE  20    BREWING:  OUTPUT SHARES IN THE MANUFACTURING BELT,
1871 AND 1891

| Areal Unit | Number of Plants | | Share of Regional Output | |
|---|---|---|---|---|
|  | 1871 | 1891 | 1871 | 1891 |
| Brant | 1 | 1 | 2.60 | 0.83 |
| Halton | 2 | 2 | 1.92 | 0.74 |
| Lincoln | 1 | 1 | 2.33 | 1.95 |
| Peel | 2 | 0 | 1.01 | -- |
| Waterloo | 13 | 10 | 8.80 | 4.07 |
| Wentworth | 9 | 4 | 8.65 | 6.31 |
| York | 13 | 10 | 26.85 | 39.03 |

## THE AGRICULTURAL IMPLEMENTS INDUSTRY

While not a giant industry, past or present, the agricultural implements industry very early started to play an important role in
Ontario's industrial development.  It is especially noteworthy
because it was probably the first secondary manufacturing industry
in Ontario to develop strong export markets outside Canada indeed,
outside North America.  Its considerable exports in the 1890's
indicate the substantial economic progress made by Ontario in the
hundred years since its development had begun.

Once again we encounter an industry that grew while its distributional pattern was changing as the result of a dilution process
(see Map 65).  From 1871, there is a marked decline in the num-

168

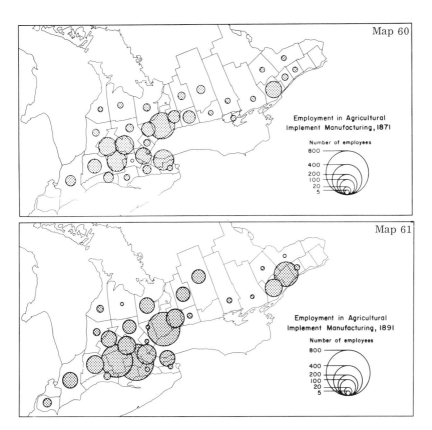

TABLE 21   AGRICULTURAL IMPLEMENTS:  CHARACTERISTICS

| Year | Plants | Capital ($) | Employment | Value of Output ($) |
|------|--------|-------------|------------|---------------------|
| 1871 | 173 | 821,242 | 2,143 | 2,291,989 |
| 1881 | 141 | 3,606,594 | 3,201 | 3,928,411 |
| 1891 | 130 | 5,687,370 | 4,029 | 6,927,887 |

ber of establishments, but in every other respect, the industry showed vigour.

In 1871, the industry was widespread, found in 33 of the 38 areal units (see Map 60).  There was no confinement of the major production areas to the manufacturing belt.  The more important areas were in central and southwestern Ontario, but just as many were outside the manufacturing belt as were in it.

169

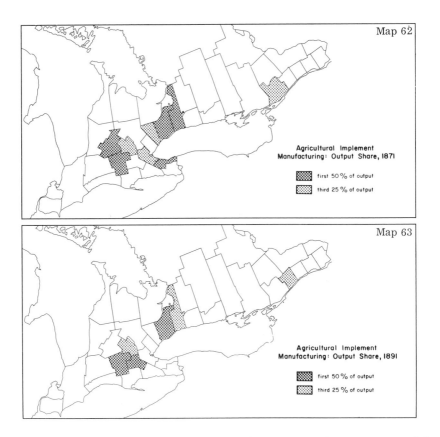

Map 62

Agricultural Implement
Manufacturing: Output Share, 1871

▨ first 50% of output

▧ third 25% of output

Map 63

Agricultural Implement
Manufacturing: Output Share, 1891

▨ first 50% of output

▧ third 25% of output

The agricultural implements industry is and was, a very different kind of industry from brewing which also changed its distribution as the result of a dilution process. The market for both
industries is and was widespread, but it is a completely different
market. North would describe the agricultural implements industry as a service industry to the export sector. In fact, it represents one of the best examples of backward linkage from the primary sector to secondary manufacturing found in Ontario. The
market was the widely distributed farming units, the distribution
of which was reflected to a considerable degree in the distribution
of the industry. For brewing, the distribution of demand changed
substantially as population concentrated in a few cities. For the
agricultural implements industry, the market remained almost as
widespread as the farming units. It is best to say almost, for
demand was likely to vary for some time with the age of settlement
and the prosperity of the farmers. There is plenty of evidence to
show that levels of mechanization in Ontario varied from first set-

170

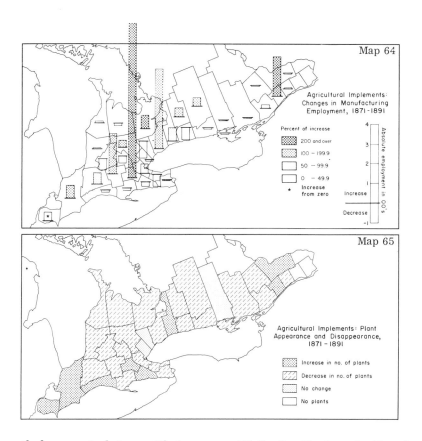

Map 64

Agricultural Implements:
Changes in Manufacturing
Employment, 1871-1891

Percent of increase

200 and over

100 – 199.9

50 – 99.9

0 – 49.9

★ Increase from zero

Absolute employment in .00's

Increase

Decrease

Map 65

Agricultural Implements: Plant
Appearance and Disappearance,
1871 – 1891

Increase in no. of plants

Decrease in no. of plants

No change

No plants

tled areas to later settled areas. While the first agricultural clearings were being made in parts of Grey and Bruce counties using hand methods of cultivation, around the head of Lake Ontario farming had entered a mixed commercial phase and was turning to mechanized methods. This being so, it is likely that there was a spatial variation in demand that endowed some areas with an initial advantage in the form of an early start. Nevertheless, demand was widespread. Although the density of farming units declined through time, farming activities remained widespread, and with increasing mechanization the density of demand throughout the farming areas probably increased. Unlike brewing, therefore, there was no important change in the distribution of the market lending strength to those developments in production processes and industry organization that encourage concentration.

Developments on the supply side alone would cause change in distributional patterns. Over the years they have indeed created an industry with large, highly mechanized, integrated plants which are as few in number as the firms in the industry. In the 1960's

171

production was almost entirely in the manufacturing belt with large plants at the following centres: Brantford, Toronto, Hamilton, and Welland. In effect, in the long run the industry represents an extreme example of dilution operating through economies of scale and agglomeration economies, with plants eliminated in many ways, including merger.

The industry started in numerous small establishments which "...were little more than blacksmiths' shops which supplied a variety of rudimentary implements for a local demand."[13] These were scattered across the province. The transition to a few large plants took a very long time and the 20 years under observation represent but a part of the transformation. Nonetheless, there was much observable change. During the 50's and 60's, many of the small workshops grew into small factories. Phillips attaches importance to the railways for this growth and points up that the railways become important in effecting some concentration in the industry. He notes that entrepreneurs made decisions to locate at various points on the railways.[14] We have, however, no idea why one point or town on the railway was chosen in preference to another. Chance factors must be considered of great importance. One of the earliest railways was the Great Western Railway, connecting Buffalo and Detroit, completed in 1855. It quickly attracted plants in the towns along its route. Phillips notes the establishment of plants at Beamsville in 1857, Hamilton in 1856, Paris in 1864, Ingersoll in 1856, and Francestown in 1857.[15] He notes that similar decisions were made in relation to other railway lines. The implication is also there that as well as conscious decisions to locate in centres on railway routes, railways passed through centres where plants were already located. This seems inevitable when plants were so widely distributed. The effect of the railways was to widen the distribution area of plants.

Completion of the Grand Trunk, between Toronto and Montreal, in 1856, opened new markets to the scattered group of small establishments already strung along the north shore of lake Ontario and the St. Lawrence. Towns such as Newcastle ..., Port Hope, Cobourg and Bowmanville, all became important implement-producing centres of the day.[16]

[13] W. G. Phillips, The Agricultural Implement Industry in Canada (Toronto: University of Toronto Press, 1956), p.38.

[14] Ibid.

[15] Ibid.

[16] Ibid.

With time railways became so widespread in Ontario that only the smallest centres were not located on them. In view of this, the railway became an ubiquitous factor of little locational significance. Since there was a time lag between construction of lines, however, this may have been important in giving some producers in certain centres an early start.

More is known about location decisions in this industry than most other Ontario industries. It seems that towns and villages became production centres in quite different ways. In the first place there were the plants that evolved out of blacksmiths' shops and other enterprises. As with many other industries they were set up wherever entrepreneurs perceived an opportunity at a local level. Craftsmen, merchants, and others, searching for economic opportunities in newly settled areas, set up small-scale businesses wherever chance factors led them to be. Other enterprises were set up for the specific purpose to manufacture agricultural implements in small, and at times, quite large factories. Denison makes the following interesting statement.

However, it can be loosely stated that most Canadian manufacturing had two general origins; one, in the gradual mechanization of small handicraft village enterprises, and the other, in undertakings like Daniel Massey's in which persons with capital to invest brought together the plant and workers required to supply the growing market. [17]

All in all it was probably a matter of chance that one centre was chosen by one producer, and some other centre chosen by another producer. Of course, demand was so widespread and plants sufficiently numerous that almost all towns became production centres of the industry. Available evidence about plant and production centre elimination suggests that luck, drive, foresight, diligence, inventive ability, financial connections, and many other factors were important in promoting the growth of some firms over others. Size of plant or production centre was not a determinant of success. Denison puts a lot of stress on the enterprise and drive of the entrepreneur in keeping a firm viable. In the long run, however, viability may have been maintained by judicious change of location. It is of great significance that two of the most successful enterprises started in small centres but in their expansion drives moved to larger centres in the centre of the manufacturing belt. One tends to suspect that it was a matter of chance that certain firms at certain small centres were successful for a

[17]Merrill Denison, Harvest Triumphant (Toronto: McClelland & Stewart Ltd., 1948), p. 36.

while, but their continued success may have been strongly related to the foresight that led them to relocate in larger centres.

Related to enterprise and drive was the success of some Canadian firms in maintaining connections with United States firms. Phillips asserts that the leading manufacturers in Ontario derived a large measure of their success from connections established with American firms. By arrangement, Ontario firms could produce American invented implements. [18] Firms with such connections, however, were neither associated with restricted areas of South Ontario, nor with centres of a certain minimum size. While several firms with American connections grew to be very large, there was no certainty of continued success. Inferior management, bad luck, and other factors exercised influence over these firms as they did over all others.

Until the latter part of the 19th century, there was no indication that proximity to the secondary manufacturing core of the region was of particular locational significance to the industry. The gradual concentration of population and manufacturing had no marked significance for this industry. Locations advantageous for shipment to farming areas would appear to have been more important than locations providing easy production relationships with other industries. Most firms seem to have been highly self-contained, producing all their needs from a few basic raw materials, some of which were ubiquitous (such as wood), and some of which were imported (iron and steel). While plants were small and incapable of supplying a regional market, a central location with regard to an agricultural area was desirable. There seems no reason why a location central to the total region would be desired until firms became very large; hence the reason why firms could prosper throughout the region.

Plant moves seem to have been easily accomplished. The Patterson Company of Richmond Hill, for example, appears to have located first in London. Later it tried Dundas, and subsequently moved to Richmond Hill. [19] Another company that was located in Paris, applied to that town for a loan. On being refused it succeeded in getting the requested capital from the town of St. Mary's to which it moved in the same year. [20] Plant moves, in

---

[18] Phillips mentions several firms with such connections. These included firms in Newcastle, Richmond Hill, Beamsville, Oshawa, Hamilton, and Port Perry (Phillips, The Agricultural Implement Industry in Canada, p. 39).

[19] Ibid., p. 177.

[20] Ibid., p. 176.

TABLE 22 AGRICULTURAL IMPLEMENTS: AVERAGE SIZE OF ESTABLISHMENT BY OUTPUT SHARE, 1871

| Output Share | Plants | Employment | Employment per Plant |
|---|---|---|---|
| First 50 per cent of output | 41 | 981 | 23.9 |
| Third 25 per cent of output | 36 | 555 | 15.4 |
| Fourth 25 per cent of output | 96 | 607 | 9.4 |

fact, were quite common. They occurred for a variety of reasons and did not by any means always favour the manufacturing belt, but there did seem to be a long-term move towards the manufacturing belt as production processes became more complex and as plants became larger.

By the standards of Ontario in 1871, this was a big and important industry. Although widespread, it was more concentrated than Map 60 might suggest. From Map 62 it can be seen that nine producing areas, mainly in central and southwest Ontario, accounted for 75 per cent of the industry's total output by value. Establishments in those areas were generally much larger. As shown by Table 22, the 96 plants in the areas producing the last 25 per cent of output were almost three times smaller on average than the 41 plants in the areas producing the first 50 per cent of output. Output-labour share ratios suggest that the smaller establishments were getting a lower output for each member of their labour force than the larger establishments. Table 23 indicates that the areas contributing the first 50 per cent of output achieved on average an output per member of labour force 160 per cent greater than the areas contributing the last 25 per cent of output.

Over the next twenty years to 1891, the industry continued to grow. Forty-three establishments went out of production. In distribution these had been widespread so that most areal units recorded a drop in number of establishments (see Map 65). The developments of the period are complex and interesting. The employment map for 1891 (Map 61) clearly shows that the industry was still widespread but showing above-average development in several areal units. Growth had been widespread, but a few areal units had recorded such considerable expansion that most growth areas were in relative decline. Grenville, York, Brant,

175

and Oxford were the outstanding areas (see Map 64). A few
companies were responsible for the prominent position of these
areas. The limited evidence available would suggest that the
enterprise of the companies was more important than any advantages of their locations in creating their prominence in the industry.

Some areas experienced no expansion of the industry. A
few of these had been important earlier in the industry's development. Their decline was not always due to plant elimination,
but to plant relocation which was a strongly developed characteristic of the industry.

In certain respects the agricultural implements industry
was behaving in ways similar to the brewing industry, while in
other respects its behaviour was strikingly different. In brewing,
the distribution pattern was more or less fixed by 1871. From
then on the only new production centres to appear were in peripheral parts of the region. Distribution changed chiefly as the
result of production concentration at the larger centres accompanied by elimination of smaller producers at smaller centres.

No such regularity was attained in the agricultural implements industry. In some cases establishment and production
centre were simultaneously eliminated. In other cases, however, only the production centre was eliminated because the
establishment moved to another production centre. Further,
elimination, growth, or decline in the industry was not strongly
related to the size of the production centres in which plants were
located. There were several reasons for these characteristics.

In the first place, the population of the production centre
did not constitute the whole or part of the market for the plant
located in it. No market advantage derived from population size
of the production centre. In brewing, a small local market, in
the sense of a small population in the production centre, increased
chances of early elimination. For the agricultural implements
industry size of centre was not important in this respect, although as the industry and plants grew it may have been important for considerations of labour, and supply and transport
facilities. Another reason for the difference lay in the product
differentiation between plants. During the seventies and eighties
the various plants of the industry were producing a very wide
range of implements. It was not the general rule for each plant,
whether large or small, to produce all types of agricultural
implements. Some firms concentrated on harvesting equipment,

176

TABLE 23    AGRICULTURAL IMPLEMENTS:  OUTPUT-LABOUR
SHARE RATIOS BY OUTPUT SHARE.  1871

| Output Share | Output-Labour Share Ratio |
| --- | --- |
| First 50 per cent of output | 1.26 |
| Third 25 per cent of output | 1.00 |
| Last 25 per cent of output | 0.78 |

others on ploughing, seeding, harrowing, or various combina-
tions of equipment.  Each plant, therefore, was not in competition with all other plants.  Each competed against the few others
making the same type of implement.  It was not really until the
20th century that large plants competed against each other in
all types of implements.  The "full line" principle did exist
during the study period, but it was not common.  Within the
various divisions of the industry, the success of a plant depended
upon quality of product, sales network, cost of product, advertising, to name but a few factors.

We are not dealing here with a simple situation of large
producers in large centres competing against small producers
in small centres.  For some time, for example, the largest
plough manufacturer was located at Exeter in Huron County.
Not until certain firms succeeded in expanding their production
to cover the full range of implements did the Exeter establishment face the danger of elimination.

For these reasons, elimination did not follow a regular
sequence that reflected population size of production centres.
It may have reflected the size and efficiency of producers in
different lines of products, but the data needed to prove or dis-
prove the point are lacking.  Prolonged and detailed investigation would be necessary to establish why some firms prospered
and grew.  There did not seem to be any strong relationship
between growth and any particular area, or, between growth and
size and type of centre.  It is most likely a matter of chance that
the two most successful companies developed in the small towns
of Beamsville and Newcastle.  It may still be a matter of chance
that both specialized in harvesting equipment, and that both
moved to larger centres in the manufacturing belt.  The Massey
Company moved from Newcastle to Toronto in 1880.  Denison

| Output Share | Employment | Plants | Average Employment per Plant | Average Capital per Plant |
|---|---|---|---|---|
| First 50 per cent | 1930 | 25 | 77.2 | 33,722 |
| Third 25 per cent | 535 | 21 | 25.5 | 10,832 |
| Last 25 per cent | 1664 | 84 | 19.8 | 5,210 |

writes that "...Toronto...was finally chosen for its better
shipping and banking facilities and larger labour and material
markets."[21] Eight years before the Harris Company had moved
its location, in this case from Beamsville to Brantford.  One
wonders if it was still a matter of chance that it was these two
companies which moved to large centres in the manufacturing
belt that succeeded in overpowering most of the other producers.
The amalgamation of enterprising management, good locations
for distribution throughout the region, large local labour market, and the availability of the services and materials of other
industries may have swung the balance in favour of these two
companies.

By the 1880's a few firms were leading the industry in size,
no matter what measure is used.  From Denison's research it
would appear that these larger firms were attempting to sell in
all parts of the province, some of them in other parts of Canada
as well as in other continents.  Each branch of the industry was
dominated by a few plants.  Denison notes:

By the middle of the 1880's more companies were manufacturing harvesting
machinery in Ontario than in the whole of the United States, but Massey and
Harris, between them, accounted for more than 60 per cent of all the sales
in the Dominion.[22]

By 1891 the successful growth of a few companies had led
to quite strong concentration in the industry.  Examination of
Map 64 shows that 75 per cent of total output by value was emanating from six areal units.  These contained a majority of the
industry's largest plants and companies.  As Table 24 shows,

[21] Denison, Harvest Triumphant, p. 69.

[22] Ibid., p. 93.

TABLE 25    AGRICULTURAL IMPLEMENTS: OUTPUT-LABOUR SHARE RATIOS
AND OUTPUT-CAPITAL SHARE RATIOS BY OUTPUT SHARES, 1891

| Share of Output | Output-Labour Share Ratio | Output-Capital Share Ratio |
|---|---|---|
| First 50 per cent | 1.29 | 1.20 |
| Third 25 per cent | 1.18 | 1.19 |
| Last 25 per cent | 0.72 | 0.58 |

TABLE 26    AGRICULTURAL IMPLEMENTS: RELATIVE DISTRIBUTION.
MANUFACTURING BELT VERSUS THE REST OF THE REGION
(All figures are percentages of regional totals)

| Magnitude Characteristic | Manufacturing Belt | | | Rest of the Region | | |
|---|---|---|---|---|---|---|
| | 1871 | 1881 | 1891 | 1871 | 1881 | 1891 |
| Establishments | 25 | 24 | 24 | 75 | 76 | 76 |
| Employees | 44 | 46 | 54 | 56 | 54 | 46 |
| Salaries and Wages | 47 | 45 | 52 | 53 | 55 | 48 |
| Value of Raw Materials | 45 | 50 | 42 | 55 | 50 | 58 |
| Value of Output | 45 | 44 | 49 | 55 | 56 | 51 |

the 25 plants contributing the first 50 per cent of output represented less than a quarter of all the plants in the industry. The
average figures of the table obscure the considerable size achieved
by a few plants. While the average employment in the first group
was 77, we learn from Denison that the Massey Company in 1887
employed 800 persons including head office staff, factory hands,
and travellers.[23] Among the areas producing the last 25 per
cent of output were some large plants well above average size for
that group. In Elgin, for example, there were nine plants employing 33 people, but in Peterborough one plant employed 80
people, and in Hamilton two plants employed 181 people. However, compared to the leaders of the industry these were modest
enterprises by 1891.

[23] Ibid., p. 100.

179

TABLE 27    AGRICULTURAL IMPLEMENTS:  AVERAGE EMPLOYMENT
PER ESTABLISHMENT

|  | 1871 | 1881 | 1891 |
|---|---|---|---|
| Manufacturing Belt | 21.5 | 43.0 | 68.35 |
| Rest of Region | 9.3 | 16.3 | 18.28 |

Table 25 leaves little doubt that the leading production areas
were on average more efficient.  The small producers responsible for the last 25 per cent of output were getting lower returns
on both labour and capital.

The manufacturing belt had more than its proportionate share
of the larger, more efficient producers.  With only 24 per cent
of the establishments it had approximately 50 per cent of the
output of the industry (see Table 26).  Table 27 shows that the
difference in average plant size increased through time.  During
the last ten years of the century this difference widened even more
as the manufacturing belt increased its total share of the industry.  The major force behind this trend was the merger of the
Massey and Harris Companies, a development that was largely
due to the wasteful competition between them in the home market.[24]  This was followed by a merger with the Patterson-
Weisner Company which itself had only recently been formed in
response to the Massey-Harris merger.  With this merger and
the acquisition of the controlling interest in the Verity Plow
Company of Exeter, Massey-Harris entered into the production
of the full range of agricultural implements.  Phillips notes:

The amount of rearrangement of plant facilities which immediately followed
the amalgamation (with Patterson-Weisner) suggests that potential savings
in production costs were an important factor considered throughout the
negotiations.[25]

These and an ensuing series of mergers and acquisitions were
followed in many cases by relocation of production facilities.
The operations of the Weisner plant in Brantford were moved
to Toronto, while the Verity plant in Exeter was moved to the
Weisner factory.  Competing lines of the amalgamated companies
were closed down.  Similar actions were taken at later dates.

[24] For full details see Phillips, The Agricultural Implement Industry in Canada, p. 52
and Denison, Harvest Triumphant, pp. 115-127.

[25] Phillips, The Agricultural Implement Industry in Canada, p. 52.  Phrase in brackets
inserted by author.

Production at Toronto and Brantford was enlarged and production processes were integrated as the result of persistent efforts to lower costs. In the 20th century, when large American companies set up plants in the Ontario manufacturing belt they indulged in activities analagous to those of Massey-Harris. The end result was the gradual elimination of the smaller establishments and further concentration of the industry in the manufacturing belt.

Although rigorous empirical verification is not available on all points, it seems as if this industry went through one of the several possible variants of the dilution process. The number of plants and the number of production sites declined as the industry grew. A relatively small number of plants was responsible for the greater part of the growth. Through luck, enterprise, favourable location, and greater efficiency they gradually eliminated less successful rivals. The end result was concentration in part of the region with production units found at several locations within the area of concentration.


ENGRAVING AND LITHOGRAPHING

In origin and distribution the engraving and lithographing industry differs markedly from the industries so far examined. Brewing developed early in response to widespread basic consumer demands. Very low thresholds were needed for plant emergence, so plants were scattered throughout the region. The agricultural implements industry was the inevitable response to a successful, profit conscious, agricultural sector that was both export and domestic market oriented. It too distributed itself widely. Through time, this and brewing concentrated.

Engraving and lithographing never followed the distribution of settlement or population. The demand for its product was not exerted by the widespread labour force of the primary sector. This was the kind of industry that could be successfully introduced only when the economic strivings of the nascent region had allowed the emergence of a more complex economic society; a more prosperous society with more demands and an increasing means to satisfy them. Engraving and lithographing awaited the attainment of thresholds that came more slowly than those for basic consumer goods and primary production equipment. The development of the book printing industry and of illustrated advertising were important prerequisites of its domestic debut.

181

The emergence of a group of people with the time, the tempera-
ment, and means to enjoy the finer things of life should not be
discounted in explaining the attainment of thresholds for this
industry.

Such preconditions would be most strongly developed in the
cities. The ties of this industry would be with the printing industry which would be most developed in the larger urban centres
with their greater demand for all forms of printed literature --
a demand emanating from manufacturers, retailers, importers,
entertainers, and others making economic use of illustrated
literature -- a demand deriving from spatial concentration of
the groups likely to consume luxury products. The highly skilled
labour requirements would be more likely found in the city, or
attracted to the city from abroad, than found in, or attracted to
a small market town. Transportation costs are of little importance. Raw material quantities are modest and the value of the
output is high. No disadvantage would accrue, therefore, from
a location in the city. The bulk of the market would be there
and outlying demand could be supplied from there. All in all,
every advantage attached to a city location and very few to a non-
city location.

The distribution of the industry in South Ontario disputes
none of these suppositions. Apart from a one-man business
found in Northumberland in 1891, the industry was to be found
only in the five largest urban centres of the region -- Toronto,
Hamilton, Ottawa, London, and Kingston.

It had taken nearly one hundred years of economic development before this industry took hold. In 1871, when the agricultural implements industry was employing over 2000 people in
173 establishments, engraving and lithographing was a tiny industry just coming into existence. There were five plants distributed among four centres. The miniscule nature of the industry is clear from Table 28 and Map 66. During the next twenty
years it made progress but still remained a small industry (see
Table 29 and Maps 67 and 68).

While this growth took place the industry exhibited a very
marked proclivity for concentration, such that by 1891 it was
more highly concentrated than any of the industries so far examined. Approximately 73 per cent of the industry's employment
was found in Toronto. When Hamilton's share is added to this,
the industry is seen to be very highly concentrated in the manufacturing belt (see Table 30).

182

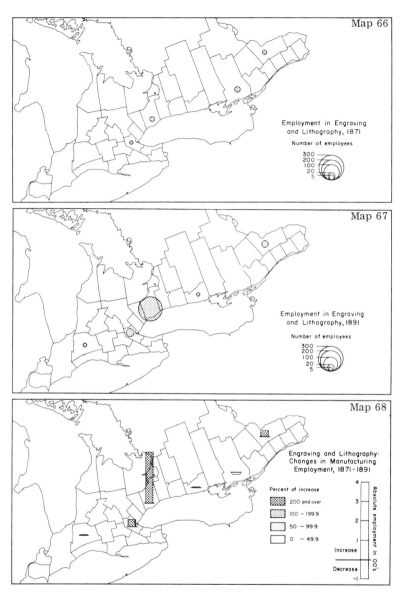

Map 66

Employment in Engraving
and Lithography, 1871

Number of employees

300
200
100
20
5

Map 67

Employment in Engraving
and Lithography, 1891

Number of employees

300
200
100
20
5

Map 68

Engraving and Lithography:
Changes in Manufacturing
Employment, 1871-1891

Percent of increase

200 and over
100 — 199.9
50 — 99.9
0 — 49.9

Absolute employment in 00's

4
3
2
1
Increase
Decrease
-1

Outside the manufacturing belt were a few plants, one in
London and five in Ottawa. These were much smaller affairs,
the average employment being six compared to nineteen in
Toronto and Hamilton.

This industry had moved into concentration in a very different way from the other industries examined. During the observed
period it grew while the number of plants increased. There was

183

TABLE 28  ENGRAVING AND LITHOGRAPHING: INDUSTRY CHARACTERISTICS
BY AREAL UNITS, 1871

| Unit | Plants | Employees | Salaries and Wages ($) | Value of Output ($) |
|------|--------|-----------|------------------------|---------------------|
| Hamilton | 1 | 4 | 2,000 | 5,000 |
| Toronto | 2 | 7 | 3,400 | 4,700 |
| Kingston | 1 | 2 | 800 | 1,500 |
| Ottawa | 1 | 3 | 2,000 | 3,000 |

TABLE 29  ENGRAVING AND LITHOGRAPHING: INDUSTRY CHARACTERISTICS,
1871-1891

| Year | Plants | Employees | Salaries and Wages ($) | Value of Output ($) |
|------|--------|-----------|------------------------|---------------------|
| 1871 | 5 | 16 | 8,200 | 14,200 |
| 1881 | 17 | 170 | 64,113 | 167,968 |
| 1891 | 24 | 364 | 114,770 | 405,020 |

no dilution, no plant and production centre elimination -- quite
the opposite.  It concentrated because of location decisions taken
from the very beginning in its development.  The dilution process
had been completely short-circuited.

SAW AND FILE CUTTING

Saw and file cutting presents another example of an industry
which did not appear in the region for several decades.  As with
engraving and lithographing, the dilution process was not experienced by this industry.  There was never a widespread
scattering of plants.  This started as, and remained, a manufacturing belt industry.

184

TABLE 30    ENGRAVING AND LITHOGRAPHING: RELATIVE DISTRIBUTION.
MANUFACTURING BELT VERSUS THE REST OF THE REGION, 1891
(All figures are percentages of regional totals)

| Magnitude Characteristic | Manufacturing Belt | Rest of Region |
|---|---|---|
| Plants | 71 | 29 |
| Employees | 89 | 11 |
| Salaries and Wages | 89 | 11 |
| Value of Raw Materials | 96 | 4 |
| Value of Output | 92 | 8 |
| Capital in Plant and Machinery | 96 | 4 |

Between 1871 and 1891 the industry grew, but remained small (see Table 31). The number of plants tripled. Other magnitude characteristics displayed a faster rate of growth, indicative of increase in the average size of establishment. In 1871, for example, the average employment per establishment was about 16. Twenty years later it was almost 22.

In 1871 three of the industry's four plants were found in the manufacturing belt, and 12 out of 13 in 1891 (see Maps 69 and 70). There was a slight diminution in the manufacturing belt's share of the industry, but if an industry starts in a small area some subsequent dispersal is likely (see Table 32).

Within the manufacturing belt the industry was very highly localized. Lincoln and York accounted for 99 per cent of total output value in 1871. During the study period Toronto gained dominance, and by 1891 55 per cent of output emanated from the six plants found there. Following Toronto with most of the remaining output were Waterloo with 22 per cent and Lincoln with 11 per cent.

Without going into a detailed study, the data for which are unavailable, there is little else relating to the objectives of the chapter to be said about this industry. In its distributional behaviour it is representative of many industries that first appeared in the region in the 70's and 80's. Chapter v gave at length reasons why new industries would increasingly favour the general zone of concentration in manufacturing, and especially

TABLE  31    SAW AND FILE CUTTING:  INDUSTRY CHARACTERISTICS,  1871-1891

| Year | Plants | Employees | Salaries and Wages ($) | Value of Output ($) |
|------|--------|-----------|------------------------|---------------------|
| 1871 | 4 | 63 | 28,775 | 96,150 |
| 1881 | 10 | 165 | 69,100 | 277,400 |
| 1891 | 13 | 282 | 118,372 | 455,580 |

TABLE  32    SAW AND FILE CUTTING:  RELATIVE DISTRIBUTION.
MANUFACTURING BELT VERSUS THE REST OF THE REGION, 1871 AND 1891
(All figures are percentages of regional totals)

| Magnitude Characteristic | Manufacturing Belt | | Rest of Region | |
|--------------------------|------|------|------|------|
|  | 1871 | 1891 | 1871 | 1891 |
| Plants | 75 | 92 | 25 | 8 |
| Employees | 97 | 78 | 3 | 22 |
| Salaries and Wages | 99 | 87 | 1 | 13 |
| Value of Raw Materials | 99 | 95 | 1 | 5 |
| Value of Output | 99 | 93 | 1 | 7 |

the larger cities contained within it.  Some dispersal could be
expected with industry growth, but it would be slight compared
to the early consumer goods industries of the region.  In 1891
many industries were found only in the manufacturing belt.  These
included the production of nuts and bolts, needles, thread, ink,
fireworks, and wall paper, to name but a few.  Many more
industries had an overwhelming concentration in the manufacturing belt; examples include bicycles, coffee and spices, iron
and steel bridges, and rubber.

Uncertainty, location of market, regional centrality, production relationships with other industries, labour market considerations, threshold levels, regional disparity of income, and

186

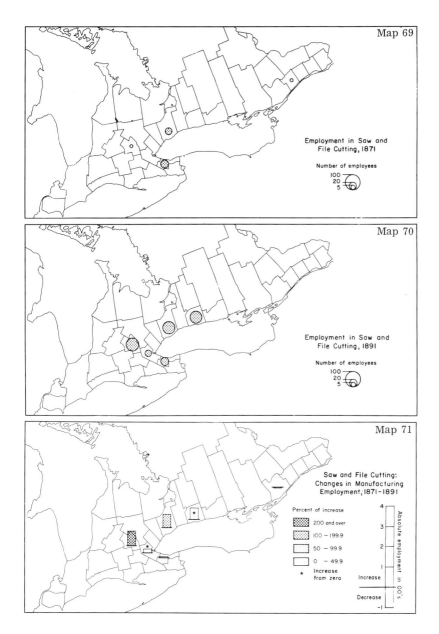

Map 69

Employment in Saw and
File Cutting, 1871

Number of employees

100
20
5

Map 70

Employment in Saw and
File Cutting, 1891

Number of employees

100
20
5

Map 71

Saw and File Cutting:
Changes in Manufacturing
Employment; 1871–1891

Percent of increase

200 and over

100 – 199.9

50 – 99.9

0 – 49.9

Increase
from zero

Absolute employment in 00's

Increase

Decrease

other factors must all be woven together to account for this different locational behaviour of many new industries.

This is what was attempted in chapter v. Unfortunately,
we can only infer that the interlinked mechanisms of process
described in that chapter were the mechanisms that produced

187

the industrial patterns found in South Ontario. It is much easier to establish the distributional patterns of reality than it is to establish beyond all doubt the operation of mechanisms accorded the responsibility for producing these patterns.

Information on manufacturing in the past is so fragmentary, it may never be possible to bridge the gap between speculative reasoning on the one hand, and the observed patterns of reality on the other. It is possible to give sound reasons why 13 of the 14 plants of the saw and file cutting industry were found in an area designated as the manufacturing belt. Most likely it will never be possible to know enough about the conditions and circumstances of the industry to be sure that our reasoning is correct. Past experience suggests that diminishing returns set in very early in attempts to determine and understand the actual location and operating decisions of the past. Yet, explanation will remain tentative until micro-process studies can be, and are undertaken.

# VIII
# Conclusion

Between 1851 and 1891 the economy of South Ontario grew and changed in structure. Population increased, most economic activities enlarged their output, and many new activities were introduced. Export-base theory of regional economic growth provides the most satisfactory explanatory framework for the changes that occurred in the economy as a whole. South Ontario's economic dynamism derived from the primary sector and its exports. These had set in motion a chain of interconnected, multiplying reactions which in total produced the structural changes observed in this study.

Within the secondary sector, the predominant concern of this work, the extent of change was no less than in the economy as a whole. Although the sector's relative share of the economy changed little, it experienced considerable absolute growth, and structural changes were clearly evident. Important structural shifts occurred in secondary manufacturing. Producer goods industries improved their relative position vis-à-vis consumer goods industries -- a strong indication that the foundations were being laid early for the more rapid industrialization of the twentieth century, and that successful development founded on the export base was taking place.

As the total economic structure and the structure of manufacturing in the region as a whole manifested maturative tendencies, the various parts of South Ontario progressed along their
separate paths of structural development. Some areas lagged
behind the general regional trends while other areas anticipated
them. Export-base theory is not designed to explain the intra-
regional variations in the growth process, and resultant variations in structure. The spatial dimensions of the economy are
ignored in its explanations of the growth mechanisms. An explanation of intra-regional structural variation was sought in
two different ways.

First, an attempt was made to establish if spatial structural
variation is a reflection of a time-lag from one part of the region
to another in the initiation of the growth processes that typify development in export-based regions. This assumes that the same
processes operate in every part of the region and that the only
cause of structural variation is the time that has been available
for the processes to operate. If the simple fact of time-lag explains structural variation, then the spatial pattern of structural
variation would correspond to that of the time-lag, which in
turn could be expected to be strongly related to the progression
of settlement through the region. In an export-based region,
which by definition is more or less unoccupied prior to its development, settlement would not be expected to occur in a
spatially haphazard manner; rather, it would spread out fairly
evenly from one or a number of points. This even pattern would
be matched by the pattern of spatial structural variation.

If such an explanation proved to be correct it would follow that
the relative distribution of activities would be explained by the same
processes that cause spatial structural variation because activities
could only appear in the region as a whole, and in particular parts
of it, as structure changes. If different areas are at different
stages of structural development, reflecting the staggered spatial
progress of export-based development, relative distribution would
be a function of the growth process.

In this way development within the region is analagous to a
handicap race in which the strong and weak competitors are never
equalized. Starters (different parts of the space economy) are
staggered by time, and the late starters are weaker by the very
fact of their late start. Later starters are also increasingly separated by distance from earlier starters, such that the last part
of the region to be settled is likely to be at the maximum possible

distance from the first settled area. Therefore, time for development decreases with distance from first settled areas.

Although irregularities attributable to variation in human characteristics and resource endowment were present, these simple notions about relations between time, growth, structure, and relative distribution found strong substantiation in the spatial and temporal variation in the structure of the South Ontario economy. Economic structure, in terms of the breakdown between the primary, secondary, and tertiary sectors, varied in a manner that strongly suggested that a time-lag effect was in operation. Also, the time-lag effect exhibited a spatial pattern that corresponded with distanace from first settled areas. As a corollary, the relative distribution of manufacturing was related to time and distance. However, when the structure of manufacturing was examined separately, structure, distance, and the relative distribution of the various groups showed a much weaker association and one that was obviously dissolving as the region prospered.

This led to a second way of explaining spatial structural variation that is particularly relevant to the structure of manufacturing. The time-lag explanation of structural variation and relative distribution ignores the possibility that different activities may have different locational requirements. It seems reasonable to propose that as the region's manufacturing structure changes through growth and diversification, different types of manufacturing with varied locational needs will appear. When locational needs can no longer be found everywhere, as is assumed by the time-lag argument, spatial variation in the structure of manufacturing will reflect the distribution of locational advantages, and these will be found increasingly in a restricted portion of the region.

Consideration of location theory and examination of events in South Ontario appear to support this argument. However, as far as manufacturing is concerned, both explanations are relevant at different times in the growth process. It appears that the changing locational requirements of manufacturing progressively affect the pattern of spatial structural variation that formed due to the time-lag factor. The structural changes in an export-based economy are such that the first economic elements to appear have locational requirements that can be met virtually anywhere within the region. Hence, activities become ubiquitous and structural variation relates to time and distance. These widespread activities exert demands that may eventually support new economic

activities which exhibit in their staggered emergence, a decreasing proclivity for spatial ubiquity. As new activities are succes-
sively added to the economy, structure changes. Change in the
total regional economy is the sum of change in the constituent
parts of the space economy, and these parts vary increasingly
in structure as the structure of the region as a whole matures.
Maturation of structure in manufacturing is an expression of the
growing ascendency of producer goods industries, but these distribute themselves in such a way that the simple connections between spatial structural variation, time-lag in development initiation, and relative distribution are eventually destroyed.

Dissolution of the relationship is produced by two related
distributional traits of manufacturing industry. First, increasingly, new activities have locational requirements that work
against ubiquitous distribution. These requirements are expressed in a spatial preference for that part of the region with
the greatest amount of activity, and with the most complex and
advanced structure -- a position reached when the structural
variation is still explicable in terms of the time-lag argument.
This area of most advanced structure and greater attraction
power is found in the first settled areas. Within it, certain
initial advantages will have promoted growth in excess of average. New additions to the manufacturing sector tend to favour
this relatively small area of the region, and perhaps some other
smaller areas of advanced development associated with major
regional centres.

Second, as the attractions of the first settled area grow,
long-established industries expand their production there faster
than elsewhere, and gradually localize there as plants in other
areas are eliminated. The combined effect of these processes
is the creation of a manufacturing core area that is structurally
more advanced than would be expected on the basis of the association between structure, time, and distance. Agglomeration
economies in the widest sense, permit the core to acquire more
and more of the region's manufacturing. The structure of this
favoured area increasingly mirrors the structure of the region
as a whole, and its economic ascendency becomes impregnable.

Localization of manufacturing in the core causes the rest of
the region to have a decreasing proportion of the region's manufacturing. Of course, it is not an area of absolute decline, and
it is by no means totally avoided by new elements or denuded of
old elements. Primary manufacturing, for example, with its ir-

192

regular distribution patterns, will favour this area, thus differ-entiating its structure from that of the core. In some cases long-established industries experience a form of dilution that does not lead to total concentration in the core alone, but to concentration in the core plus a few other areas in the rest of the region. This further contributes to the reasons for increasing spatial structural variation.

The new elements added to the region also provide a reason for structural variability. Outside the core, chance factors lead to the appearance in sporadic form of new activities that are mainly found in the core. The absence of regularity in the spa-tial patterns of the few new activities found outside the core fur-ther confuses the pattern of structural variability. In many parts of the region manufacturing development is so slight that it requires but a small infusion of a new element to greatly alter the structure of those parts. When manufacturing is disaggre-gated into its smallest subdivisions, that is, individual indus-tries like those examined in chapter vii, the randomness in dis-tributional behaviour is quite apparent. In 1891 there was one saw and file-cutting establishment outside the manufacturing core. For reasons unknown it was located in Durham County. Thus the structure of this area was differentiated from the struc-ture of surrounding areas. This establishment could have lo-cated somewhere else, and so the pattern of structural varia-bility would have been different.

The operation of these processes caused a remarkably early stabilization of the basic spatial economic structure of South Ontario. The time-lag effect had clearly given the first settled areas distinct growth advantages by 1851. From then on, the railways, and the agglomerative tendencies of new activities, in spiralling interaction with a spatially variable resource en-dowment and with certain initial economic advantages related to political decisions taken before and after 1851, endowed part of the first settled areas with continually increasing advantages in the development race. The forces which created the present preeminence of the area around the head of Lake Ontario were indisputably launched by 1891, the last year of the study period. What was not so certain was the speed at which they would oper-ate. This depended on unpredictable events both inside and out-side Ontario -- the development of the west, the effects of the world wars, and the impacts of technological change, all of which have at least been partially researched by workers in geography and other disciplines.

Many of the industries which would contribute to the creation of the Ontario manufacturing belt were still to be introduced, but the basic outlines of the belt, and indeed, of South Ontario's economic geography of the twentieth century had been set down. Some unforseeable spatial influences were still to emerge. The spatial pattern of American investment in manufacturing in this century encouraged considerable economic growth in certain border areas. But on the whole the American presence in Canadian manufacturing has reinforced the trends already evident in the 1890's rather than worked against them.

# Appendix

## Classification of manufacturing by markets for output and areal allocation of data

All manufacturing activities, occupations and trades employed in the study were allocated to one or more of the following twelve subdivisions:

Secondary

| | |
|---|---|
| Consumer | food, drink, tobacco |
| | consumer sundries |
| | clothing and footwear |
| | household goods |
| | consumers durables |
| | |
| Producer | construction materials |
| | supplies to primary and tertiary sectors |
| | investment goods |
| | unfinished |

Primary food

construction

unfinished producer

## DEFINITIONS

The most fundamental division in the classification is that between primary and secondary manufacturing.

### Primary Manufacturing.
The biggest difference between the classifications adopted by Dales[1] and by Shaw[2] is the former's introduction of primary manufacturing. His rationale for its use was that "...some manufacturing enterprises are so closely related to the Primary Sector industries that supply their raw materials that they are in effect extensions of the Primary Sector of the economy, and therefore conceptually different from the rest of manufacturing industry."[3] Further, it is very useful in probing Canadian growth to differentiate industries which are more closely related to the Canadian staple industries than to manufacturing as normally understood in highly industrialized areas.[4] This reasoning was accepted as was the following definition by Dales.

Primary manufacturing industries are industries engaged in the processing of domestic natural products (including hydro electricity as a natural product) up to the point where the output of the industry is economically transportable over long distances. A corollary of this definition is that no primary manufacturing industry processes a natural product that enters into interregional or international trade in any significant volume.[5]

### Consumer and Producer Goods.
The groups employed by Dales and Shaw followed several of the guidelines set down by Simon Kuznets in Commodity Flow and Capital Formation.[6]

The following definitions of groups and criteria for delimiting groups were developed by Kuznets.[7]

---

[1]J. H. Dales, "Estimates of Canadian Manufacturing Output by Markets, 1870-1915," Papers, Canadian Political Science Association, Conference on Statistics 1962 and 1963.

[2]W. H. Shaw, Value of Commodity Output Since 1869 (New York: National Bureau of Economic Research, 1947).

[3]Dales, "Estimates of Canadian Manufacturing Output by Markets," Appendix 1, p. 77.

[4]Ibid.

[5]Ibid.

[6]Simon Kuznets, Commodity Flow and Capital Formation, vol. 1 (New York: National Bureau of Economic Research, 1938).

[7]Shaw, Value of Commodity Output Since 1869, p. 6.

Consumer: Commodities, whether finished or unfinished, that when finished and at their destination, are used by households or large ultimate consuming units.

Producer: Commodities, whether finished or unfinished, that when finished and at their destination, are used by business agencies in the production process.

The criteria listed below could be used to subdivide consumer and producer goods. These are Kuznets' definitions slightly modified by Shaw. [8] Durability or non-durability of commodities was most important.

Durable: Commodities that, without marked change, and retaining their essential physical identity are ordinarily employed in their ultimate use three or more years. Examples: a steam engine, a dynamo, a bed, table, or chair.

Nondurable: Commodities that, without marked change, and retaining their essential physical identity, are ordinarily employed in their ultimate use less than three years. They are further classified into:

Semidurable: Commodities that, without marked change and retaining their essential physical identity are ordinarily employed in their ultimate use from six months to three years.
Examples: automobile tires, clothing, shoes.

Perishable: Commodities that, without marked change and retaining their essential physical identity, are ordinarily employed in their essential physical identity, are ordinarily employed in their ultimate use less than six months.
Examples: bread, cigarettes.

Kuznets also distinguished between finished and unfinished commodities.

Finished: Commodities, whether durable or nondurable in the form in which, without significant alteration, they are employed in their ultimate use.

Unfinished: Commodities that, whether durable or nondurable are not yet in the form in which they are employed in their ultimate use.

Kuznets went one stage further by introducing a distinction between goods at destination and goods in circulation. All commodities at destination, consumer and producer, are finished. Both consumer and producer goods in circulation can be either finished or unfinished. With this division Kuznets created a more complex classification than was used by either

[8]Ibid., pp. 5-6.

Shaw or Dales. He was differentiating unfinished goods on the basis of the use and durability of the goods in which they would be incorporated. For example, a screw intended for incorporation in a television set would be an unfinished consumers durable in circulation, while a screw intended for incorporation in a tractor would be an unfinished producers durable in circulation.

Shaw and Dales did not go to this level of detail. Their subdivision of goods at destination (all finished) was the same as Kuznets'. Divisions were made on the basis of the consumer-producer and the durable-nondurable criteria. They recognized, however, only one category of goods in circulation, namely, unfinished producer goods (intermediate goods in Shaw's classification), thereby narrowing Kuznets' definition of consumer goods, and altering his definition of producer goods. In their classifications, any unfinished goods, in the sense of goods that are yet to be incorporated into final consumer or producer goods, are regarded as unfinished producer goods. A bottle cap used in brewing is as much an unfinished producer good as a switch that is to be fitted to a machine tool. Kuznets, on the other hand, would put these goods into different categories.

With their criteria Dales and Shaw had only five major groups (excluding Dales' primary manufacturing). These were:

Consumer perishable
Consumer semidurable
Consumer durable
Producer durable
Intermediate or unfinished producer

In some cases these were further subdivided to differentiate substantially different categories of products. Consumer perishables have two distinct groups: the food, drink, and tobacco commodities, and consumer sundries. Consumer semidurables are composed of clothing and footwear, and household goods. Producer durables are broken into three groups: supplies to primary and tertiary sectors, construction materials, and investment goods. It should be noted that Shaw included "supplies to primary and tertiary sectors" in his unfinished goods category while Dales included it in finished producer goods. Since Dales was dealing with Canada, his step and classification were adopted.

Dales and Shaw outline their allocation procedures in detail. The former discusses the differences between Canadian and American data and explains his procedures for handling a data situation much less favourable than that faced by Shaw. There is no need to repeat Dales' statements. The following list of industries shows their allocation between the groups of the classification. Where an industry or occupation is divided between one or more groups, percentages are included as well as the year when the percentage applies. In any one census year only a certain proportion of the industries and occupations are employed. The names of industries changed between censuses and new industries were added. The list includes all industries encountered over the 40-year period. Many of them were in use for one census only.

Consumer: food, drink, tobacco

areated water
bakeries
bakers
baking powder 70% (70-80-90)
baking powder & flavouring extract 70%
breweries
brewers
cigar factories
cocoa and chocolate
coffee and spice
confectionery
confectioners
cordial and syrup making
distilleries
distillers
flour and grist mills 100% (60)
                    98% (70)
                    96% (80)
                    93% (90)
ginger beer makers
grist mills 100% (50)
meat curing
oatmeal mills
pickle making
preserved food
preserved fruit and jelly
sausage makers
soda water makers
sorghum syrup factories
sugar manufacturers & refiners (95%-60)
tobacconists
tobacconists and cigar makers
vinegar factories
vinegar makers
yeast factories 70%

Consumer: sundries

art needle works 50%
blacking factories
blacking manufacturers
brooms and brushes

broom makers
brush makers
button factories 20% (70)
              15% (80)
              10% (90)
chandlers
chemicals establishments 66% (70-80-90)
comb factories
comb makers
fire-kindler factories
fireworks
linseed oil factories 70% (70)
                   60% (80-90)
lubricating oil factories 70% (70)
                       60% (80-90)
match factories
match makers
methylated spirits
needle factories 50%
oil refineries 70% (70)
            60% (80-90)
oil manufacturers 90% (50)
               80% (60)
paper pattern factories
paraffine and wax works 70% (70)
                     60% (80-90)
patent medicine manufacturing
printing offices 50%
printers, publishers, editors
   reporters 60% (50)
           55% (60)
sandpaper 20%
soap and candle making
soap makers
tallow chandlers
wax candle and taper factories
washing compound making

Consumer: clothing and footwear

boots and shoes
boot and shoemakers
cordwainers

199

corset factories
dressmakers
dressmakers and milliners
dressmaking and millinery
furriers
furriers and hatters
glove and mitt making
glover
hatters
hoisery manufacturing
knitting factories
milliners
oil clothing
seamstresses
shirt, collar, and tie making
shirtmakers
shoelace factories
tailors
tailoresses
tailors and clothiers
underwear factories
wig making

Consumer: household goods
            (semi-durables)

alter linen
artificial flowers
bellows making 20%
bellows makers 20%
braid and elastic factories 50%
celluloid goods
china decorating works
clock and watch makers
cloth manufacturers 90% (50)
                    80% (60)
cutlery
cutlers
edge tools 20%
edge tool makers 20%
electrotyping
embroidery factories
embroiderers
enamel works
fancy goods factories
glassworks 25%
glassmakers 25%
gold and silversmiths
goldsmiths
horn and bone works
horse blankets 66%
Indian manufactures
India Rubber factories 10%
Japanware manufacturers
jewellers
jewellers and watchmakers
lace factories 85%
lace makers 90% (50)

last and peg factories (20%)
mathematical instr. making 60%
mathematical instr. makers 60%
pail makers
pail and tub factories
potters
potteries
regalia factories
rubber goods 10%
sail making
sail makers
shoddy mills 70% (70)
            60% (80-90)
silk manufacturers 70%
spoon makers
sporting goods
straw works
tent and awning factory
terra cotta works
toy factories
toy makers
umbrella and parasol mfg.
umbrella makers
weavers 90% (50)
        80% (60)
        70% (70)
        60% (80-90)
wood cloth making 70% (70)
                60% (80-90)
woollen factories 90% (50)
                80% (60)
woollen mills 60%

Consumer: durables

band box makers
bicycle factories
billiard table making 20%
boat building
boat builders
brass founders 15% (50)
brass founders & finishers 10% (60)
bronze monumental works
cabinet & furniture 85% (70-80-90)
cabinetmakers 95% (50)
            90% (60)
carpets; carpet makers
carriages 66% (70-80-90)
carriage makers 75% (50)
                70% (60)
carriage trimmers 66%
chair makers 95% (50)
            90% (60)

coffins and caskets
floor oil cloth
furnaces and stoves (5% of
        foundries & machine working)
invalid chairs and baby carriages

lamp and chandelier making
lantern factories
looking-glass makers
mat and rug making
mattress making
mattress makers
mirror and mantel making
musical instrument making
musical instrument makers
oar makers
oil-cloth making
oil-cloth manufacturers
organ builders
piano makers
picture frame making
sheepskin mat factory
spinning wheel factory
spring bed factories
stove makers
taxidermists
trunk makers
trunk and box making 70% (70-80)
                            100% (90)
trunk, box, & valise making 70% (70-80)
                                100% (90)
wallpaper factories
washing machine and wringer factories
window shades

Finished Producer Goods: construction
                                  materials

bellfoundries
coppersmithing 60%
coppersmiths 60%
foundries 10%
foundries and machinists 10%
foundries and machine working 10%
lath mills
nail and tack factories 34%
nailers 34%
nut and bolt works 34%
paint and varnish works 75%
paving material factories
planing and moulding mills
plumbers' supplies
rivet factories 34%
roofing felt
roofing material
screw factories 34%
stained glass works
tin and sheet iron working 60%

Finished Producer Goods: supplies to
primary and tertiary sectors

axe makers
bone crushing mills
cartridge case making

dynamite factories
edge tools 80%
edge tool makers 85%
fishing tackle manufacturing 85%
gunpowder mills
net making
net makers
opium factories
pot and pearl asheries
potash manufacturers
prepared cattle food
rope makers
rope and twine manufacturing
sack makers 50%
saw and file cutting
saw makers
sand paper 80%
stationery factories
superphosphate works
surgical appliances
whip factories
whip makers

Finished Producer Goods:
Investment goods

agricultural implements
billiard table making 80%
beekeepers' supplies
bellows making 80%
bellows makers 80%
boiler makers
boiler making
brass founders and finishers 15%
cabinet & furniture 15% (70-80-90)
cabinet makers 5% (50)
                   10% (60)
car and locomotive works
car builders
carriages 34% (70-80-90)
carriage makers 25% (50)
                   30% (60)
carriage trimmers 34%
caulkers 50%
chain makers 50%
chair makers 5% (50)
               10% (60)
electrical appliances 66%
electrical supplies 66%
elevator factories
emery wheel factories
engine building, engine builders
fanning mill manufacturers
fire-proof safes
foundries 60%
foundries and machine working 60%
foundries and machinists 60%
fire engine manufacturers

horse blankets and bags 34%
iron and steel bridge works
last factories
last makers
last and peg factories 80%
lathe makers
mathe. instr. making 40%
mathe. instr. makers 40%
metal cornices and signs
needle factories 50%
optical instruments
plane makers
pump factories
pump makers
pump and windmill factories
plough makers
rake makers
railway cars
railway supplies
refrigerator factories
rolling stock
saddle and harness 34% (70-80-90)
saddlers and harness makers 30% (50-60)
safe and vault works
safe makers
scale factories
scale makers
sewing machine factories 34%
shipyards
shipbuilders
shipwrights
show case making
smut machine manufacturing
spade manufacturers
steel barb fence factories
street car works
street lamp factories
sythe makers
wagon makers
wagon and cart makers
upholsterers 5% (50)
             10% (60)
ventilator factories

Unfinished Producer Goods

artistic materials
baking powder 30% (70-80-90)
baking powder & flavouring extract 30%
bank note engraving
bark extract works
basket making
basket makers
belt and hose factories
block making
block makers
book binding
book binders

braid and elastic factories
brass fitting foundries
brass founders
brass founders and finishers
button factories 80% (70)
                 85% (80)
                 90% (90)
carriage top making
carving and guilding
carvers and guilders
cheese box factories
chemicals establishments 34%
chickory kilns
cigar box factories
cloth manufacturers 10% (50)
                    20% (60)
copperine factories
coppersmithing 40%
coppersmiths 40%
cooperage
coopers
cork cutting
cotton factories 10% (70)
                 20% (80)
                 30% (90)
dyeing
dyers
dyers and scourers
electro-stereotyping
electrical appliances 34%
electrical supplies 34%
engravers
engraving and lithographing
engravers supplies
facing companies
feather factories
fittings and foundry work
flax mills
flour and grist mills 2% (70)
                      4% (80)
                      7% (90)
foundries (30%)
foundries and machine working 30%
foundries and machinists 30%
fringe and tassel factories
fringe makers
galvanized iron works
glass makers 70%
glass works 70%
glue making
glue makers
glyercine works
gold leaf factories
hoop makers
hub and spoke works
Indian rubber factories 90%
ink factories
iron smelting and steel working

202

iron and brass fittings
lace factories 15%
lace makers 10%
leather lace factory
linseed oil factories 30% (70)
                40% (80-90)
lithographers
lubricating oil factories 30% (70)
                40% (80-90)
maltsters
miscellaneous
nail and tack factories 66%
nailors 66%
nickle plating
nut and bolt works 66%
oil manufacturers 10% (50)
              20% (60)
oil refineries 30% (70)
          40% (80-90)
packing case factories
paint and varnish works 25%
paper, bag, and box
paper factories
paper makers
paraffin and wax works 30% (70)
            40% (80-90)

patent leather dresser
pattern and mould factories
pattern makers
piano action factories
plate works
plume making
press, stamp, and dye works
printing offices 50%
printers, publishers, editors
   (reporters)      40% (50)
                45% (60)
printers, and publishing office 50%
rivet factories 66%
rolling mills
rubber factories
rubber goods 90%
sack makers 50%
screw factories 66%
ship material making
shoddy mills 30% (70)
         40% (80-90)
shook and fish box making
silk manufacturing
smelting works
spinners
spring and axle factories
spring makers
starch factories
starch makers
sugar manufacturers & refiners 5%
tallow factories

tanners
tanneries
tin and sheet iron working
tinplate workers
trunk and box making 30%
trunk, box & valise factories 30%
turners
type founders
type foundries
wadding factories
wax making
weavers 10% (50)
        20% (60)
        30% (70)
        40% (80-90)
wire works
wire workers
wood turning
wool cloth making 30% (70)
            40% (80-90)
woollen factories 10% (50)
          20% (60)
woollen mills 40% (90)
woollen yarn factories
yeast factories

Primary: food, drink, tobacco

butter factories
cheese factories
cider making
creameries
dried fruit and vegetables
fish curing
fruit and vegetable canning
hop curing
native wine making
preserved articles of food
tobacco processing
wine making

Primary: construction materials

asbestos and minerals
brick and tile
brickmakers
cement mills
gypsum mills
lime kilns
lime burners
marble cutters
plaster and stucco factories
saw mills
scutching mills
shingle mills
shingle makers
stave mills
stave makers
stone cutters

stone and marble cutting
stucco makers

Primary: unfinished producer goods

carding and fulling mills
charcoal burning
charcoal burners
mica cutting
pulp mills
quartz crusing mills
salt works

Industries were allocated to the groups for each areal unit
of the study area (38 in all). Before this could be accomplished,
however, the census industries and occupations had to be organized in areal units with constant boundaries during the study
period. This led to considerable data manipulation because the
boundaries of the units for which data were presented changed
substantially from one census to another. In some years completely different areal units were used. This was not a serious
problem if the units could be aggregated to fit the boundaries of
counties.

The use of counties as the study units was really imposed,
because the censuses of 1851 and 1861 used counties as their
smallest data presentation units. In the censuses of 1871, 1881,
and 1891, the data on manufacturing industries were presented
for census districts which for the most part lie wholly within
county boundaries. In 1871 and 1881 only a few census districts
overlapped county boundaries. Problems created by these over-
laps were handled in two ways.

In some cases the industries listed for the census district
were allocated between the counties on which the census district
overlapped. This could be done by relating directory data for
towns, villages, and townships to the census data. Unfortunately,
only employment data could be directly handled in this way because the business directories consulted contained little or no
information on sales, values of raw materials, capital, etc.
The alternative to re-allocation of the census data was combination of the counties involved in the overlap. Where possible
combination was avoided in those cases where the counties which
would have been combined were believed to be substantially different in structure and development. In other cases combination
was avoided if the resulting areal unit was going to be very large.
One census district, for example, overlapped on the counties of
Peel, Simcoe, and Wellington. A unification of these would have

brought together greatly different areas settled at widely separated dates, and thus have rendered impossible worthwhile spatial analysis. There were instances, however, when the areal extent of overlap was considerable. If it seemed that the spatial analysis would not suffer greatly, the counties involved in the overlap of the census district were combined. Carleton-Russell and Kent-Lambton are cases in point.

The census districts of 1871 and 1881 were much the same and gave rise to approximately the same amount of data manipulation. The census of 1891, however, gave rise to a greater amount of manipulation. In southwestern Ontario many of the census districts had been changed and overlapped county boundaries. There was no alternative but to disaggregate the census district totals and allocate employment in industries to the counties involved in the overlap.

# Bibliography

ACKERMAN, EDWARD A. Geography as a Fundamental Research Discipline. Department of Geography Research Paper no. 53. Chicago: Department of Geography, University of Chicago, 1958.

ADAMS, WALKER. The Structure of American Industry: Some Case Studies. New York: The Macmillan Co., 1950.

ALCHIAN, ARMEN, A. "Uncertainty, Evolution and Economic Theory." Journal of Political Economy 58 (1950): 211-221.

ALONSO, WILLIAM. "Location Theory." In Regional Development and Planning, eds. John Friedmann and William Alonso. Cambridge, Mass.: The MIT Press, 1964, pp. 78-106.

BAIN, J. S. "Economies of Scale, Concentration, and the Conditions of Entry in Twenty Manufacturing Industries." American Economic Review 44 (1954): 15-39.

--------. Barriers to New Competition. Cambridge, Mass.: Harvard University Press, 1956.

BALDAMUS, W. "Mechanization, Utilization and Size of Plant." Economic Journal 63 (1953): 50-69.

BALDWIN, R. E. "Patterns of Development in Newly Settled Regions." Manchester School of Economic and Social Studies 24 (1956): 161-179.

BERTRAM, G. W. "Economic Growth in Canadian Industry, 1870-1915: The Staple Model and the Take-off Hypothesis." The Canadian Journal of Economics and Political Science 29 (1963): 159-184.

BLADEN, V. W. An Introduction to Political Economy. Toronto: University of Toronto Press, 1956.

BLAIR, John M. "Technology and Size." The American Economic Review 38 (1948): 121-152.

BREITHAUPT, W. H. "Waterloo County History." Ontario Historical Society Papers and Records 17 (1919): 43-47.

BROWN, L. A History of Simcoe 1829-1929. Simcoe, Ontario: 1929.

BUCKLEY, K. "The Role of the Staple Industries in Canada's Economic Development." Journal of Economic History 18 (1958): 439-450.

BURROWS, C. A. The Annals of the Town of Guelph 1827-1877. Guelph: 1877.

CAIRNCROSS, A. K. "The Stages of Economic Growth." In Factors in Economic Development, by Cairncross. London: Allen and Unwin Ltd , 1962, pp. 131-144.

CAMU, P.; WEEKS, E. P.; AND SAMETZ, Z. W. Economic Geography of Canada. Toronto: Macmillan of Canada, 1964.

CANADA. Census 1851-52; 1860-61; 1870-71; 1880-81; 1890-91.

--------. Department of the Interior. Economic Survey of Peterborough County. Ottawa: King's Printer, 1931.

--------. Dominion Bureau of Statistics. The Manufacturing Industries of Canada, 1961, Section G, Geographical Distribution. Ottawa: Queen's Printer, 1964.

CANADIAN DOMINION DIRECTORY. Montreal: John Lovell, 1871.

CARELESS, J. M. S. The Union of the Canadas. Toronto· McClelland & Stewart Ltd.. 1967.

CAVES. R. E. AND HOLTON. R. H. The Canadian Economy· Prospect and Retrospect. Cambridge, Mass.: Harvard University Press. 1961.

CHAMBERS, E. J. AND BERTRAM. G. W. "Localization and Specialization in Manufacturing in Central Canada. 1870-1890." Paper delivered at Canadian Political Science meeting, Conference on Statistics. Charlottetown. P.E.I.. 1964.

CHENERY, H. B. AND CLARK. P. G. Interindustry Economics. New York: John Wiley and Sons, Inc., 1959.

CHISHOLM, M. Rural Settlement and Land Use. Hutchinson University Library, 1962.

--------. Geography and Economics. London: Bell & Sons Ltd., 1966.

CHORLEY, R. J. AND HAGGETT. P., EDS. Frontiers in Geographical Teaching. London: Methuen, 1965.

CITY OF LONDON AND COUNTY OF MIDDLESEX DIRECTORY, 1871-1872. Strathroy, Ontario: Mackintosh and Company, 1872.

COCHRAN, T. C. The Pabst Brewing Company. New York: New York University Press, 1948.

CONNON, T. R. Elora. Elora: Elora "Express" and the Fergus "News Record," 1930.

COOMBS, A. E. History of the Niagara Peninsula and the Welland Canal. Toronto: Historical Publishers' Association, 1930.

COOPER, R. T. "Furniture." In A Century of Industrial Development in Ontario, Studies in Selected Industries. Toronto· Ontario Department of Economics and Development, 1965.

COUNTY OF HURON GAZETTEER AND GENERAL DIRECTORY, 1869-70. Hamilton: Joseph Sutherland & Company, 1870.

COWAN, Hugh. Canadian Achievement in the Province of Ontario Volume 1: The Detroit River District. Algonquin Historical Society of Canada, 1929.

CRAIG, GERALD M. Upper Canada: The Formative Years 1784-1841. Toronto· McClelland & Stewart, 1963.

CRUIKSHANK, E. A. "A Country Merchant in Upper Canada, 1800-1812." Ontario Historical Society Papers and Records 25 (1929): 145-190.

CUMMINGS, L. P. Geography of Guyana. London and Glasgow: Collins, 1965.

DALES, J. H. "Fuel, Power and Industrial Development in Central Canada." American Economic Review 43 (1953): 181-198.

--------. Hydroelectricity and Industrial Development: Quebec 1898-1940. Cambridge: Harvard University Press, 1957.

--------. "A Comparison of Manufacturing Industry in Quebec and Ontario." In Canadian Dualism, ed. M. Wade. Toronto: University of Toronto Press, 1960, pp. 203-222.

--------. "Estimates of Canadian Manufacturing Output by Markets, 1870-1995." Papers, Canadian Political Science Association, Conference on Statistics 1962 and 1963.

DENISON, MERRILL. Harvest Triumphant. Toronto: McClelland & Stewart Ltd., 1948.

--------. The Barley and the Stream. Toronto: McClelland & Stewart Ltd., 1955.

DIX, ERNEST. "United States Influences on the Agriculture of Prince Edward County Ontario." Economic Geography 26 (1950): 179-182.

DOMINION BREWERS ASSOCIATION. Facts on the Brewing Industry of Canada. Ottawa, 1940.

DONALD, W. S. The Canadian Iron and Steel Industry. Boston: Houghton Mifflin, 1915.

EASTERBROOK, W. T. AND AITKEN. H. G. Canadian Economic History. Toronto: The Macmillan Co. of Canada Ltd.. 1956.

EASTERBROOK, W. T. AND WATKINS. M. H., EDS. Approaches to Canadian Economic History. Toronto: McClelland & Stewart Ltd.. 1967.

ESTALL, R. C. AND BUCHANAN, R. O. Industrial Activity and Economic Geography. London: Hutchinson University Library, 1961.

FAIRBANK, J. K.; ECKSTEIN, A.; AND YANG, L. S. "Economic Change in Early Modern China: An Analytic Framework." Economic Development and Cultural Change 9 (1960): 1-26.

FIRESTONE, O. J. Canada's Economic Development, 1867-1953. Income and Wealth, Series VII. London: Bowes and Bowes, 1958.

--------. "Development of Canada's Economy, 1850-1890." In Trends in the American Economy in the Nineteenth Century. Princeton: Princeton University Press, 1960, pp. 217-252.

FLORENCE, P. SARGENT. Investment, Location and Size of Plant. National Institute of Economic and Social Research. Cambridge: Cambridge University Press, 1948.

--------. The Logic of British and American Industry. London: Routledge & Kegan Paul Ltd., 1953.

FOGEL, R. W. Railroads and American Economic Growth. Baltimore: Johns Hopkins Press, 1964.

FRIEDMANN, JOHN. "Locational Aspects of Economic Development." Land Economics 32 (1956): 213-227.

FRIEDMANN, JOHN AND ALONSO, WILLIAM, EDS. Regional Development and Planning. Cambridge, Mass.: The MIT Press, 1964.

GENTILCORE, R. LOUIS "The Beginnings of Settlement in the Niagara Peninsula (1782-1792). " The Canadian Geographer 7 (1963): 72-82.

GILMOUR, JAMES M. "The Economic Geography of the Pulp and Paper Industry in Ontario. " Unpublished master's dissertation, Department of Geography, University of Toronto, 1964.

--------. "The Joint Anarchy of 'Confidentiality' and Definitional Change. " Canadian Geographer 10 (1966): 40-48.

GLAZEBROOK, G. P. de T. A History of Transportation in Canada. 2 vols. The Carleton Library No. 11. Toronto: McClelland & Stewart, 1964.

GOLLEDGE, R. G. "The New Zealand Brewing Industry. " The New Zealand Geographer 19 (1963): 7-24.

GUILLET, EDWIN C. Pioneer Inns and Taverns. 4 vols. Toronto: Ontario Publishing Co. Ltd., 1956.

--------. Pioneer Days in Upper Canada. Toronto: University of Toronto Press, Canadian University Paperbacks Edition, 1964.

HAGGETT, PETER. "Changing Concepts in Economic Geography. " In Frontiers in Geographical Teaching, eds. R. J. Chorley and Peter Haggett. London: Methuen, 1965, pp. 101-117.

--------. Locational Analysis in Human Geography. London: Edward Arnold Ltd., 1965.

HAMILTON, F. E. IAN. "Models in Industrial Location. " In Models in Geography, eds. R. J. Chorley and Peter Haggett. London: Methuen 1967, pp. 361-424.

HAMMILL, J. D. "Early History of Meaford and its District. " Ontario Historical Society Papers and Records 18 (1920): 42-43.

HARTMAN, C. W. "Early History of the Beaver \ alley. " Ontario Historical Society Papers and Records 18 (1920): 37-41.

HIRSCHMAN, ALBERT O. The Strategy of Economic Development. New Haven: Yale University Press, 1958.

HOOVER, EDGAR M. Location Theory and the Shoe and Leather Industries. Harvard Economic Studies 55. Cambridge, Mass.: Harvard University Press, 1937.

--------. The Location of Economic Activity. Paperback Edition. New York: McGraw-Hill, 1963.

HOSELITZ, BERT F. Theories of Economic Growth, ed. Hoselitz. New York: The Free Press of Glencoe, 1960.

INNIS, HAROLD. The Fur Trade in Canada: An Introduction to Canadian Economic History. New Haven: Yale University Press, 1930.

--------. The Cod Fishery: The History of an International Economy. New Haven: Yale University Press, 1940.

INNIS, M. Q. "The Industrial Development of Ontario, 1783-1820. " Ontario Historical Society Papers and Records 32 (1936).

--------. An Economic History of Canada. Toronto: Ryerson Press, 1954.

ISARD, WALTER. Location and Space Economy. Cambridge, Mass.: The MIT Press, 1956.

--------. Methods of Regional Analysis. Cambridge, Mass.: The MIT Press, 1960.

ISARD, W. AND KUENNE, R. "The Impact of Steel Upon the Greater New York – Philadelphia Region: A Study in Aggolomeration Projection." Review of Economics and Statistics 35 (1953): 289-301.

JOHNSTON, C. M. Brant County: A History, 1784-1945. Toronto: Oxford University Press, 1967.

JONES, J. C. H. "Mergers and Competition: The Brewing Case." The Canadian Journal of Economics and Political Science 33 (1967): 551-568.

JONES, R. L. History of Agriculture in Ontario, 1613-1880. Toronto: University of Toronto Press, 1946.

KAPLAN, A. D. H. "The Influence of Size of Firms on the Functioning of the Economy." American Economic Review 40 (1930): 74-84.

KEEBLE, D. E. "Models of Economic Development." In Models in Geography, eds. R. J. Chorley and Peter Haggett. London: Methuen and Company, 1967.

KERR, DONALD AND SPELT, JACOB. The Changing Face of Toronto. Memoir 11. Ottawa: Geographical Branch, Mines and Technical Surveys, 1965.

KIERSTEAD, B. S. The Theory of Economic Change. Toronto: The Macmillan Co. of Canada Ltd., 1948.

KINDLEBERGER, C. P. Foreign Trade and the National Economy, New Haven: Yale University Press, 1962.

KING. L. J. "Approaches to Location Analysis." The East Lakes Geographer 2 (1966): 1-16.

KIRKCONNELL, Watson. Victoria County (Centennial History). Lindsay. Ontario: Watchman-Warder Press. 1921.

KLEIN. L. R. "A Model of Japanese Economic Growth." Econometrica 29 (1961): 277-292.

LITHWICK, N. H. AND PAQUET. GILLES. "Urban Growth and Regional Contagion." In Urban Studies: A Canadian Perspective. eds. Lithwick and Paquet. Toronto: Methuen, 1968, pp.18-39.

LÖSCH, AUGUST. The Economics of Location. New Haven: Yale University Press. 1954. An English translation by William H. Woglom of Die Raumliche Ordnung der Wirtschaft.

LOVELL'S BUSINESS AND PROFESSIONAL DIRECTORY OF THE PROVINCE OF ONTARIO FOR 1882. Montreal: John Lovell & Son, 1882.

MACKINTOSH, W. A. The Economic Background of Dominion Provincial Relations. Appendix III of the Royal Commission Report on Dominion-Provincial Relations. Edited and introduced by J. H. Dales. Carleton Library, No. 13. Toronto: McClelland & Stewart, 1964.

MAIN, O. W. The Canadian Nickel Industry. Toronto: University of Toronto Press, 1955.

MASTERS, D. C. The Rise of Toronto 1850-1890. Toronto: University of Toronto Press, 1958.

MATHIAS, PETER. "Industrial Revolution in Brewing." Explorations in Entrepreneurial History 5 (1953): 208-224.

McCAFFERTY, E. D. Henry J. Heinz. Privately published by the Heinz Company in 1923.

McCARTY, H. H. AND LINDBERG, J. B. A Preface to Economic Geography. Englewood Cliffs, N. J.: Prentice-Hall Inc., 1966.

210

McILWRAITH, T. F. "Accessibility and Rural Land Utilization in the Yonge Street Area of Upper Canada." Unpublished master's dissertation, Department of Geography, University of Toronto, 1966.

McKENZIE, RUTH. Leeds and Grenville. Toronto: McClelland & Stewart, 1967.

MEINIG, D. W. "A Comparative Historical Geography of Two Railnets: Columbia Basin and South Australia." Annals of the Association of American Geographers 52 (1962): 392-413.

MIDDLETON, JESSE EDGAR, et al. The Municipality of Toronto: A History. 3 vols. Toronto: Dominion Publishing Company, 1923.

MIERNYK, W. H. The Elements of Input-Output Analysis. New York: Random House, 1965.

MORRILL, RICHARD L. "Simulation of Central Place Patterns Over Time." Proceedings of the IGU Symposium in Urban Geography: Lund 1960. Lund Studies in Geography, Series B, Human Geography, No. 24. Lund: C.W.K. Gleerup, 1962.

MORTON, W. L. The Critical Years. Toronto: McClelland & Stewart Ltd., 1964.

MYINT, H. The Economics of the Developing Countries. London: Hutchinson University Library, 1964.

MYRDAL, GUNNAR. Economic Theory and Underdeveloped Regions. London: Gerald Duckworth, 1957.

--------. Economic Theory and Underdeveloped Regions. London: Methuen, University Paperbacks, 1963.

NATIONAL ACADEMY OF SCIENCES. The Science of Geography. Report of the ad hoc Committee on Geography, Earth Sciences Division. NAS-NRC Publication 1277. Washington D.C.: National Academy of Sciences-National Research Council, 1965.

NORTH, D. C. "Location Theory and Regional Economic Growth." Journal of Political Economy 63 (1955): 243-258.

--------. "A Reply." Journal of Political Economy 64 (1956): 165-168.

--------. "A Note on Professor Rostow's 'Take-off' into Self-Sustained Growth." Manchester School of Economic and Social Studies 26 (1958): 68-75.

--------. The Economic Growth of the United States, 1790-1860. Englewood Cliffs, N. J.: Prentice-Hall, 1961.

ONTARIO. Department of Economics and Development. A Century of Industrial Development in Ontario. Toronto, 1965.

--------. Royal Commission on Liquor Traffic. "Minutes of Evidence Taken in the Province of Ontario." Sessional Papers vol.15, Sessional Paper 21 (2 parts) Fourth Session of the 7th Parliament of the Dominion of Canada, Session 1894.

-------- "The Report Upon the Inspection of Liquor Licenses for the Year 1902." Presented to the Ontario Legislature 21 March 1903. Sessional Papers vol. 35, Part IX, Sessional Paper 44. First Session, 10th Legislature of the Province of Ontario, Session 1903.

OTTESON, S. F. Physical Distribution Management. New York: The Macmillan Co., 1961.

OXFORD GAZETTEER AND GENERAL BUSINESS DIRECTORY 1870-71. Toronto: Hunter, Rose & Company, 1870.

PATNI, R. L. "A New Method for Measuring Locational Changes in a Manufacturing Industry." Economic Geography 44 (1968): 210-217.

PENROSE, EDITH TILTON. The Theory of the Growth of the Firm. Oxford: Basil Blackwell, 1959.

PERLOFF, H. AND WINGO, L. JR. "Natural Resource Endowment and Regional Economic Growth." In Regional Development and Planning, eds. John Friedmann and William Alonso. Cambridge, Mass.: The MIT Press, 1964, pp. 215-239.

PERROUX, F. "Note sur la notion de pôle de croissance." Economie Appliquée 8 (1955): 307-320.

PFISTER, RICHARD L. "External Trade and Regional Growth: A Case Study of the Pacific Northwest." Economic Development and Cultural Change 11 (1963): 134-151.

PHILLIPS, ALMARIN. "Concentration Scale and Technological Change in Manufacturing Industries, 1899-1939." Journal of Industrial Economics 4 (1956): 179-193.

PHILLIPS, W. G. The Agricultural Implement Industry in Canada. Toronto: University of Toronto Press, 1956.

PREBISCH, R. The Economic Development of Latin America and Its Principal Problems. Lake Success, 1950.

--------. "Commercial Policy in the Underdeveloped Countries." American Economic Review 49 (1959): 251-273.

PRED, ALLAN. The External Relations of Cities During 'Industrial Revolution.' Department of Geography Research Paper No. 76. Chicago: Dept. of Geography, University of Chicago, 1962.

--------. "Industrialization, Initial Advantage and American Metropolitan Growth." Geographical Review 55 (1965): 158-185.

--------. "Manufacturing in the American Mercantile City: 1800-1840." Annals of the Association of American Geographers 56 (1966): 307-338.

--------. "Some Locational Relationships Between Industrial Inventions, Industrial Innovations and Urban Growth." The East Lakes Geographer 2 (1966): 45-70.

--------. The Spatial Dynamics of U.S. Urban-Industrial Growth, 1800-1914: Interpretive and Theoretical Essays. Cambridge, Mass.: The MIT Press, 1966.

PROVINCE OF ONTARIO GAZETEER AND DIRECTORY. Toronto: The Might Directory Company of Toronto Ltd., 1895.

RAWSTRON, E. M. "Three Principles of Industrial Location." Transactions and Papers, Institute of British Geographers (1958): 135-142.

RAY, MICHAEL D. Market Potential and Economic Shadow. Department of Geography Research Paper No. 101. Chicago: Dept. of Geography, University of Chicago, 1965.

RAYNAULD, ANDRE. The Canadian Economic System. Toronto: The Macmillan Co. of Canada Ltd., 1967.

REEDS, LLOYD G. "Agricultural Regions of Southern Ontario, 1880-1951." Economic Geography 35 (1959): 219-227.

RETALLACK, JOAN. "The Changing Distribution of Wheat in Southern Ontario, 1850-1890." Unpublished master's dissertation, Department of Geography, University of Toronto, 1966.

212

REVILLE, F. D. History of the County of Brant. 2 vols. Brantford, Ontario: Brant Historical Society, 1920.

RICHARDS, J. HOWARD. "Population and the Economic Base in Northern Hastings County, Ontario." Canadian Geographer 2 (1958): 23-34.

ROBINSON, E. A. G. The Structure of Competitive Industry. Chicago: University of Chicago Press, 1958.

ROSENBLUTH, GIDEON. Concentration in Canadian Manufacturing Industries. A Study by the National Bureau of Economic Research, New York. Princeton: Princeton University Press, 1957.

ROSTOW, W. W. "The Take-Off into Self-Sustained Growth." Economic Journal 66 (1956): 25-48.

--------. "The Stages of Economic Growth." Economic History Review, Second Series 12 (1959): 1-16.

--------. The Stages of Economic Growth: A Non-Communist Manifesto. Cambridge: Cambridge University Press, 1960.

SCOTT, JAMES. The Settlement of Huron County. Toronto: The Ryerson Press, 1966.

SHAW, W. H. Value of Commodity Output Since 1869. New York: National Bureau of Economic Research, 1947.

SMITH, CALEB, A. "Survey of the Empirical Evidence on Economies of Scale." In Business Concentration and Price Policy. A report of the National Bureau of Economic Research, New York. Princeton: Princeton University Press, 1955, pp. 213-238.

SPELT, JACOB. The Urban Development in South Central Ontario. Assen: Van Gorcum, 1955.

STEINDHL, JOSEPH. Small and Big Business. Institute of Statistics, Monograph no. 1. Oxford: Basil Blackwell, 1945.

STIGLER, G. T. "The Division of Labour is Limited by the Extent of the Market." Journal of Political Economy 59 (1951): 185-193.

STONE, LEROY O. Urban Development in Canada. A Census Monograph. Ottawa: Dominion Bureau of Statistics, Census Division, 1967.

SYMONS, LESLIE. Agricultural Geography. London: G. Bell & Sons Ltd., 1967.

TAAFE, E. J.; MORRILL, R. L.; AND GOULD, P. R. "Transport Expansion in Underdeveloped Countries: A Comparative Analysis." Geographical Review 53 (1963): 503-529.

TATTERSALL, J. N. "Exports and Economic Growth: The Pacific Northwest 1880 to 1960." Papers and Proceedings of the Regional Science Association (1962): 215-234.

TAYLOR, GRIFFITH. Canada. 2nd. ed. revised. London: Methuen, 1950.

TAYLOR, IAIN C. "Components of Population Change, Ontario 1850-1940." Unpublished master's dissertation, Department of Geography, University of Toronto, 1967.

TEMPLIN, HUGH. Fergus: The Story of a Little Town. Fergus, Ontario: Fergus News Record, 1933.

THE CANADA DIRECTORY. By Robert W. S. Mackay. Montreal: John Lovell, 1852.

THE ECONOMIC ATLAS OF ONTARIO, ed. W. G. Dean. Toronto: University of Toronto Press for the Government of Ontario, 1969.

THE PROVINCE OF ONTARIO GAZETEER AND DIRECTORY   Toronto:  Robertson
& Cook, 1869.

TIEBOUT, C. M.  "Exports and Regional Economic Growth."  Journal of Political
Economy 64 (1956):  160-164.

--------.  "Location Theory, Empirical Evidence and Economic Evolution."  Papers
and Proceedings of the Regional Science Association 3 (1957):  74-86.

THOMAS, MORGAN.  "The Export Base and Development Stages Theories of Regional
Economic Growth."  Land Economics 40 (1964):  421-432.

THOMPSON, JOHN.  "A New Method of Measuring Manufacturing."  Annals of the
Association of American Geographers 45 (1945):  416-436.

TUCKER, GILBERT N.  The Canadian Commercial Revolution, 1845-1851.  Carleton
Library, No. 19.  Toronto:  McClelland & Stewart, 1964.

ULLMAN, EDWARD L.  "Regional Development and the Geography of Concentration."
Papers and Proceedings of the Regional Science Association 4 (1958):  179-198.

URQUART, M. C. AND BUCKLEY, K., EDS.  Historical Statistics of Canada.  Toronto:
Cambridge University Press, 1965.

VAIZEY, JOHN.  The Brewing Industry, 1886-1951.  London:  Sir Issac Pitman & Sons
Ltd., 1960.

WALKER, D. F.  "The Role of Coal as a Location Factor in the Development of
Manufacturing Industry in Southern Ontario 1871-1921."  Unpublished master's
dissertation, Department of Geography, University of Toronto, 1967.

WARKENTIN, JOHN.  "Southern Ontario:  A view From the West."  Canadian Geographer
10 (1966):  157-171.

WARKENTIN, JOHN, ED.  Canada, A Geographical Interpretation.  Toronto:  Methuen
Publications, 1967.

WATKINS, MELVILLE.  "A Staple Theory of Economic Growth."  The Canadian Journal
of Economics and Political Science 29 (1963):  141-158.

WATSON, J. WREFORD.  Canada:  Problems and Prospects.  Toronto:  Longmans
Canada Ltd., 1968.

WEBER, ALFRED.  Theory of the Location of Industries.  Chicago:  University of
Chicago Press, 1929.  An English translation of Uber den Standort der Industrien,
with introduction and notes by Carl J. Friedrich.

WILLIAMS, MICHAEL.  "Delimiting the Spread of Settlement:  Examination of Evidence
in South Australia."  Economic Geography 42 (1966):  336-355.

YOUNG, ALLYN.  "Increasing Returns and Economic Progress."  Economic Journal
38 (1928):  527-542.